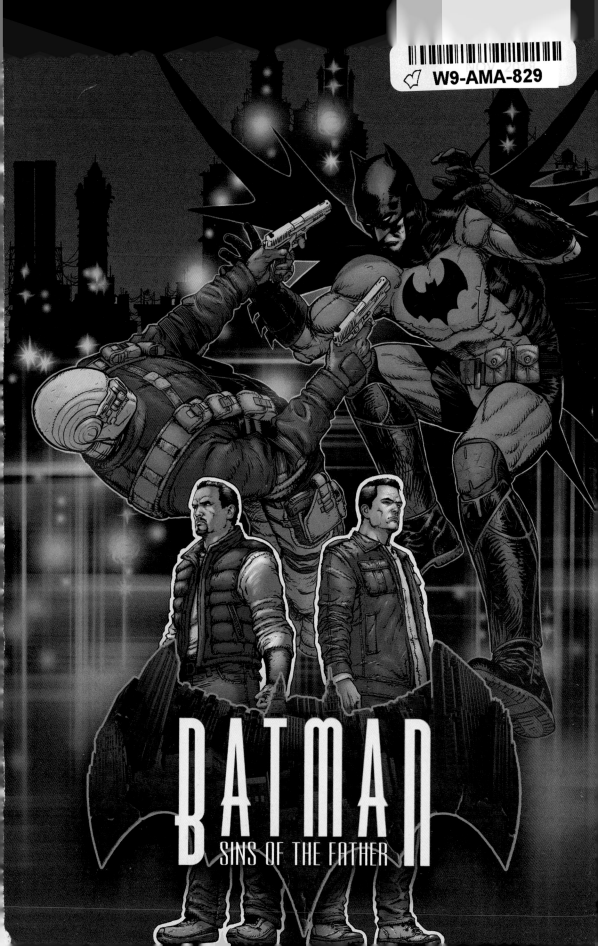

BATMAN
SINS OF THE FATHER

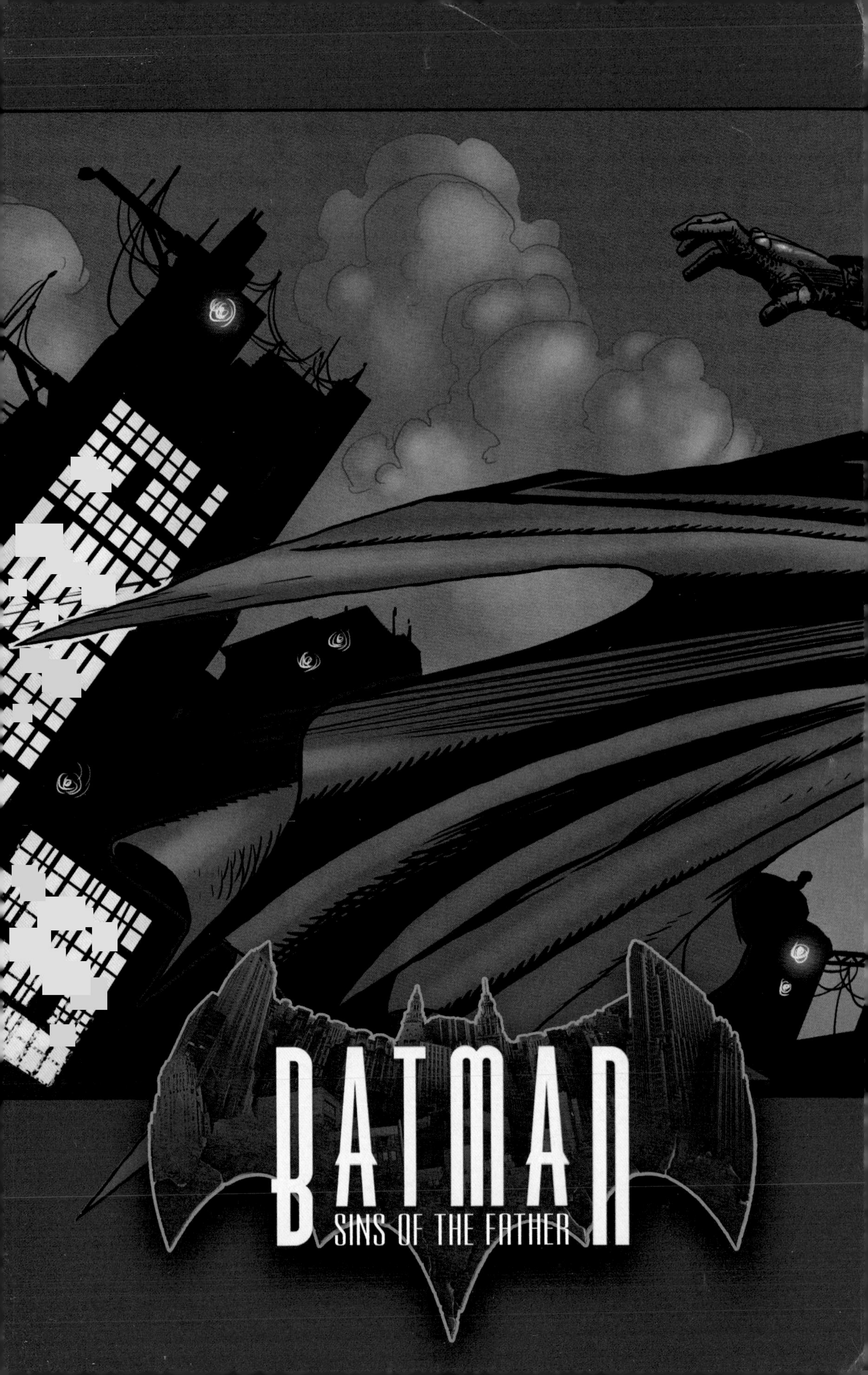
BATMAN
SINS OF THE FATHER

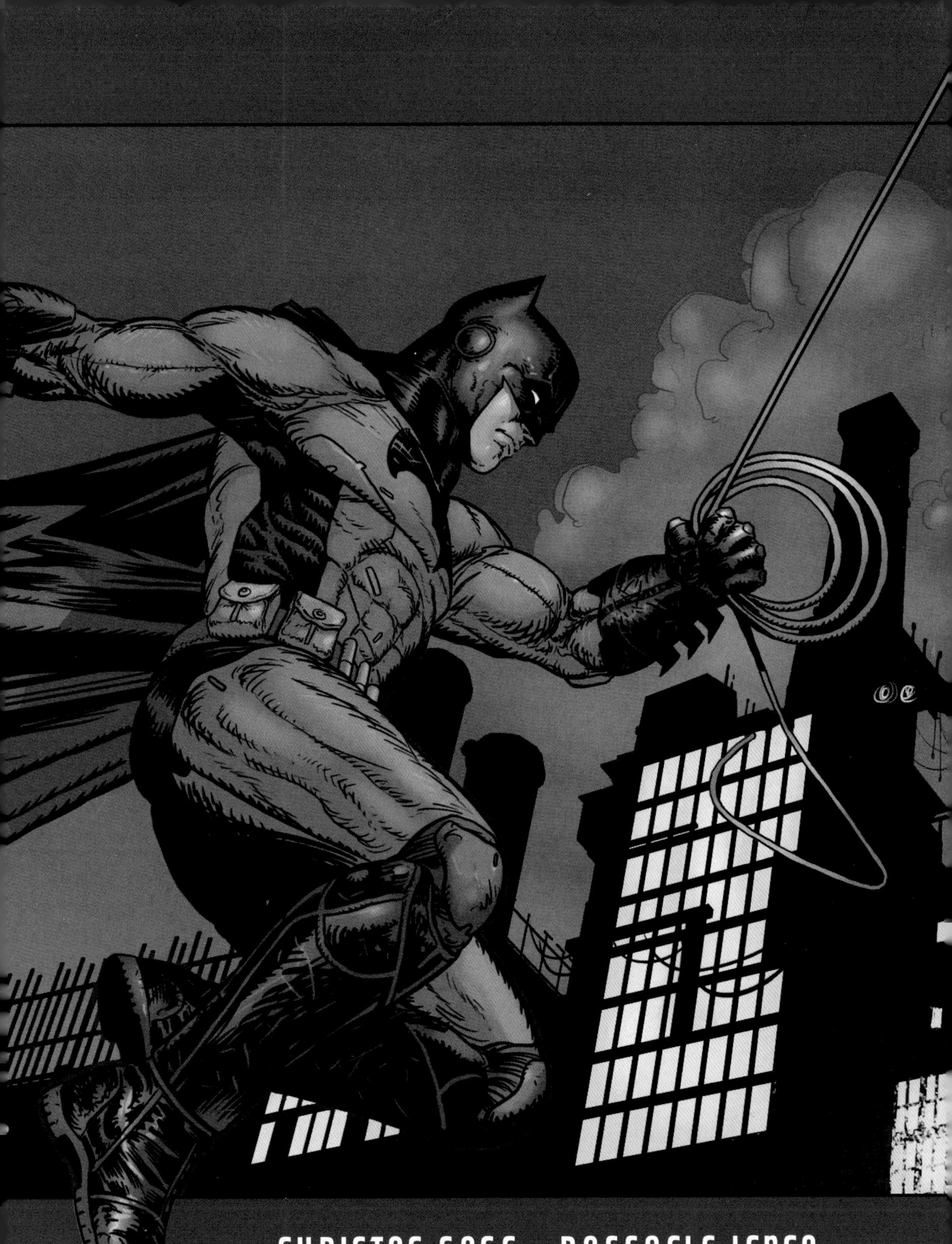

Writer **CHRISTOS GAGE** **RAFFAELE IENCO** Artist

Colorist **GUY MAJOR** **JOSH REED** Letterer

RAFFAELE IENCO and **GUY MAJOR** Collection cover artists

BATMAN created by **BOB KANE** with **BILL FINGER**

JIM CHADWICK *Editor - Original Series*
LIZ ERICKSON *Assistant Editor - Original Series*
JEB WOODARD *Group Editor - Collected Editions*
ERIKA ROTHBERG *Editor - Collected Edition*
STEVE COOK *Design Director - Books*
CURTIS KING JR. *Publication Design*

BOB HARRAS *Senior VP - Editor-in-Chief, DC Comics*
PAT McCALLUM *Executive Editor, DC Comics*

DAN DiDIO *Publisher*
JIM LEE *Publisher & Chief Creative Officer*
AMIT DESAI *Executive VP - Business & Marketing Strategy,*
   Direct to Consumer & Global Franchise Management
BOBBIE CHASE *VP & Executive Editor,*
   Young Reader & Talent Development
MARK CHIARELLO *Senior VP - Art, Design & Collected Editions*
JOHN CUNNINGHAM *Senior VP - Sales & Trade Marketing*
BRIAR DARDEN *VP - Business Affairs*
ANNE DePIES *Senior VP - Business Strategy, Finance & Administration*
DON FALLETTI *VP - Manufacturing Operations*
LAWRENCE GANEM *VP - Editorial Administration & Talent Relations*
ALISON GILL *Senior VP - Manufacturing & Operations*
JASON GREENBERG *VP - Business Strategy & Finance*
HANK KANALZ *Senior VP - Editorial Strategy & Administration*
JAY KOGAN *Senior VP - Legal Affairs*
NICK J. NAPOLITANO *VP - Manufacturing Administration*
LISETTE OSTERLOH *VP - Digital Marketing & Events*
EDDIE SCANNELL *VP - Consumer Marketing*
COURTNEY SIMMONS *Senior VP - Publicity & Communications*
JIM (SKI) SOKOLOWSKI *VP - Comic Book*
   Specialty Sales & Trade Marketing
NANCY SPEARS *VP - Mass, Book, Digital Sales & Trade Marketing*
MICHELE R. WELLS *VP - Content Strategy*

BATMAN: SINS OF THE FATHER

Published by DC Comics. Compilation and all new material Copyright
© 2018 DC Comics. All Rights Reserved. Originally published in single
magazine form in BATMAN: SINS OF THE FATHER 1-6 and online as
BATMAN: SINS OF THE FATHER Digital Chapters 1-12. Copyright © 2018
DC Comics. All Rights Reserved. All characters, their distinctive likenesses
and related elements featured in this publication are trademarks of DC
Comics. The stories, characters and incidents featured in this publication
are entirely fictional. DC Comics does not read or accept unsolicited
submissions of ideas, stories or artwork.

DC Comics
2900 West Alameda Ave., Burbank, CA 91505
Printed by Times Printing, LLC, Random Lake, WI, USA. 10/5/18.
First Printing. ISBN: 978-1-4012-8423-7

Library of Congress Cataloging-in-Publication Data is available.

MIX
Paper from
responsible sources
FSC® C015572
www.fsc.org

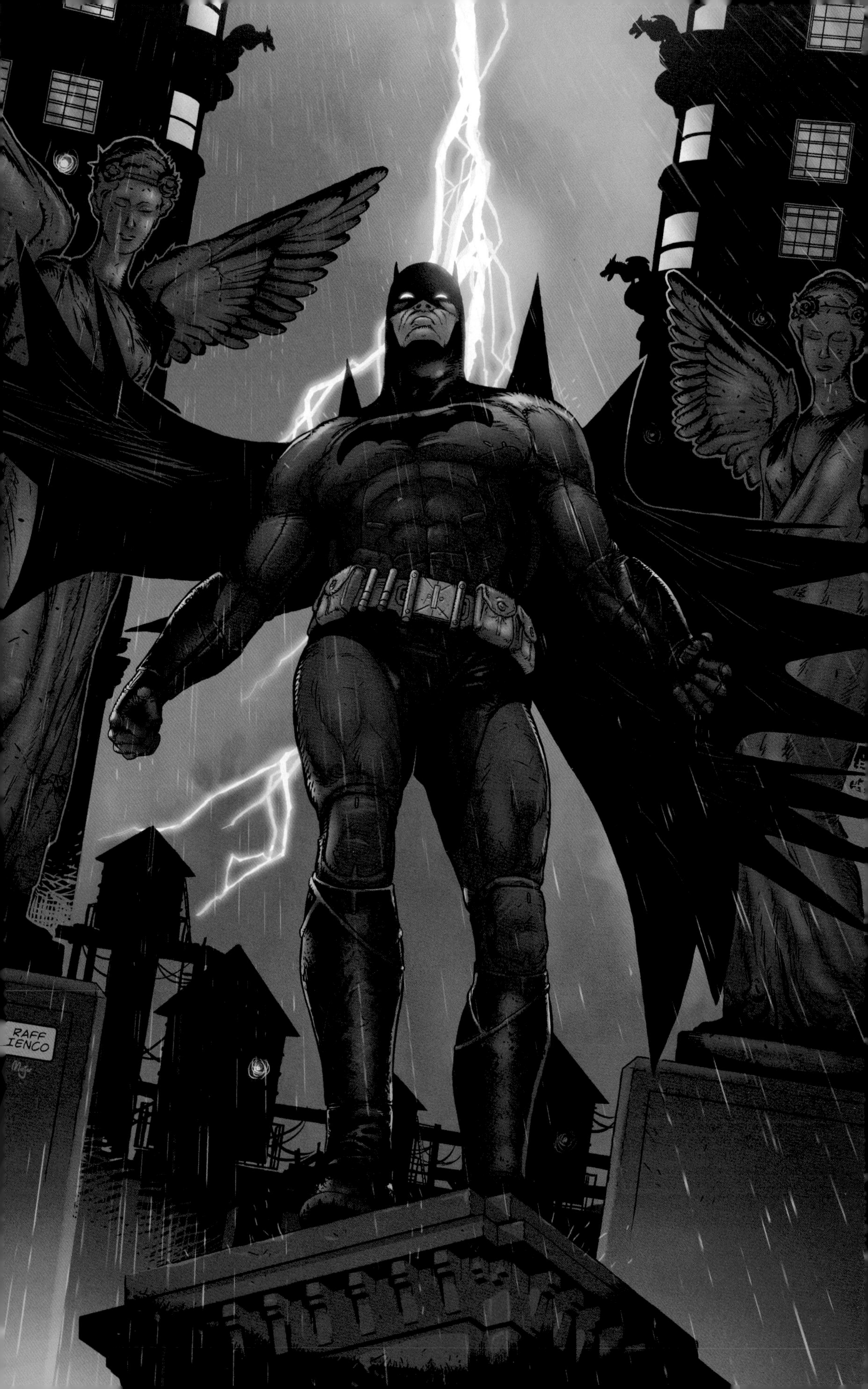
RAFF
IENCO

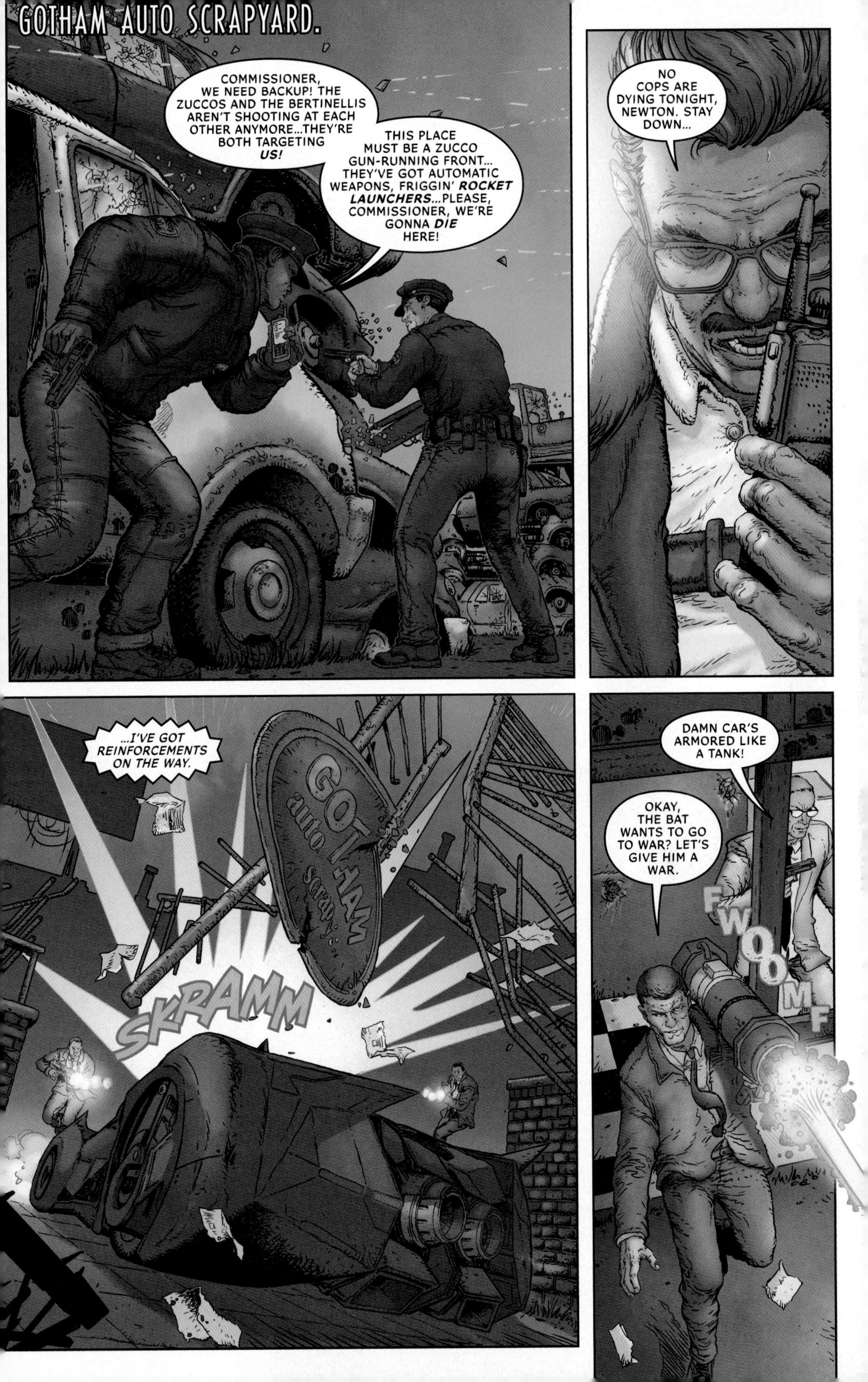
GOTHAM AUTO SCRAPYARD.
COMMISSIONER, WE NEED BACKUP! THE ZUCCOS AND THE BERTINELLIS AREN'T SHOOTING AT EACH OTHER ANYMORE...THEY'RE BOTH TARGETING US!
THIS PLACE MUST BE A ZUCCO GUN-RUNNING FRONT... THEY'VE GOT AUTOMATIC WEAPONS, FRIGGIN' ROCKET LAUNCHERS...PLEASE, COMMISSIONER, WE'RE GONNA DIE HERE!
NO COPS ARE DYING TONIGHT, NEWTON. STAY DOWN...
...I'VE GOT REINFORCEMENTS ON THE WAY.
SKRAMM
DAMN CAR'S ARMORED LIKE A TANK!
OKAY, THE BAT WANTS TO GO TO WAR? LET'S GIVE HIM A WAR.
FWOOMF

BAWHOOOM

HELL YEAH!!

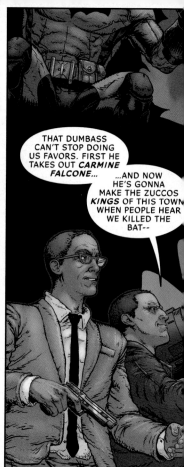

THAT DUMBASS CAN'T STOP DOING US FAVORS. FIRST HE TAKES OUT *CARMINE FALCONE*...

...AND NOW HE'S GONNA MAKE THE ZUCCOS *KINGS* OF THIS TOWN WHEN PEOPLE HEAR WE KILLED THE BAT--

GORDON, KEEP YOUR PEOPLE BACK. I'M ON SCENE AND HANDLING THE SITUATION.

CAREFUL. SOUNDS LIKE THEY'VE GOT AN IMPRESSIVE ARSENAL.

--MURRGH!

SSSSS

SO DO I.

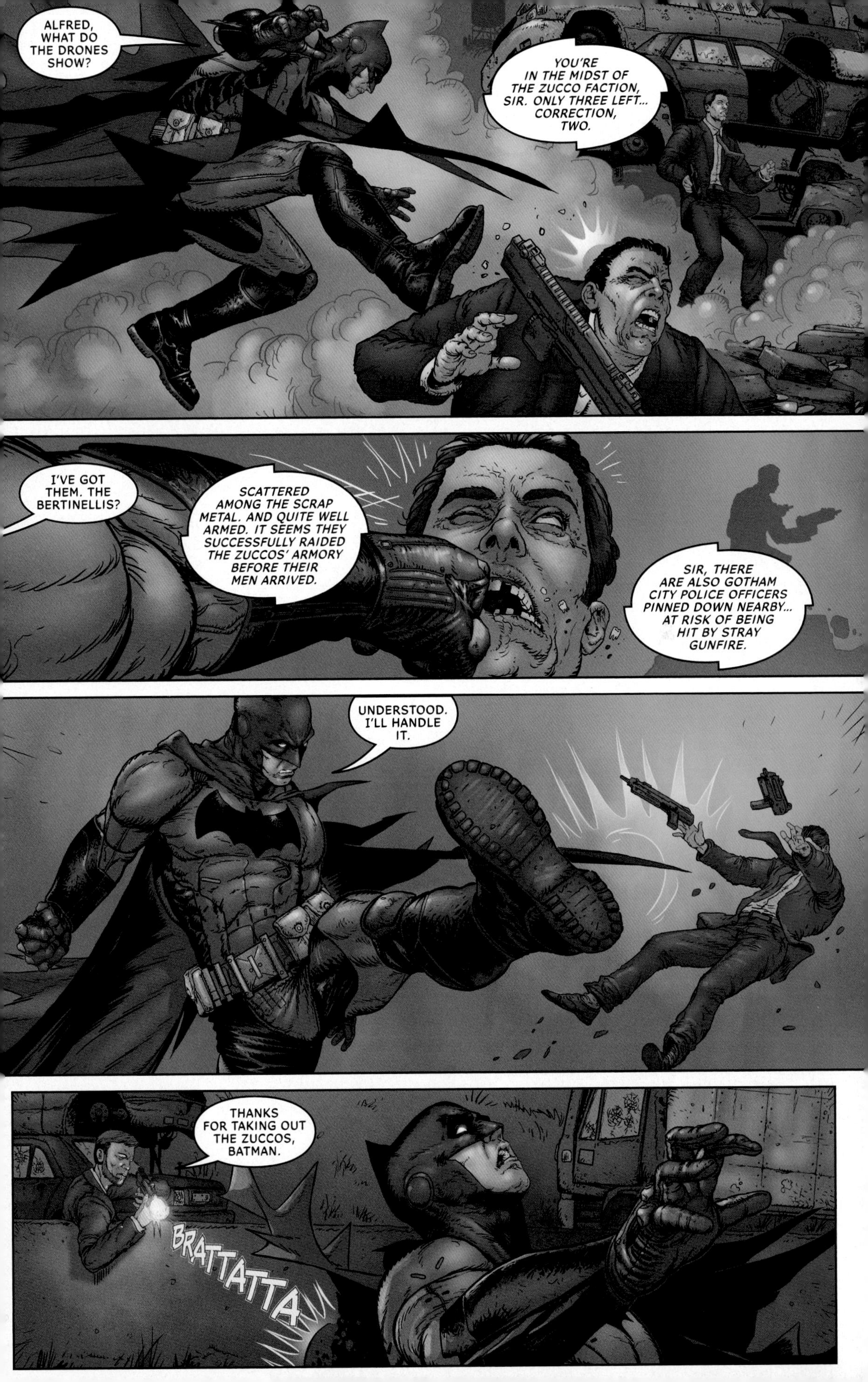
ALFRED, WHAT DO THE DRONES SHOW?
YOU'RE IN THE MIDST OF THE ZUCCO FACTION, SIR. ONLY THREE LEFT... CORRECTION, TWO.
I'VE GOT THEM. THE BERTINELLIS?
SCATTERED AMONG THE SCRAP METAL. AND QUITE WELL ARMED. IT SEEMS THEY SUCCESSFULLY RAIDED THE ZUCCOS' ARMORY BEFORE THEIR MEN ARRIVED.
SIR, THERE ARE ALSO GOTHAM CITY POLICE OFFICERS PINNED DOWN NEARBY... AT RISK OF BEING HIT BY STRAY GUNFIRE.
UNDERSTOOD. I'LL HANDLE IT.
THANKS FOR TAKING OUT THE ZUCCOS, BATMAN.
BRATTATTA

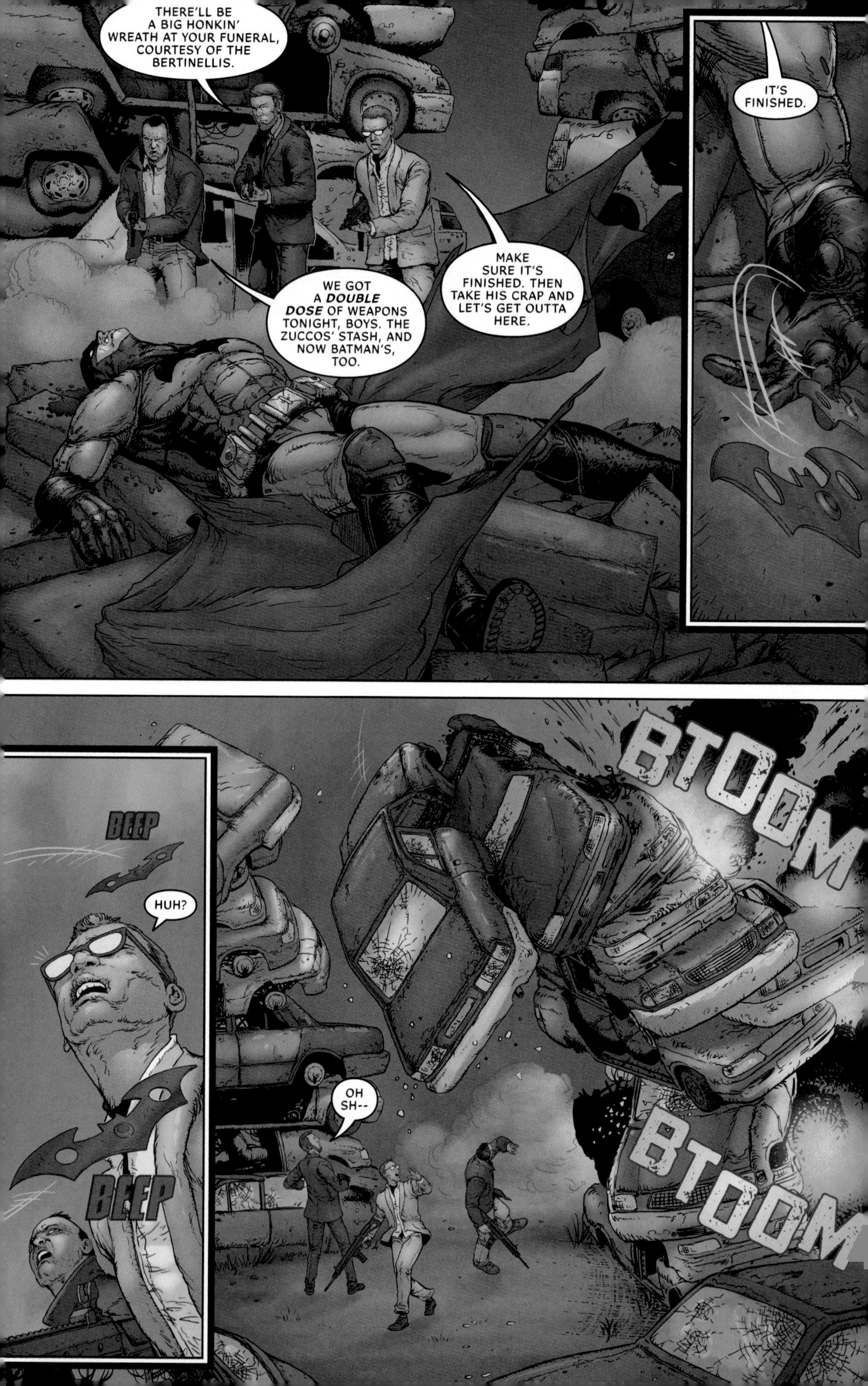

THERE'LL BE A BIG HONKIN' WREATH AT YOUR FUNERAL, COURTESY OF THE BERTINELLIS.
WE GOT A ***DOUBLE DOSE*** OF WEAPONS TONIGHT, BOYS. THE ZUCCOS' STASH, AND NOW BATMAN'S, TOO.
MAKE SURE IT'S FINISHED. THEN TAKE HIS CRAP AND LET'S GET OUTTA HERE.
IT'S FINISHED.
BEEP
HUH?
BEEP
OH SH--
BTOOM
BTOOM

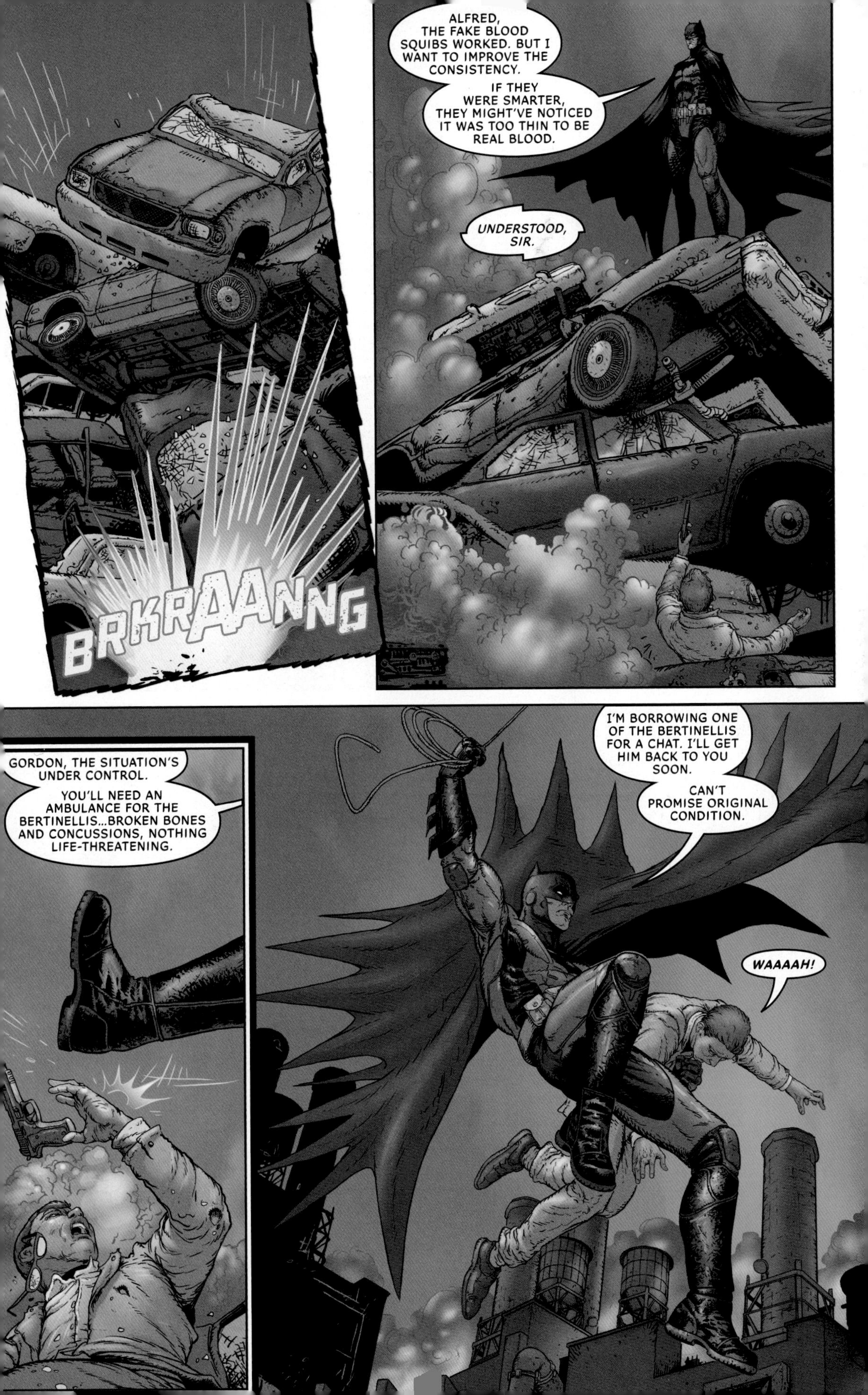
BRKRAANNG
ALFRED, THE FAKE BLOOD SQUIBS WORKED. BUT I WANT TO IMPROVE THE CONSISTENCY.
IF THEY WERE SMARTER, THEY MIGHT'VE NOTICED IT WAS TOO THIN TO BE REAL BLOOD.
UNDERSTOOD, SIR.
GORDON, THE SITUATION'S UNDER CONTROL.
YOU'LL NEED AN AMBULANCE FOR THE BERTINELLIS...BROKEN BONES AND CONCUSSIONS, NOTHING LIFE-THREATENING.
I'M BORROWING ONE OF THE BERTINELLIS FOR A CHAT. I'LL GET HIM BACK TO YOU SOON.
CAN'T PROMISE ORIGINAL CONDITION.
WAAAAH!

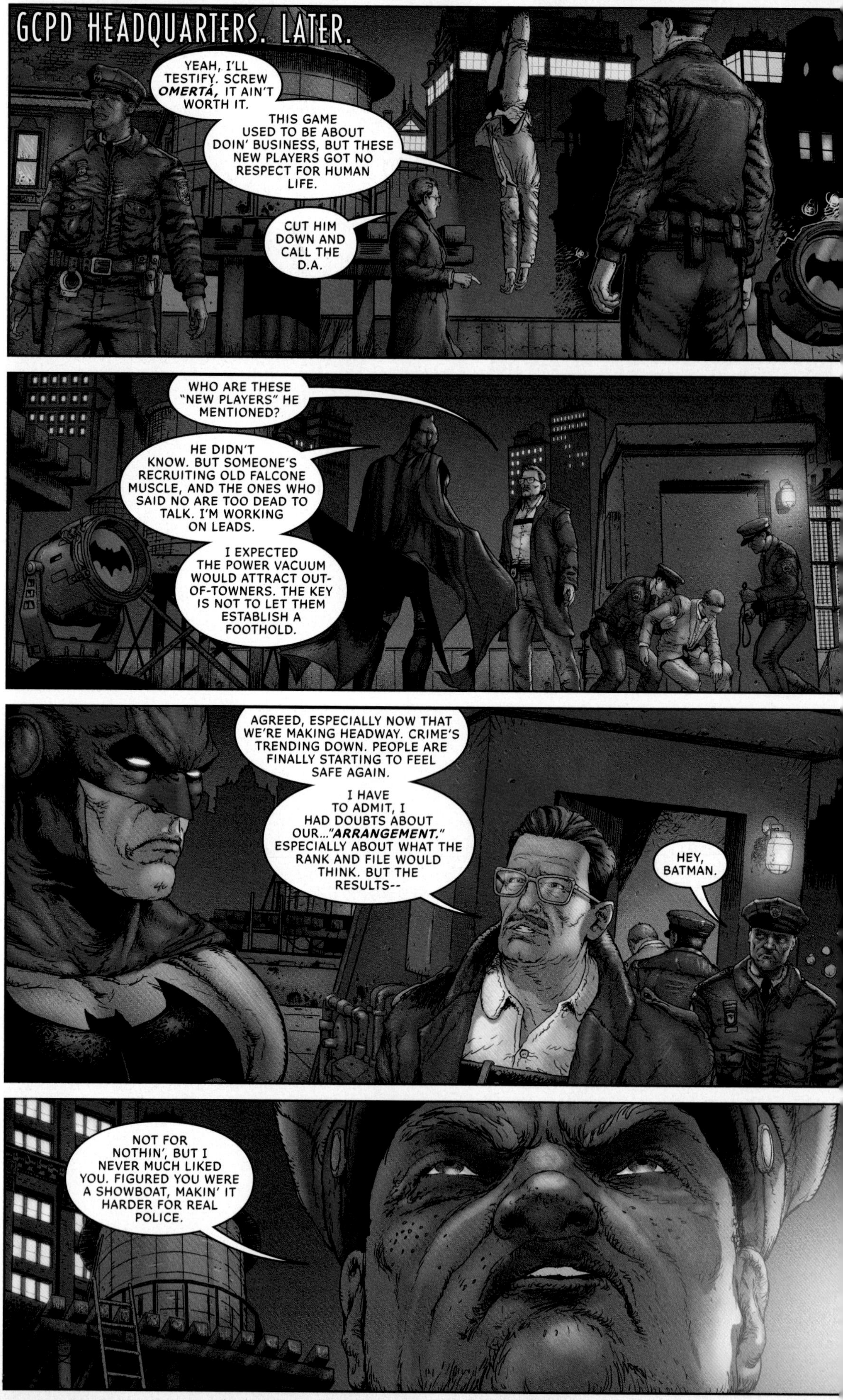
GCPD HEADQUARTERS. LATER.
YEAH, I'LL TESTIFY. SCREW OMERTÀ, IT AIN'T WORTH IT.
THIS GAME USED TO BE ABOUT DOIN' BUSINESS, BUT THESE NEW PLAYERS GOT NO RESPECT FOR HUMAN LIFE.
CUT HIM DOWN AND CALL THE D.A.
WHO ARE THESE "NEW PLAYERS" HE MENTIONED?
HE DIDN'T KNOW. BUT SOMEONE'S RECRUITING OLD FALCONE MUSCLE, AND THE ONES WHO SAID NO ARE TOO DEAD TO TALK. I'M WORKING ON LEADS.
I EXPECTED THE POWER VACUUM WOULD ATTRACT OUT-OF-TOWNERS. THE KEY IS NOT TO LET THEM ESTABLISH A FOOTHOLD.
AGREED, ESPECIALLY NOW THAT WE'RE MAKING HEADWAY. CRIME'S TRENDING DOWN. PEOPLE ARE FINALLY STARTING TO FEEL SAFE AGAIN.
I HAVE TO ADMIT, I HAD DOUBTS ABOUT OUR..."ARRANGEMENT." ESPECIALLY ABOUT WHAT THE RANK AND FILE WOULD THINK. BUT THE RESULTS--
HEY, BATMAN.
NOT FOR NOTHIN', BUT I NEVER MUCH LIKED YOU. FIGURED YOU WERE A SHOWBOAT, MAKIN' IT HARDER FOR REAL POLICE.

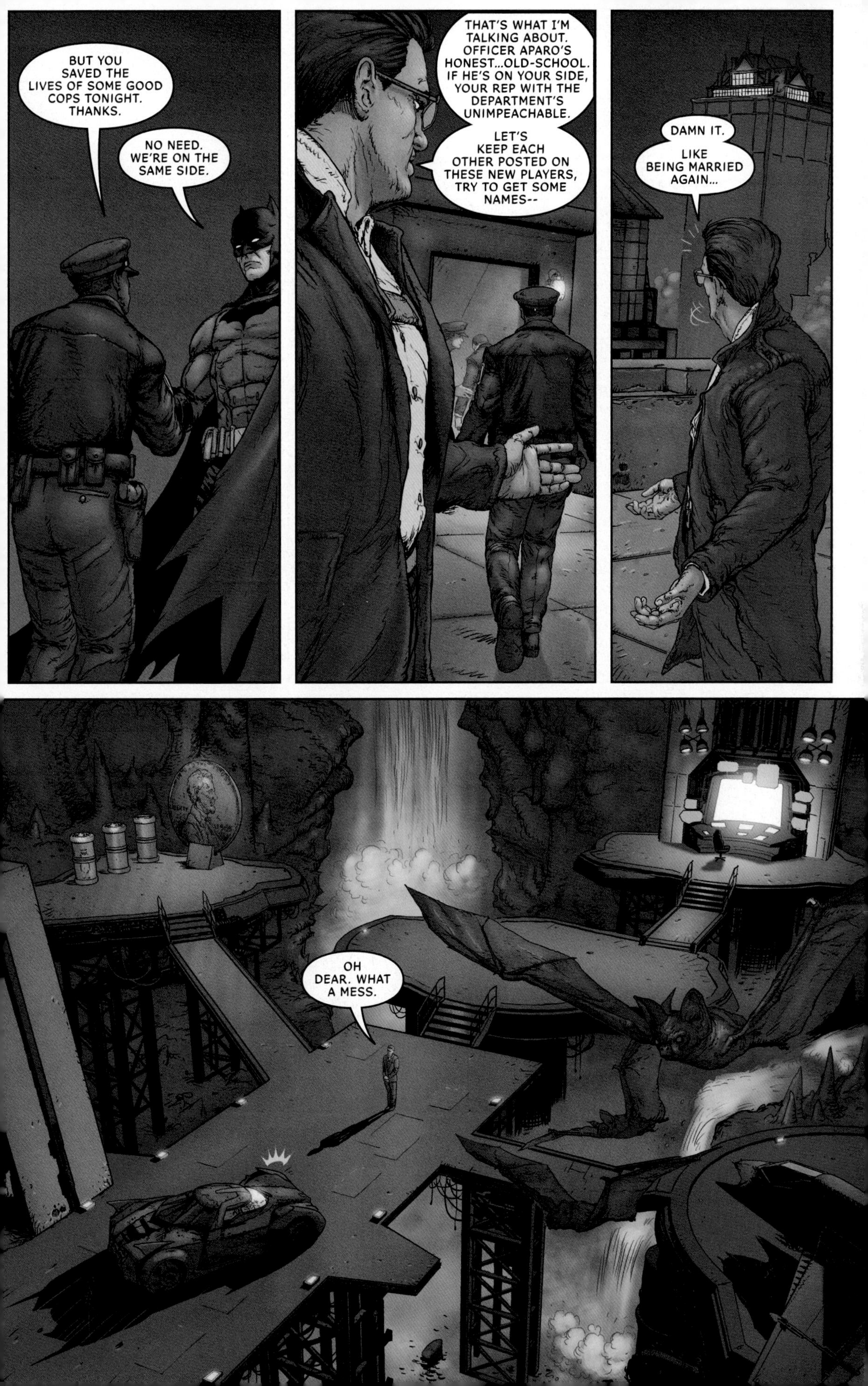
BUT YOU SAVED THE LIVES OF SOME GOOD COPS TONIGHT. THANKS.
NO NEED. WE'RE ON THE SAME SIDE.
THAT'S WHAT I'M TALKING ABOUT. OFFICER APARO'S HONEST...OLD-SCHOOL. IF HE'S ON YOUR SIDE, YOUR REP WITH THE DEPARTMENT'S UNIMPEACHABLE.
LET'S KEEP EACH OTHER POSTED ON THESE NEW PLAYERS, TRY TO GET SOME NAMES--
DAMN IT.
LIKE BEING MARRIED AGAIN...
OH DEAR. WHAT A MESS.

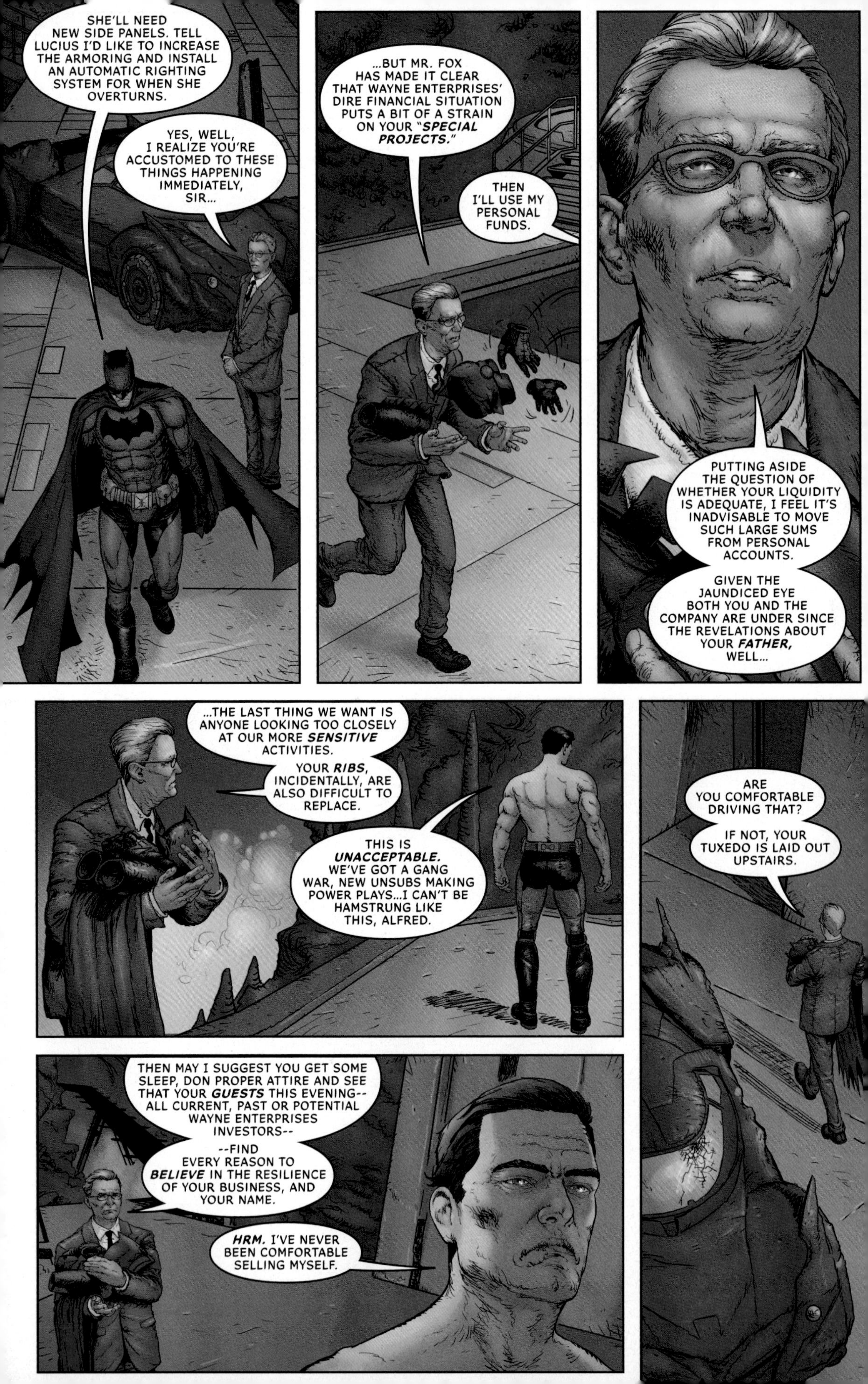
SHE'LL NEED NEW SIDE PANELS. TELL LUCIUS I'D LIKE TO INCREASE THE ARMORING AND INSTALL AN AUTOMATIC RIGHTING SYSTEM FOR WHEN SHE OVERTURNS.
YES, WELL, I REALIZE YOU'RE ACCUSTOMED TO THESE THINGS HAPPENING IMMEDIATELY, SIR...
...BUT MR. FOX HAS MADE IT CLEAR THAT WAYNE ENTERPRISES' DIRE FINANCIAL SITUATION PUTS A BIT OF A STRAIN ON YOUR "*SPECIAL PROJECTS.*"
THEN I'LL USE MY PERSONAL FUNDS.
PUTTING ASIDE THE QUESTION OF WHETHER YOUR LIQUIDITY IS ADEQUATE, I FEEL IT'S INADVISABLE TO MOVE SUCH LARGE SUMS FROM PERSONAL ACCOUNTS.
GIVEN THE JAUNDICED EYE BOTH YOU AND THE COMPANY ARE UNDER SINCE THE REVELATIONS ABOUT YOUR *FATHER,* WELL...
...THE LAST THING WE WANT IS ANYONE LOOKING TOO CLOSELY AT OUR MORE *SENSITIVE* ACTIVITIES.
YOUR *RIBS,* INCIDENTALLY, ARE ALSO DIFFICULT TO REPLACE.
THIS IS *UNACCEPTABLE.* WE'VE GOT A GANG WAR, NEW UNSUBS MAKING POWER PLAYS...I CAN'T BE HAMSTRUNG LIKE THIS, ALFRED.
THEN MAY I SUGGEST YOU GET SOME SLEEP, DON PROPER ATTIRE AND SEE THAT YOUR *GUESTS* THIS EVENING-- ALL CURRENT, PAST OR POTENTIAL WAYNE ENTERPRISES INVESTORS--
--FIND EVERY REASON TO *BELIEVE* IN THE RESILIENCE OF YOUR BUSINESS, AND YOUR NAME.
HRM. I'VE NEVER BEEN COMFORTABLE SELLING MYSELF.
ARE YOU COMFORTABLE DRIVING THAT?
IF NOT, YOUR TUXEDO IS LAID OUT UPSTAIRS.

BRUCE, THIS EVENT COULD VERY WELL DETERMINE WHETHER *WAYNE ENTERPRISES* LIVES OR DIES...

...SO TRY TO LOOK A BIT LESS LIKE YOU'RE BEING *TORTURED.*

SORRY, REGINA. I KEEP REMEMBERING THE LAST TIME I HAD A PARTY HERE...FOR *HARVEY DENT'S* MAYORAL CAMPAIGN.

THAT'S WHEN EVERYTHING STARTED TO GO TO HELL. WHEN I FOUND OUT MY FATHER WAS...NOT THE MAN I THOUGHT.

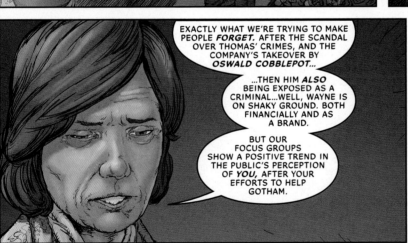

EXACTLY WHAT WE'RE TRYING TO MAKE PEOPLE *FORGET.* AFTER THE SCANDAL OVER THOMAS' CRIMES, AND THE COMPANY'S TAKEOVER BY *OSWALD COBBLEPOT...*

...THEN HIM *ALSO* BEING EXPOSED AS A CRIMINAL...WELL, WAYNE IS ON SHAKY GROUND. BOTH FINANCIALLY AND AS A BRAND.

BUT OUR FOCUS GROUPS SHOW A POSITIVE TREND IN THE PUBLIC'S PERCEPTION OF *YOU,* AFTER YOUR EFFORTS TO HELP GOTHAM.

WELL...NO. I'M NOT ABOVE THAT.

GOOD. SO SMILE. MINGLE. WHO KNOWS, YOU MIGHT EVEN HAVE *FUN.*

OH MY GOD, *BRUCE WAYNE?* I HAVE BEEN ABSOLUTELY *DYING* TO MEET YOU.

WHICH, LIKE IT OR NOT, MAKES YOU OUR SHOW PONY. I NEED YOU TO CONVINCE OUR INVESTORS, BUSINESS PARTNERS AND THE PRESS THAT WAYNE ENTERPRISES IS *STRONGER THAN EVER.*

IN OTHER WORDS, LIE.

COME NOW, BRUCE. DON'T TELL ME YOU'RE ABOVE DECEIVING PEOPLE FOR A GREATER GOOD.

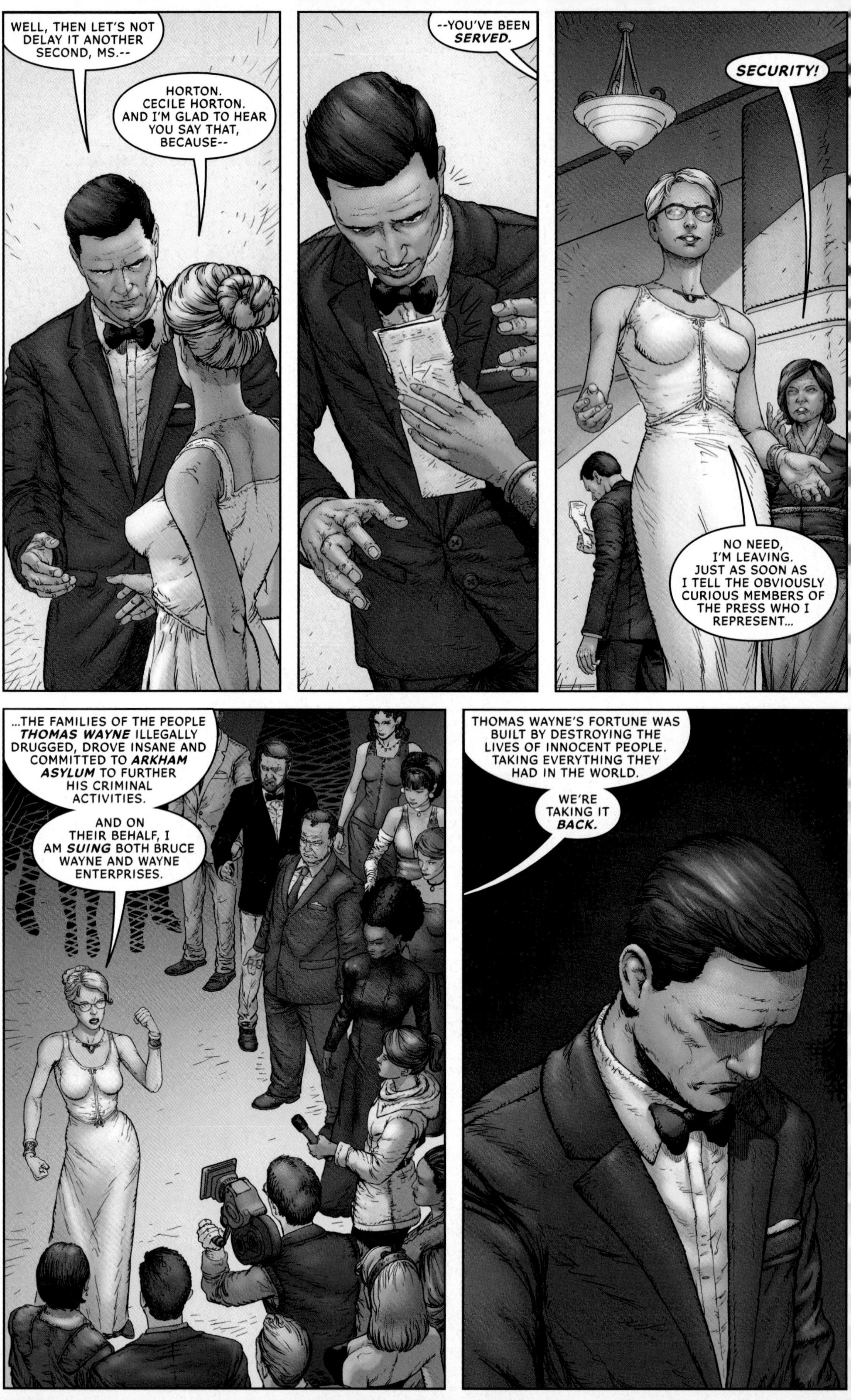
WELL, THEN LET'S NOT DELAY IT ANOTHER SECOND, MS.--
HORTON. CECILE HORTON. AND I'M GLAD TO HEAR YOU SAY THAT, BECAUSE--
--YOU'VE BEEN *SERVED.*
SECURITY!
NO NEED, I'M LEAVING. JUST AS SOON AS I TELL THE OBVIOUSLY CURIOUS MEMBERS OF THE PRESS WHO I REPRESENT...
...THE FAMILIES OF THE PEOPLE *THOMAS WAYNE* ILLEGALLY DRUGGED, DROVE INSANE AND COMMITTED TO *ARKHAM ASYLUM* TO FURTHER HIS CRIMINAL ACTIVITIES.
AND ON THEIR BEHALF, I AM *SUING* BOTH BRUCE WAYNE AND WAYNE ENTERPRISES.
THOMAS WAYNE'S FORTUNE WAS BUILT BY DESTROYING THE LIVES OF INNOCENT PEOPLE. TAKING EVERYTHING THEY HAD IN THE WORLD.
WE'RE TAKING IT *BACK.*

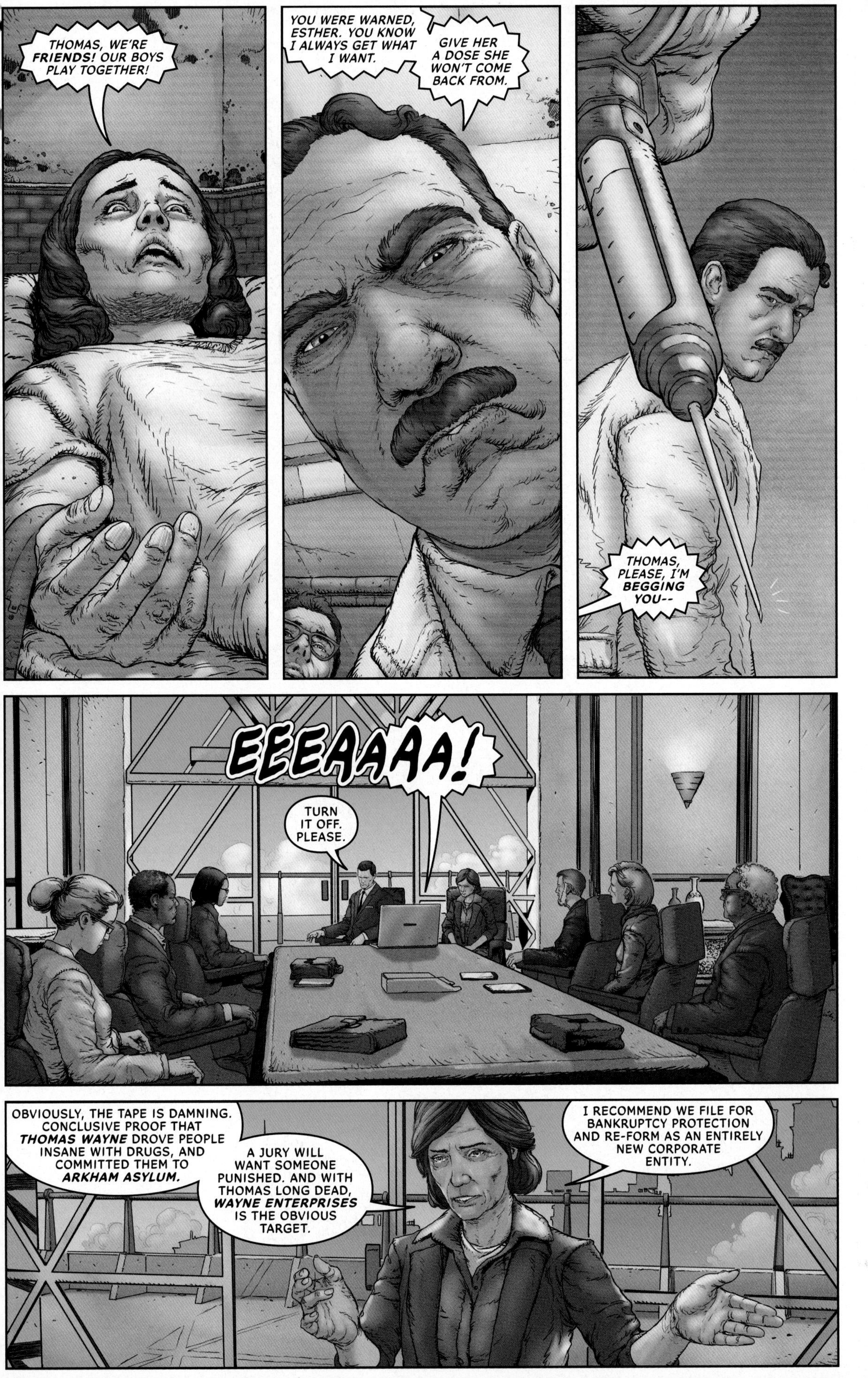
THOMAS, WE'RE FRIENDS! OUR BOYS PLAY TOGETHER!
YOU WERE WARNED, ESTHER. YOU KNOW I ALWAYS GET WHAT I WANT.
GIVE HER A DOSE SHE WON'T COME BACK FROM.
THOMAS, PLEASE, I'M BEGGING YOU--
EEEAAAA!
TURN IT OFF. PLEASE.
OBVIOUSLY, THE TAPE IS DAMNING. CONCLUSIVE PROOF THAT THOMAS WAYNE DROVE PEOPLE INSANE WITH DRUGS, AND COMMITTED THEM TO ARKHAM ASYLUM.
A JURY WILL WANT SOMEONE PUNISHED. AND WITH THOMAS LONG DEAD, WAYNE ENTERPRISES IS THE OBVIOUS TARGET.
I RECOMMEND WE FILE FOR BANKRUPTCY PROTECTION AND RE-FORM AS AN ENTIRELY NEW CORPORATE ENTITY.

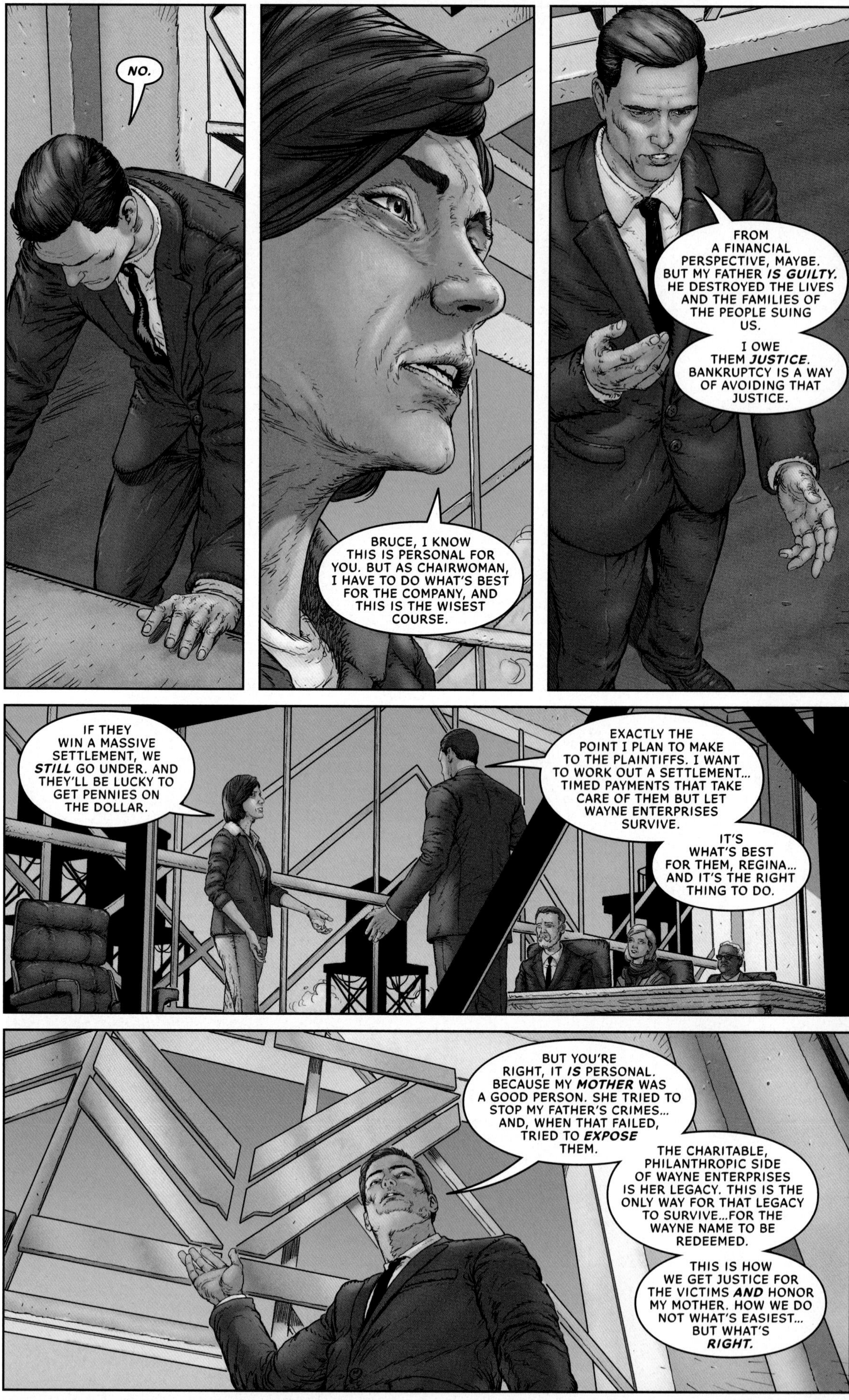
NO.
BRUCE, I KNOW THIS IS PERSONAL FOR YOU. BUT AS CHAIRWOMAN, I HAVE TO DO WHAT'S BEST FOR THE COMPANY, AND THIS IS THE WISEST COURSE.
FROM A FINANCIAL PERSPECTIVE, MAYBE. BUT MY FATHER *IS GUILTY.* HE DESTROYED THE LIVES AND THE FAMILIES OF THE PEOPLE SUING US.
I OWE THEM *JUSTICE*. BANKRUPTCY IS A WAY OF AVOIDING THAT JUSTICE.
IF THEY WIN A MASSIVE SETTLEMENT, WE *STILL* GO UNDER. AND THEY'LL BE LUCKY TO GET PENNIES ON THE DOLLAR.
EXACTLY THE POINT I PLAN TO MAKE TO THE PLAINTIFFS. I WANT TO WORK OUT A SETTLEMENT... TIMED PAYMENTS THAT TAKE CARE OF THEM BUT LET WAYNE ENTERPRISES SURVIVE.
IT'S WHAT'S BEST FOR THEM, REGINA... AND IT'S THE RIGHT THING TO DO.
BUT YOU'RE RIGHT, IT *IS* PERSONAL. BECAUSE MY *MOTHER* WAS A GOOD PERSON. SHE TRIED TO STOP MY FATHER'S CRIMES... AND, WHEN THAT FAILED, TRIED TO *EXPOSE* THEM.
THE CHARITABLE, PHILANTHROPIC SIDE OF WAYNE ENTERPRISES IS HER LEGACY. THIS IS THE ONLY WAY FOR THAT LEGACY TO SURVIVE...FOR THE WAYNE NAME TO BE REDEEMED.
THIS IS HOW WE GET JUSTICE FOR THE VICTIMS *AND* HONOR MY MOTHER. HOW WE DO NOT WHAT'S EASIEST... BUT WHAT'S *RIGHT.*

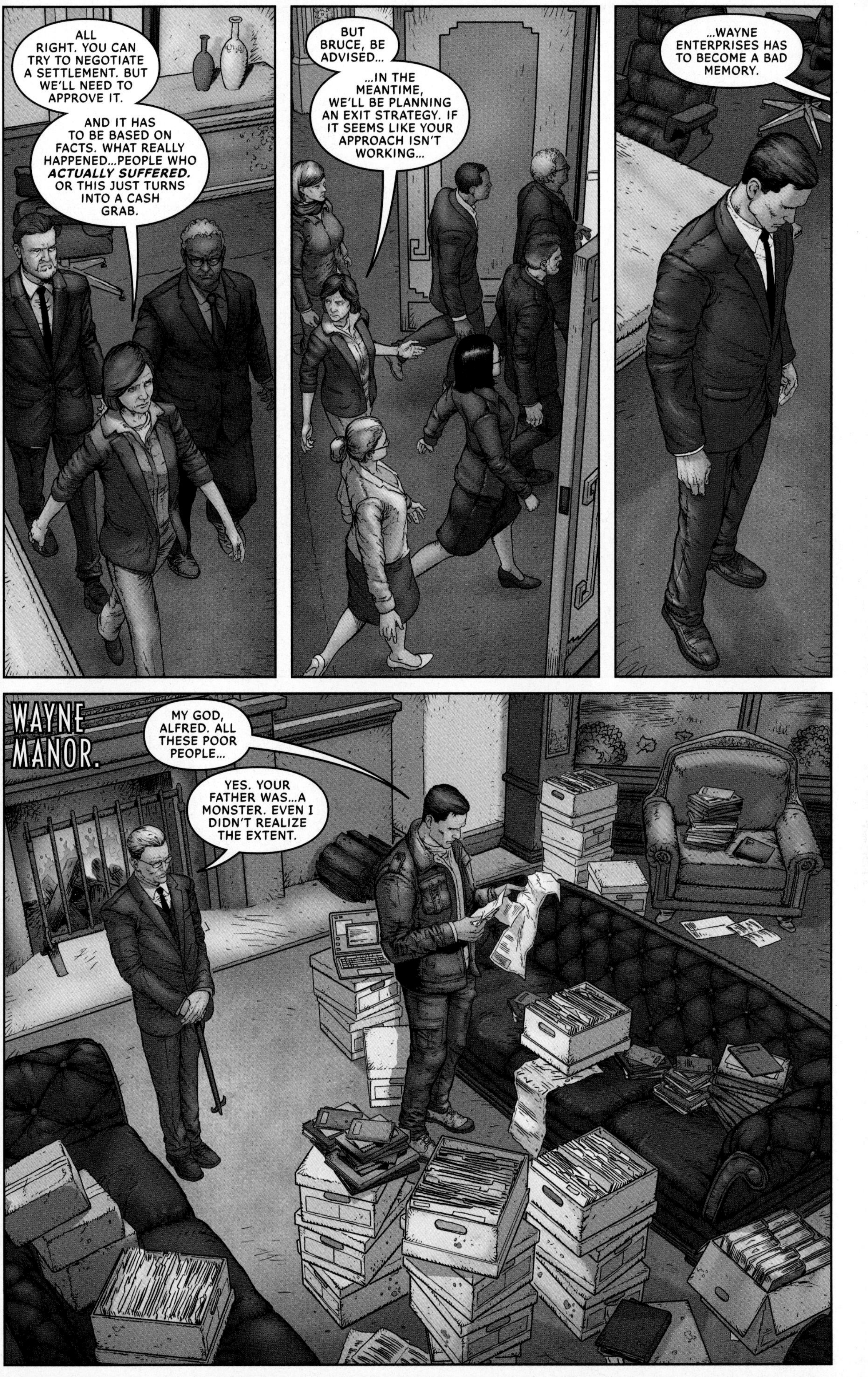
ALL RIGHT. YOU CAN TRY TO NEGOTIATE A SETTLEMENT. BUT WE'LL NEED TO APPROVE IT.
AND IT HAS TO BE BASED ON FACTS. WHAT REALLY HAPPENED...PEOPLE WHO ***ACTUALLY SUFFERED.*** OR THIS JUST TURNS INTO A CASH GRAB.
BUT BRUCE, BE ADVISED...
...IN THE MEANTIME, WE'LL BE PLANNING AN EXIT STRATEGY. IF IT SEEMS LIKE YOUR APPROACH ISN'T WORKING...
...WAYNE ENTERPRISES HAS TO BECOME A BAD MEMORY.
WAYNE MANOR.
MY GOD, ALFRED. ALL THESE POOR PEOPLE...
YES. YOUR FATHER WAS...A MONSTER. EVEN I DIDN'T REALIZE THE EXTENT.

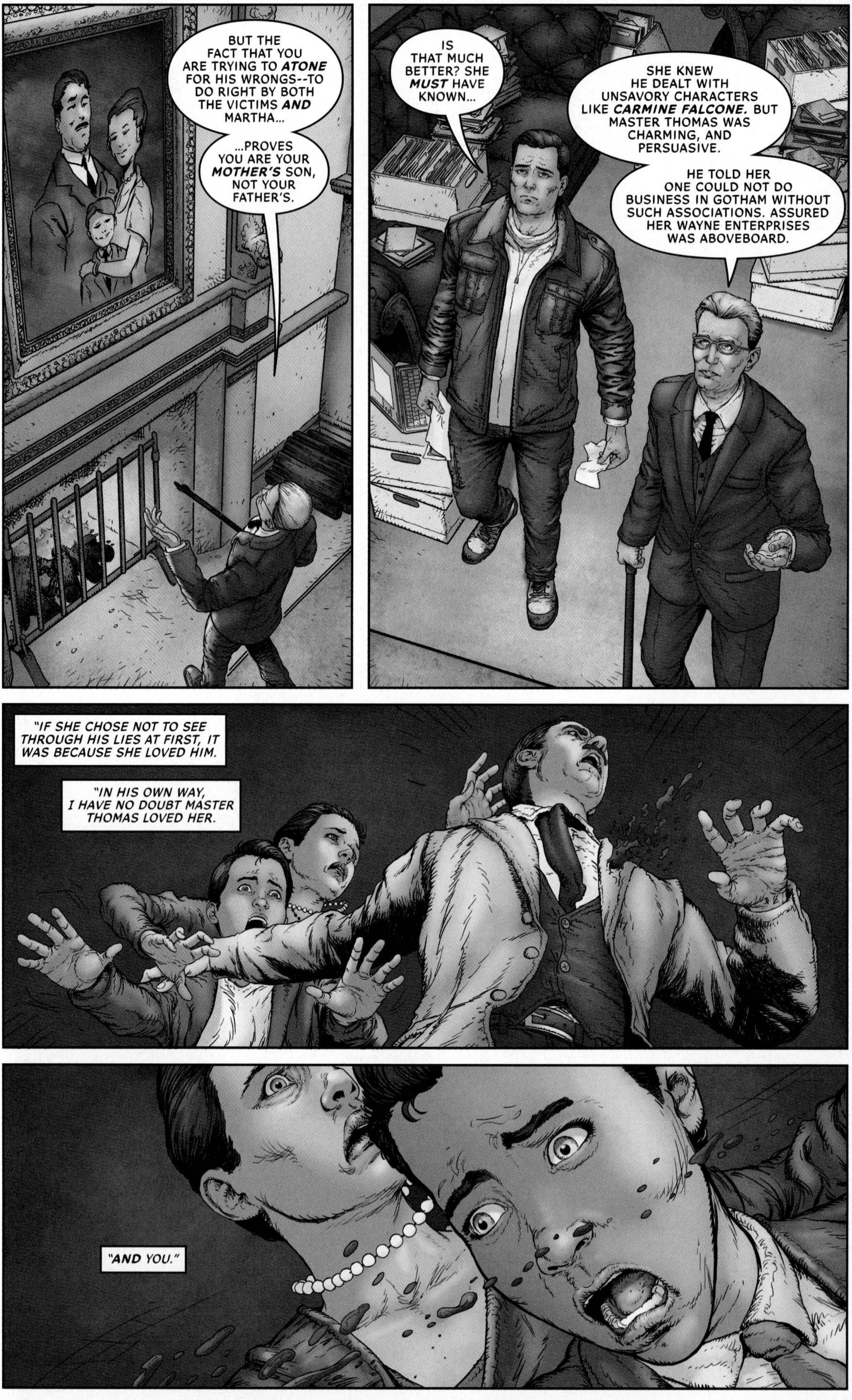

BUT THE FACT THAT YOU ARE TRYING TO ATONE FOR HIS WRONGS--TO DO RIGHT BY BOTH THE VICTIMS AND MARTHA...
...PROVES YOU ARE YOUR MOTHER'S SON, NOT YOUR FATHER'S.
IS THAT MUCH BETTER? SHE MUST HAVE KNOWN...
SHE KNEW HE DEALT WITH UNSAVORY CHARACTERS LIKE CARMINE FALCONE. BUT MASTER THOMAS WAS CHARMING, AND PERSUASIVE.
HE TOLD HER ONE COULD NOT DO BUSINESS IN GOTHAM WITHOUT SUCH ASSOCIATIONS. ASSURED HER WAYNE ENTERPRISES WAS ABOVEBOARD.
"IF SHE CHOSE NOT TO SEE THROUGH HIS LIES AT FIRST, IT WAS BECAUSE SHE LOVED HIM.
"IN HIS OWN WAY, I HAVE NO DOUBT MASTER THOMAS LOVED HER.
"AND YOU."

I'M SURE THE PEOPLE HE TOOK AWAY FROM THEIR FAMILIES LOVED THEM, TOO.

I'VE BEEN A COWARD, ALFRED. AVOIDED DELVING INTO THE FULL DETAILS OF WHAT MY FATHER DID BECAUSE IT WAS TOO PAINFUL. *NO MORE.*

I COMPILED A LIST OF PEOPLE WHO WORKED AT ARKHAM BACK THEN. I WANT YOU TO ASK THEM TO MEET ME AT WAYNE TOWER.

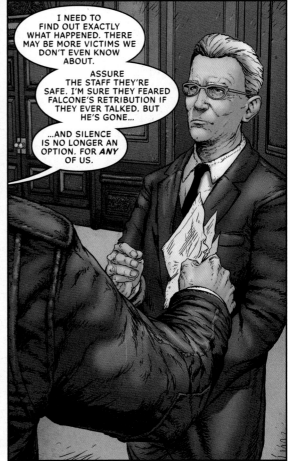

I NEED TO FIND OUT EXACTLY WHAT HAPPENED. THERE MAY BE MORE VICTIMS WE DON'T EVEN KNOW ABOUT.

ASSURE THE STAFF THEY'RE SAFE. I'M SURE THEY FEARED FALCONE'S RETRIBUTION IF THEY EVER TALKED. BUT HE'S GONE...

...AND SILENCE IS NO LONGER AN OPTION. FOR *ANY* OF US.

YOU'RE NOT IN TROUBLE. ANY ABETTING OF CRIMES WAS DONE UNDER DURESS...

...YOU KNEW WHAT MY FATHER AND FALCONE WOULD DO TO YOU IF YOU DISOBEYED. BUT THEY'RE DEAD.

AS FOR THE POLICE, THE STATUTE OF LIMITATIONS HAS PASSED.

NO ONE WANTS TO HURT YOU. I JUST NEED TO KNOW THE TRUTH...SO I CAN START TO *ATONE* FOR MY FATHER'S SINS.

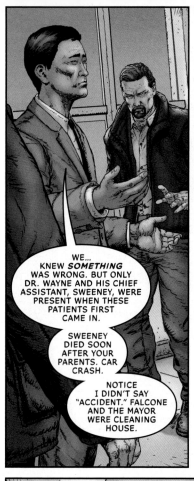

WE... KNEW *SOMETHING* WAS WRONG. BUT ONLY DR. WAYNE AND HIS CHIEF ASSISTANT, SWEENEY, WERE PRESENT WHEN THESE PATIENTS FIRST CAME IN.

SWEENEY DIED SOON AFTER YOUR PARENTS. CAR CRASH.

NOTICE I DIDN'T SAY "ACCIDENT." FALCONE AND THE MAYOR WERE CLEANING HOUSE.

SHUT UP, BEN. THIS IS A *TRAP.* HE'S TRYING TO GET US TO INCRIMINATE OURSELVES, SO HE AND HIS ONE PERCENT BUDDIES CAN PIN IT ALL ON US!

I SWEAR TO YOU, THAT'S NOT--

KRESSH

DOWN!!

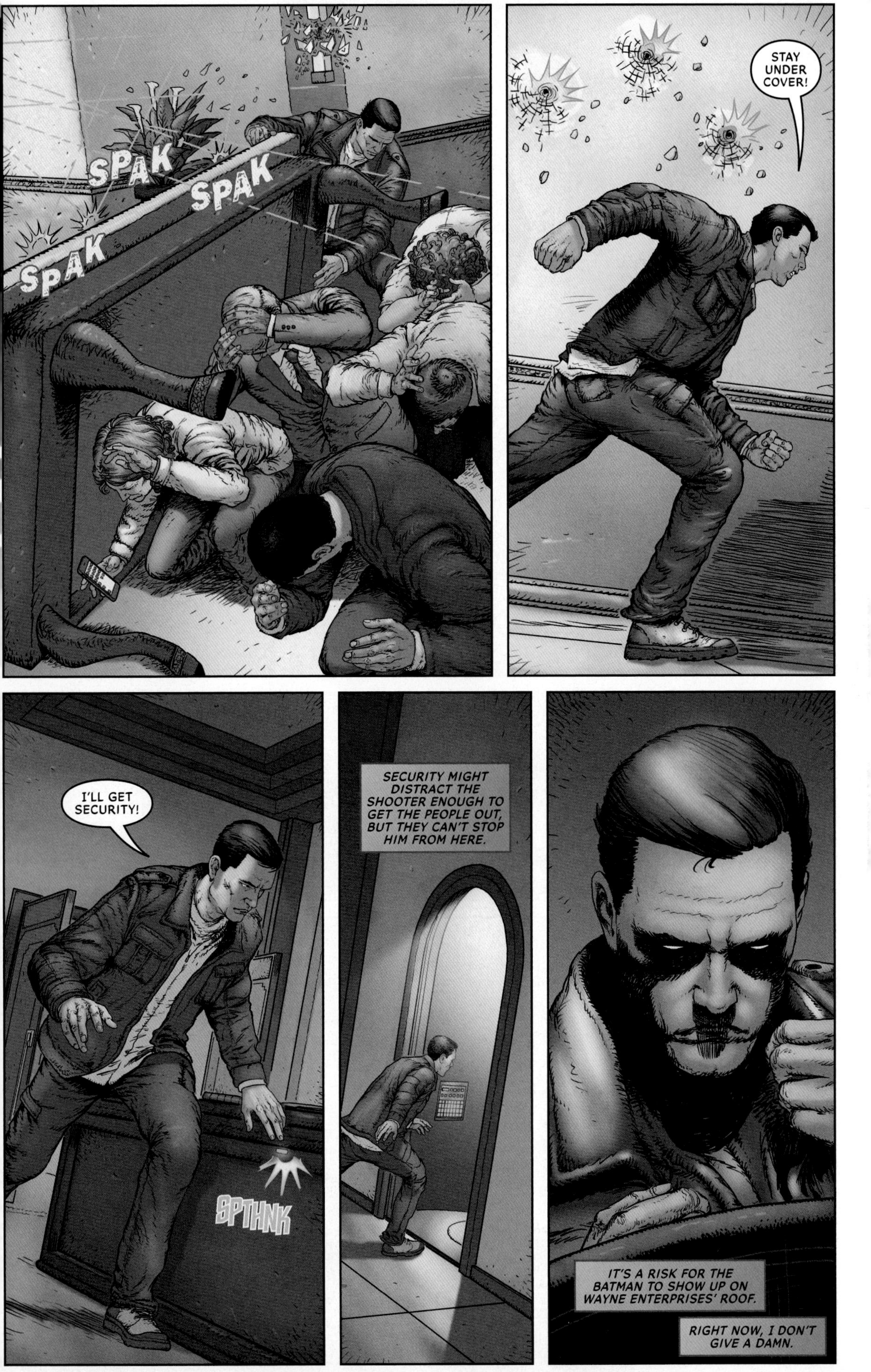
SPAK
SPAK
SPAK
STAY UNDER COVER!
I'LL GET SECURITY!
SPTHNK
SECURITY MIGHT DISTRACT THE SHOOTER ENOUGH TO GET THE PEOPLE OUT, BUT THEY CAN'T STOP HIM FROM HERE.
IT'S A RISK FOR THE BATMAN TO SHOW UP ON WAYNE ENTERPRISES' ROOF.
RIGHT NOW, I DON'T GIVE A DAMN.

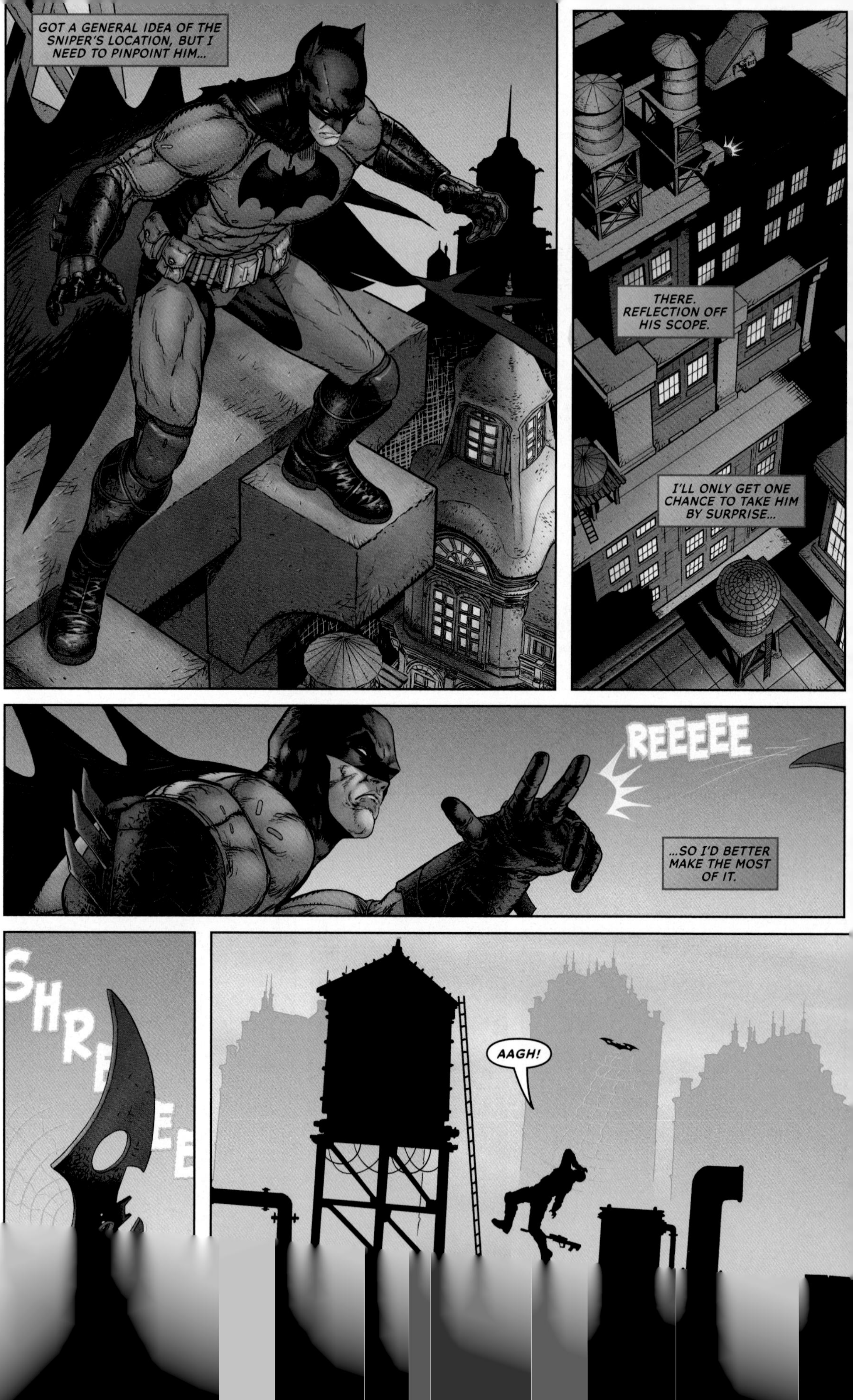
GOT A GENERAL IDEA OF THE SNIPER'S LOCATION, BUT I NEED TO PINPOINT HIM...
THERE. REFLECTION OFF HIS SCOPE.
I'LL ONLY GET ONE CHANCE TO TAKE HIM BY SURPRISE...
REEEEE
...SO I'D BETTER MAKE THE MOST OF IT.
SHREEEE
AAGH!

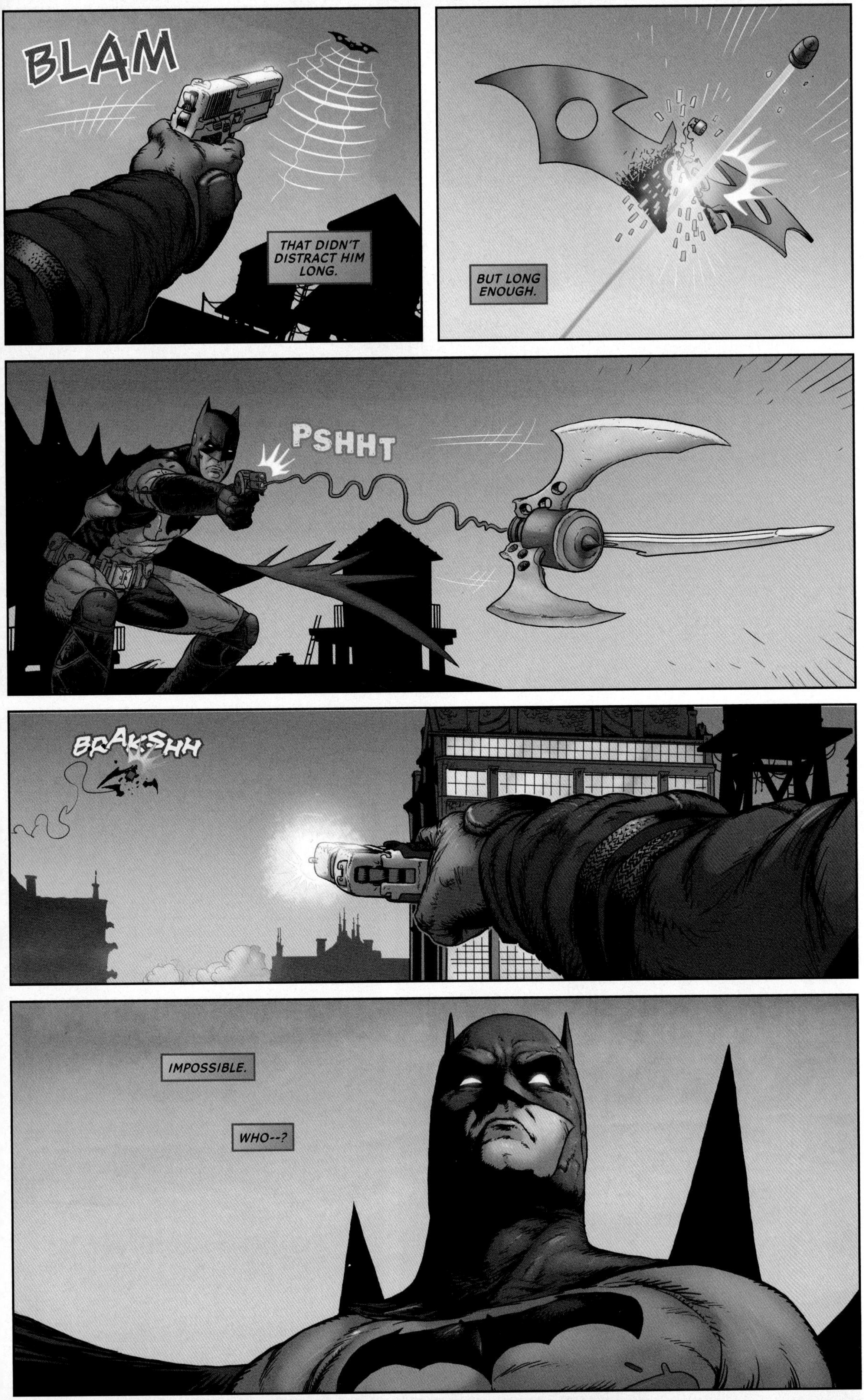
BLAM
THAT DIDN'T DISTRACT HIM LONG.
BUT LONG ENOUGH.
PSHHT
BRAKSHH
IMPOSSIBLE.
WHO--?

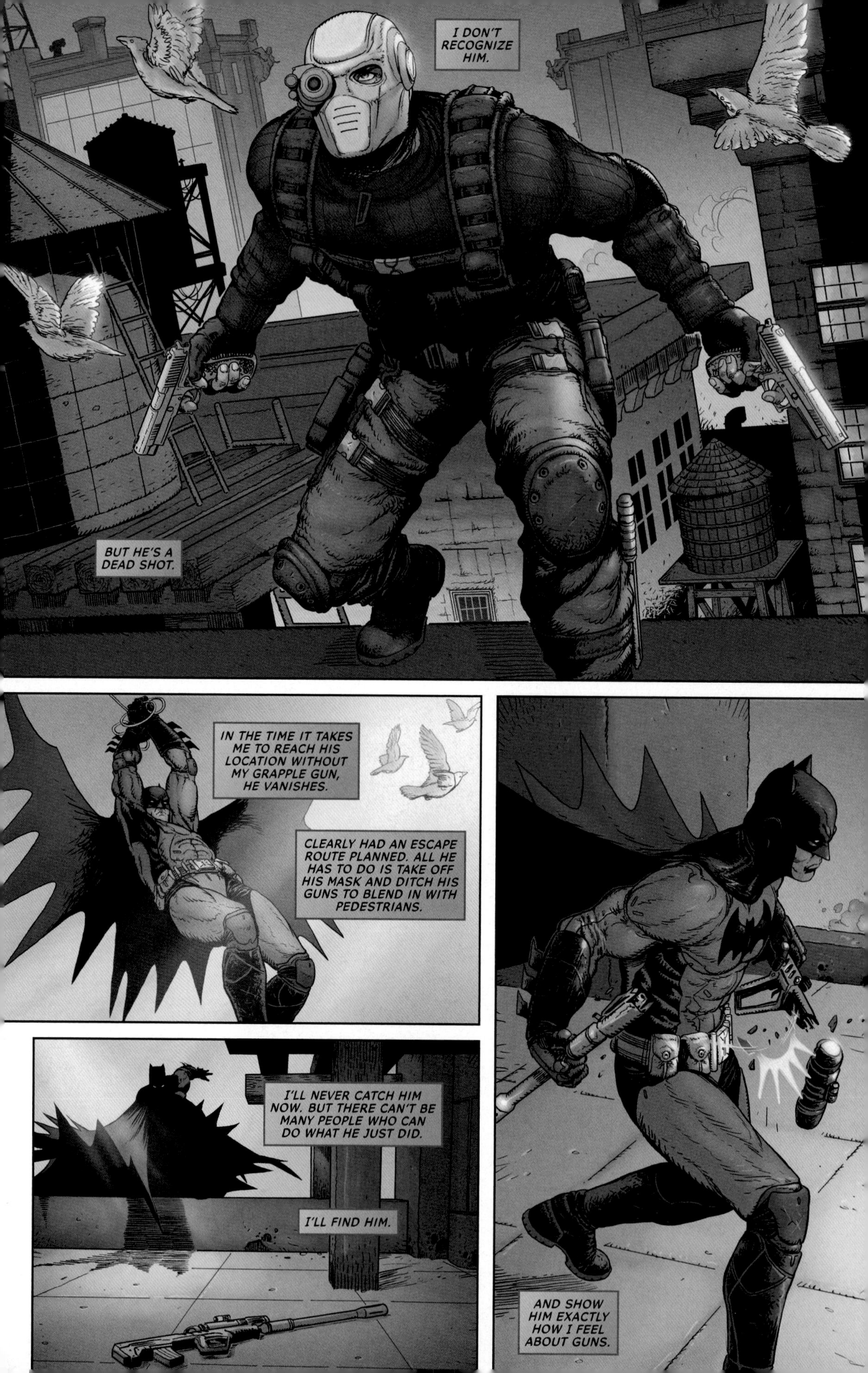
I DON'T RECOGNIZE HIM.
BUT HE'S A DEAD SHOT.
IN THE TIME IT TAKES ME TO REACH HIS LOCATION WITHOUT MY GRAPPLE GUN, HE VANISHES.
CLEARLY HAD AN ESCAPE ROUTE PLANNED. ALL HE HAS TO DO IS TAKE OFF HIS MASK AND DITCH HIS GUNS TO BLEND IN WITH PEDESTRIANS.
I'LL NEVER CATCH HIM NOW. BUT THERE CAN'T BE MANY PEOPLE WHO CAN DO WHAT HE JUST DID.
I'LL FIND HIM.
AND SHOW HIM EXACTLY HOW I FEEL ABOUT GUNS.

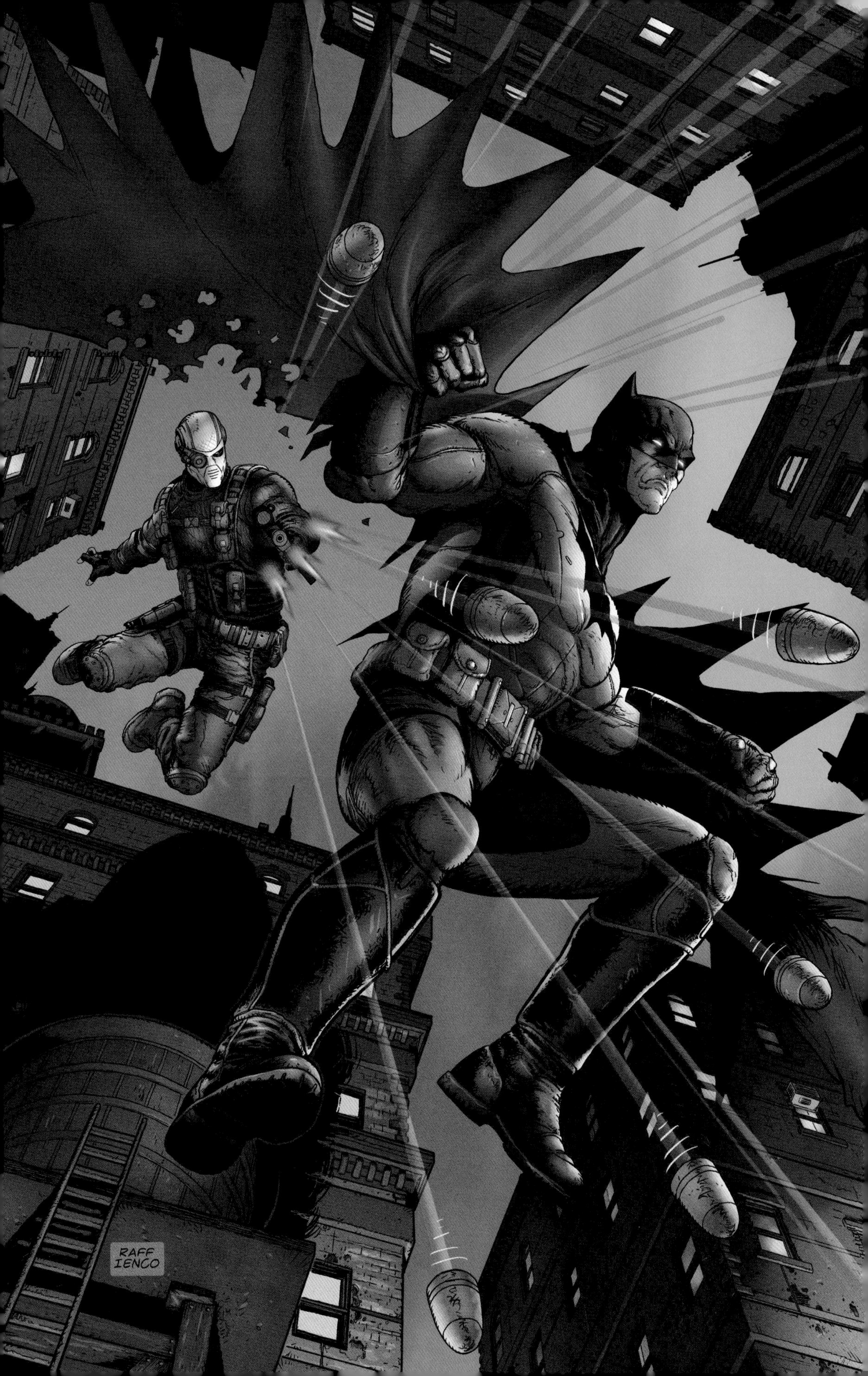
RAFF
IENCO

A SECURITY CAMERA CAUGHT THIS IMAGE OF THE SHOOTER. DOESN'T GIVE US MUCH TO GO ON.

HE'S OBVIOUSLY HIGHLY SKILLED. WELL EQUIPPED. MAYBE EX-MILITARY, POSSIBLY A PROFESSIONAL ASSASSIN.

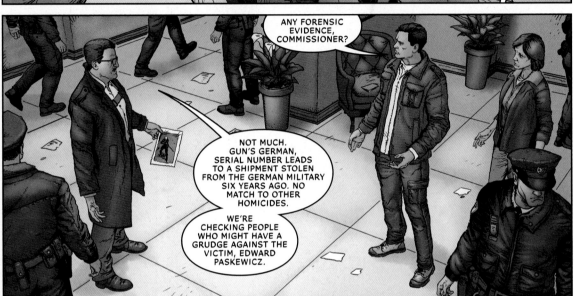

ANY FORENSIC EVIDENCE, COMMISSIONER?

NOT MUCH. GUN'S GERMAN, SERIAL NUMBER LEADS TO A SHIPMENT STOLEN FROM THE GERMAN MILITARY SIX YEARS AGO. NO MATCH TO OTHER HOMICIDES.

WE'RE CHECKING PEOPLE WHO MIGHT HAVE A GRUDGE AGAINST THE VICTIM, EDWARD PASKEWICZ.

HE WAS HEAD OF SECURITY AT ARKHAM ASYLUM FOR TWENTY YEARS, SO IT'S NOT A SHORT LIST.

PASKEWICZ WASN'T THE ONLY TARGET. THE SHOOTER FIRED AT BEN HAGIWARA NEXT, AND KEPT TRYING FOR OTHERS.

ALL FORMER ARKHAM EMPLOYEES.

I REALIZE THIS SOUNDS SELF-SERVING, BUT IF BRUCE WON'T SAY IT, I WILL.

NO ONE HAD MORE REASON TO HATE THE PEOPLE IN THAT ROOM THAN THE GROUP *SUING US.*

THOMAS WAYNE DROVE THEIR FAMILY MEMBERS INSANE AND COMMITTED THEM TO THE ASYLUM. EVERYONE IN THE SHOOTER'S LINE OF FIRE WAS ON STAFF AT THE TIME.

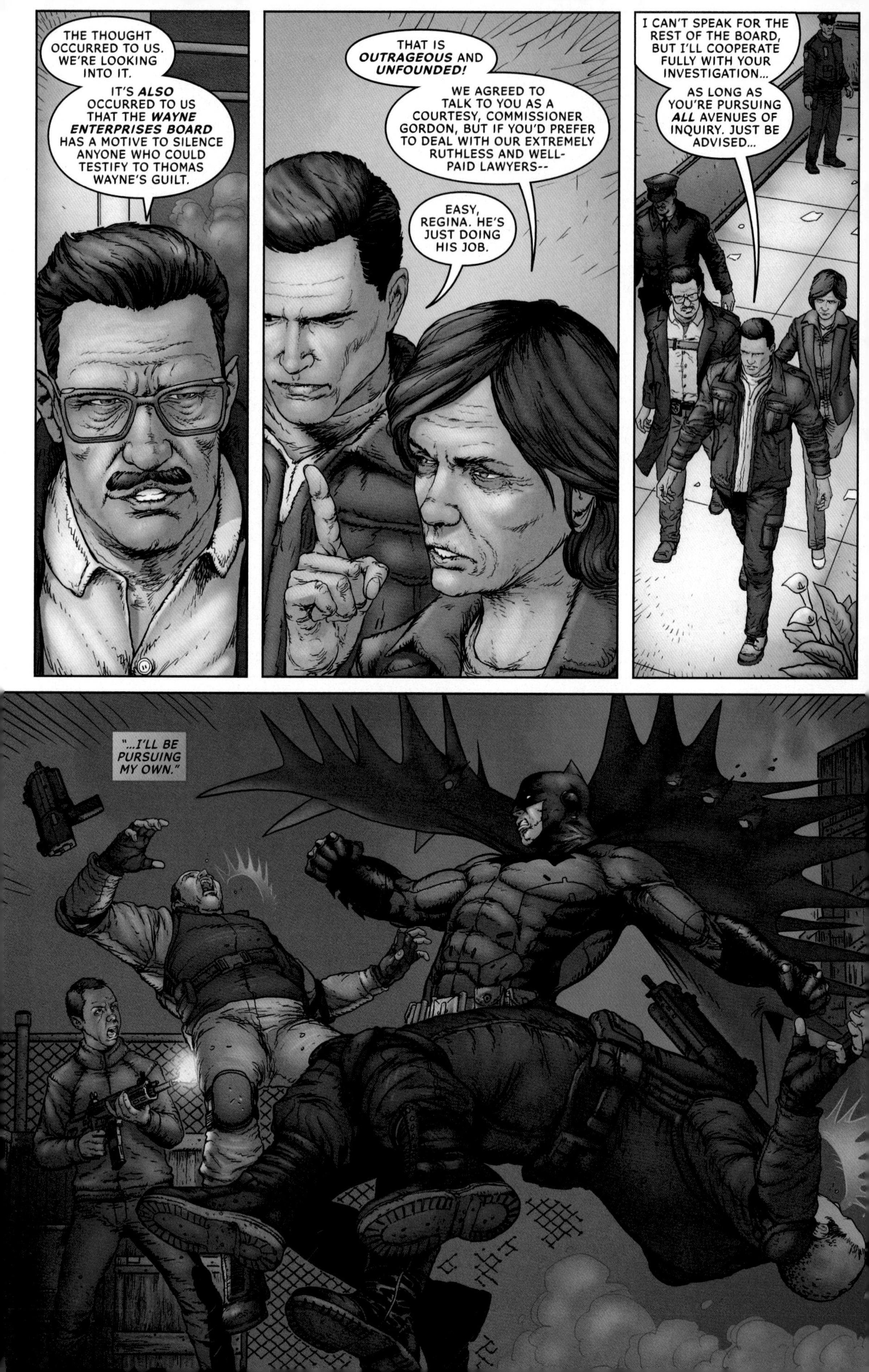
THE THOUGHT OCCURRED TO US. WE'RE LOOKING INTO IT.
IT'S *ALSO* OCCURRED TO US THAT THE ***WAYNE ENTERPRISES BOARD*** HAS A MOTIVE TO SILENCE ANYONE WHO COULD TESTIFY TO THOMAS WAYNE'S GUILT.
THAT IS ***OUTRAGEOUS*** AND ***UNFOUNDED!***
WE AGREED TO TALK TO YOU AS A COURTESY, COMMISSIONER GORDON, BUT IF YOU'D PREFER TO DEAL WITH OUR EXTREMELY RUTHLESS AND WELL-PAID LAWYERS--
EASY, REGINA. HE'S JUST DOING HIS JOB.
I CAN'T SPEAK FOR THE REST OF THE BOARD, BUT I'LL COOPERATE FULLY WITH YOUR INVESTIGATION...
AS LONG AS YOU'RE PURSUING ***ALL*** AVENUES OF INQUIRY. JUST BE ADVISED...
"...I'LL BE PURSUING MY OWN."

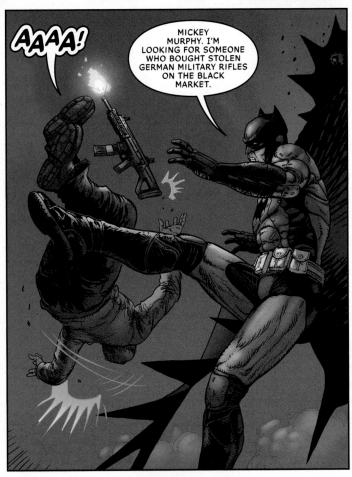

AAAA!

MICKEY MURPHY. I'M LOOKING FOR SOMEONE WHO BOUGHT STOLEN GERMAN MILITARY RIFLES ON THE BLACK MARKET.

N-NOT FROM ME. BUY AMERICAN, SELL AMERICAN, THAT'S MY MOTTO.

IF IT WASN'T YOU, WHO?

I'D ADVISE AGAINST LYING. YOU'VE GOT ONE KNEE AND TWO ELBOWS LEFT.

TRUTH? COULDA BEEN ANYONE.

GOTHAM'S ALWAYS A SELLER'S MARKET. NOW, WITH A MOB WAR ON AND NEW PLAYERS FLOODING IN TO PICK UP THE PIECES? TOWN'S A *GOLD MINE.*

WHO ARE THESE "NEW PLAYERS"?

DUNNO. THEY'RE STAYING ON THE DOWN-LOW...BUT THROWING MONEY AROUND LIKE CONFETTI.

I DID HEAR ABOUT A JAPANESE ARMS DEALER, *MORI*...NEW IN TOWN. BEEN SELLING FOREIGN MERCH THAT "FELL OFF" MILITARY TRANSPORT TRUCKS.

UNLIKELY. THIS GUN WAS STOLEN SIX YEARS AGO.

HEH. THIS IS *GOTHAM.*

ONE GUN IN SIX YEARS? THAT'S A NEEDLE IN A *SKYSCRAPER-SIZED* HAYSTACK.

MORE DEAD ENDS. THE SHOOTER LOOKS AND ACTS LIKE A PRO, BUT HIS APPEARANCE AND M.O. DON'T MATCH ANY KNOWN HIT MEN.

I DON'T WISH TO CAST ASPERSIONS ON THE PLAINTIFFS IN THE LAWSUIT, BUT REGINA ZELLERBACH MAY HAVE A POINT ABOUT A REVENGE MOTIVE.

DON'T FORGET, SIR... *YOU* WERE IN THAT ROOM AS WELL.

I WAS UNDER THE IMPRESSION THE PEOPLE YOUR FATHER COMMITTED WERE WEALTHY.

I'VE CHECKED THE PLAINTIFFS... DISCREETLY.

MOST ARE OLD. NO ONE FITS THE SHOOTER'S PROFILE. AND THEY DON'T HAVE THE FINANCIAL MEANS TO HIRE A PROFESSIONAL.

AT THE TIME. BUT AFTER HE INSTITUTIONALIZED THE BREADWINNERS AND DESTROYED THEIR FAMILIES' REPUTATIONS...

...HE MADE IT HIS MISSION TO CRUSH THEIR BUSINESSES. WHICH HE'D THEN ACQUIRE FOR PENNIES ON THE DOLLAR.

HOW COULD HE--

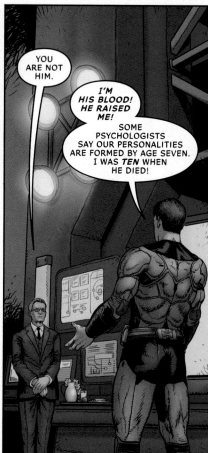

YOU ARE NOT HIM.

I'M *HIS BLOOD! HE RAISED ME!*

SOME PSYCHOLOGISTS SAY OUR PERSONALITIES ARE FORMED BY AGE SEVEN. I WAS *TEN* WHEN HE DIED!

MY FATHER BRUTALLY CRUSHED HIS ENEMIES AND THREW THEM IN ARKHAM ASYLUM.

THE APPLE DOESN'T FALL FAR FROM THE TREE.

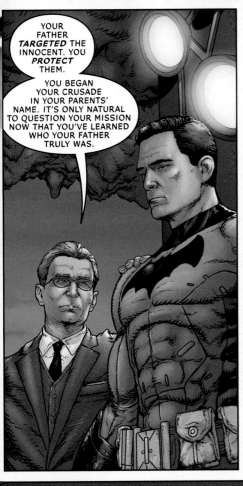

YOUR FATHER *TARGETED* THE INNOCENT. YOU *PROTECT* THEM.

YOU BEGAN YOUR CRUSADE IN YOUR PARENTS' NAME. IT'S ONLY NATURAL TO QUESTION YOUR MISSION NOW THAT YOU'VE LEARNED WHO YOUR FATHER TRULY WAS.

BUT I'D IMAGINE YOUR MOTIVES DON'T MATTER TO THE PEOPLE OF GOTHAM.

ONLY THE *RESULTS.*

COUNT ON ALFRED TO VERBALLY SLAP ME IN THE FACE WHEN I NEED IT.

I WAS MAKING THIS ABOUT ME, INSTEAD OF THE VICTIMS.

MAYBE THE SELF-CENTERED PLAYBOY IS LESS OF A MASK THAN I'D LIKE TO THINK.

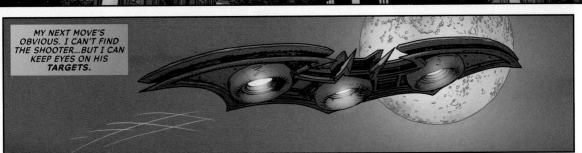

MY NEXT MOVE'S OBVIOUS. I CAN'T FIND THE SHOOTER...BUT I CAN KEEP EYES ON HIS *TARGETS.*

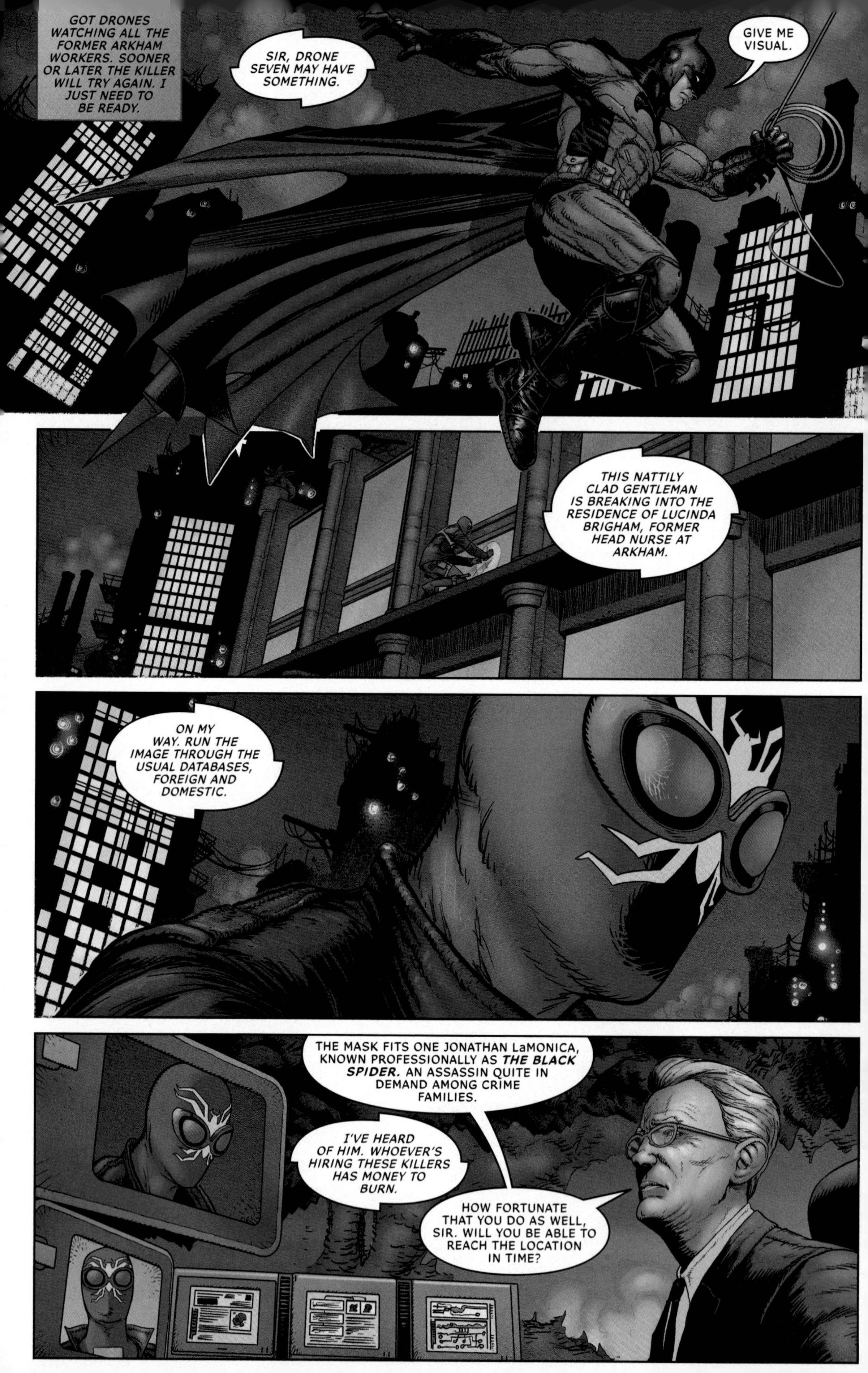
GOT DRONES WATCHING ALL THE FORMER ARKHAM WORKERS. SOONER OR LATER THE KILLER WILL TRY AGAIN. I JUST NEED TO BE READY.
SIR, DRONE SEVEN MAY HAVE SOMETHING.
GIVE ME VISUAL.
THIS NATTILY CLAD GENTLEMAN IS BREAKING INTO THE RESIDENCE OF LUCINDA BRIGHAM, FORMER HEAD NURSE AT ARKHAM.
ON MY WAY. RUN THE IMAGE THROUGH THE USUAL DATABASES, FOREIGN AND DOMESTIC.
THE MASK FITS ONE JONATHAN LaMONICA, KNOWN PROFESSIONALLY AS THE BLACK SPIDER. AN ASSASSIN QUITE IN DEMAND AMONG CRIME FAMILIES.
I'VE HEARD OF HIM. WHOEVER'S HIRING THESE KILLERS HAS MONEY TO BURN.
HOW FORTUNATE THAT YOU DO AS WELL, SIR. WILL YOU BE ABLE TO REACH THE LOCATION IN TIME?

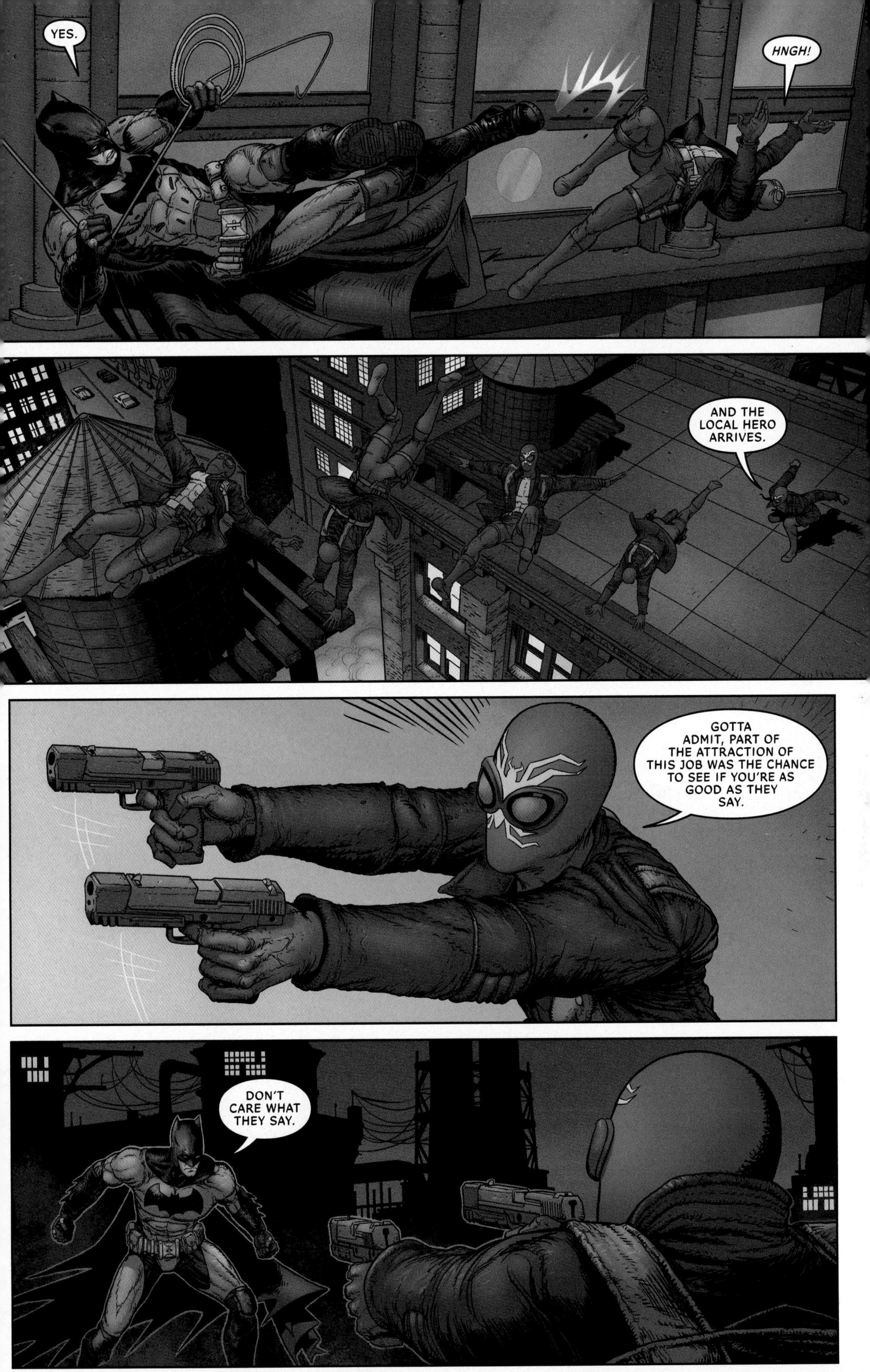
YES.
HNGH!
AND THE LOCAL HERO ARRIVES.
GOTTA ADMIT, PART OF THE ATTRACTION OF THIS JOB WAS THE CHANCE TO SEE IF YOU'RE AS GOOD AS THEY SAY.
DON'T CARE WHAT THEY SAY.

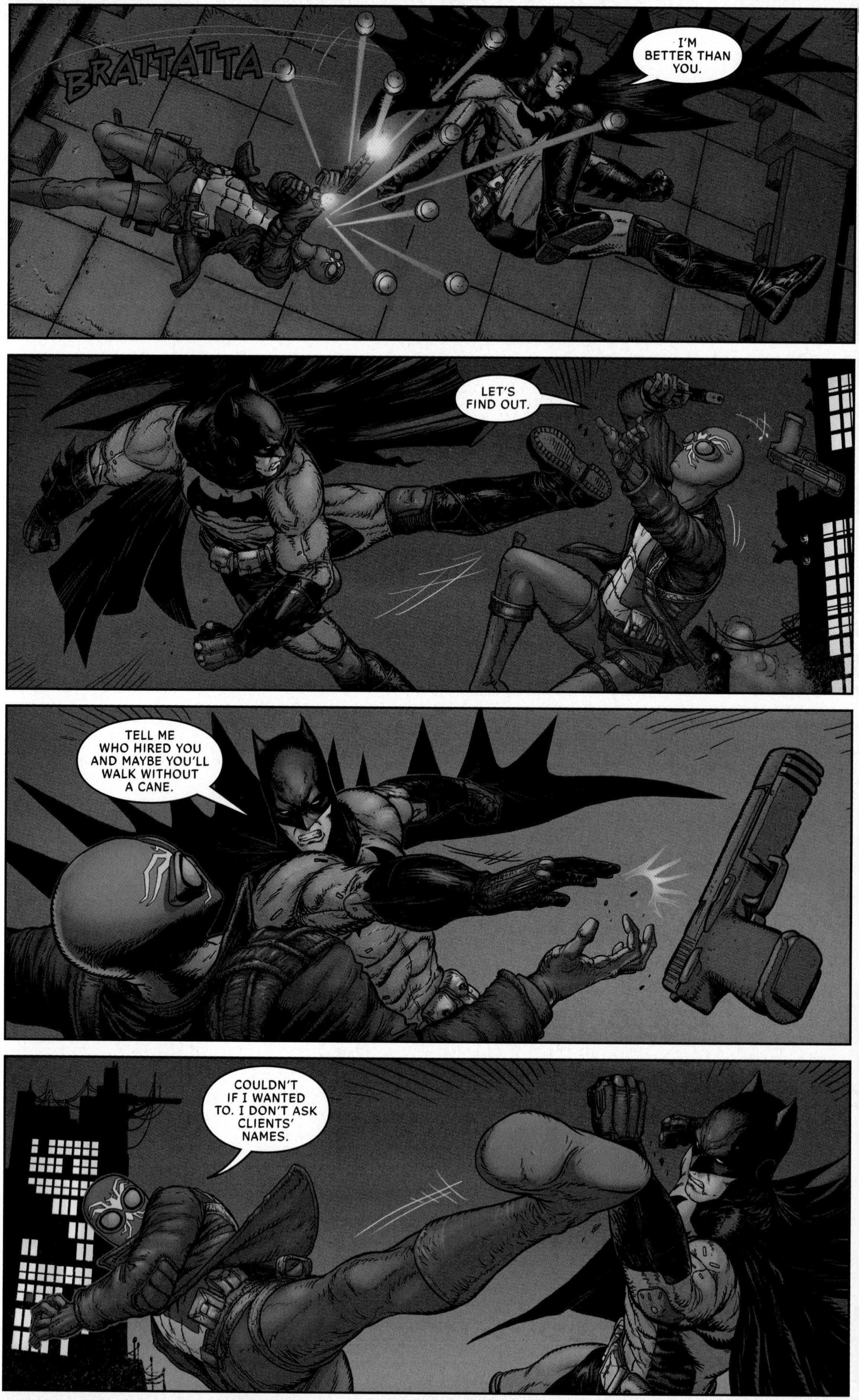
BRATTATTA
I'M BETTER THAN YOU.
LET'S FIND OUT.
TELL ME WHO HIRED YOU AND MAYBE YOU'LL WALK WITHOUT A CANE.
COULDN'T IF I WANTED TO. I DON'T ASK CLIENTS' NAMES.

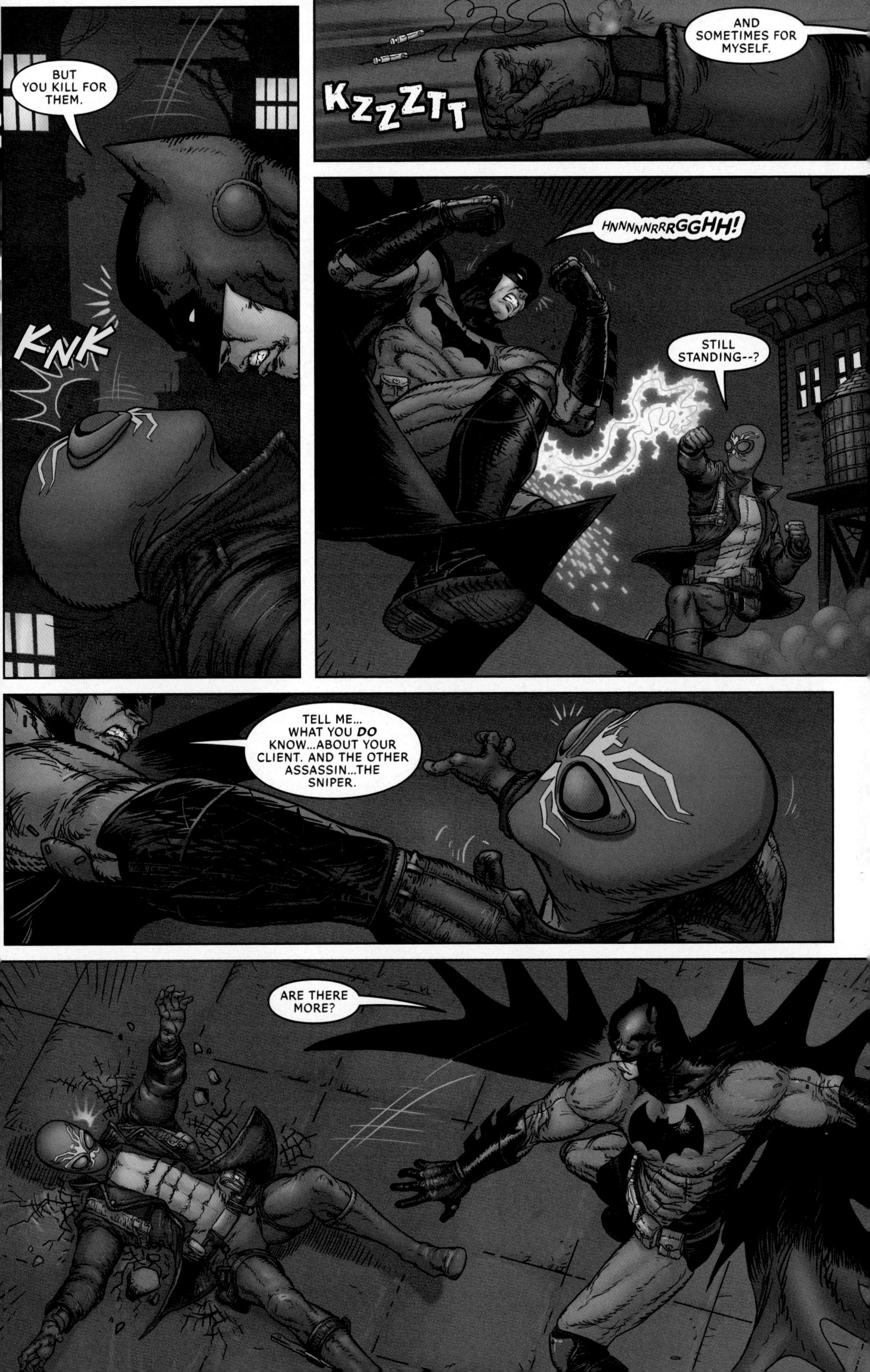
BUT YOU KILL FOR THEM.
KNK
AND SOMETIMES FOR MYSELF.
KZZZTT
HNNNNNRRRGGHH!
STILL STANDING--?
TELL ME... WHAT YOU DO KNOW...ABOUT YOUR CLIENT. AND THE OTHER ASSASSIN...THE SNIPER.
ARE THERE MORE?

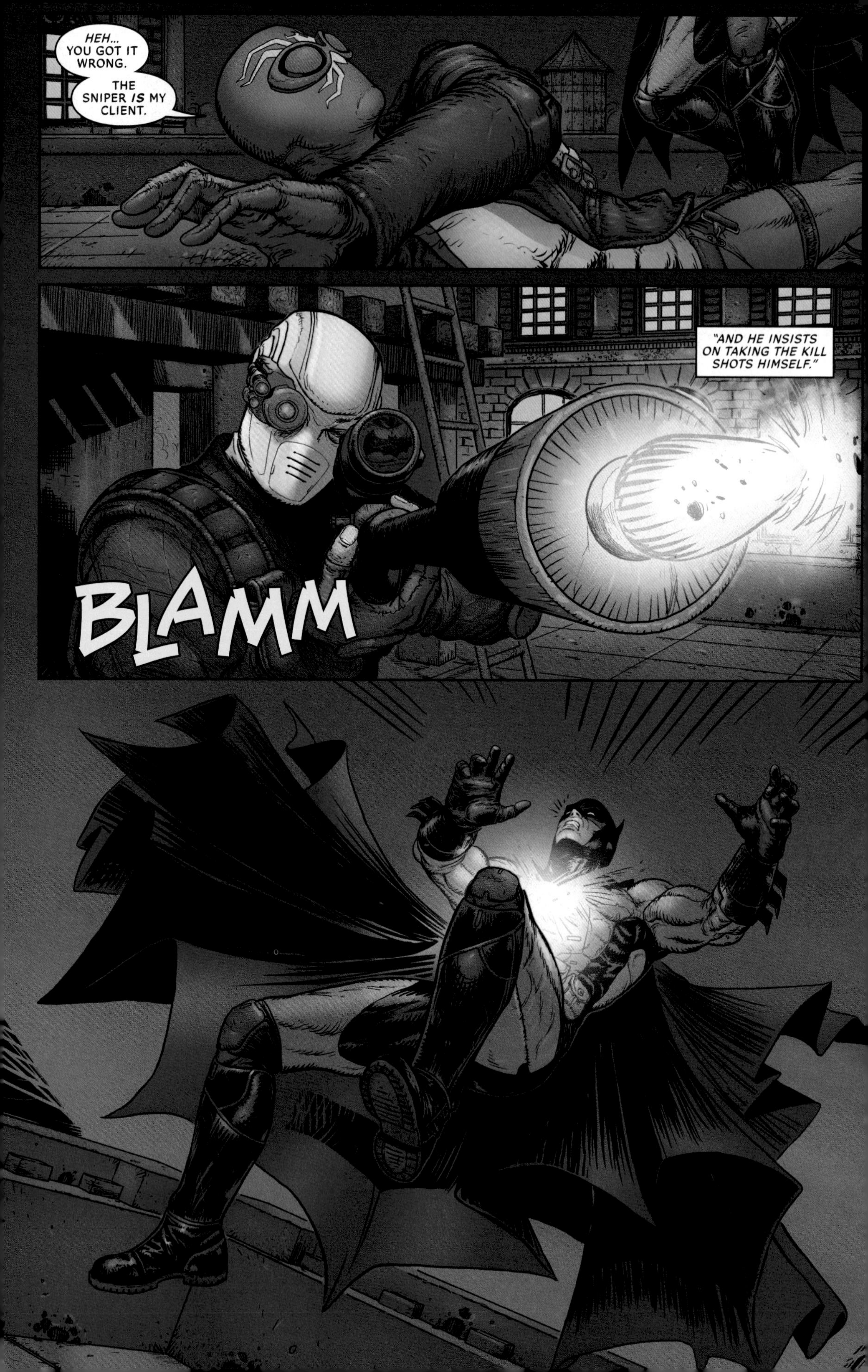
HEH... YOU GOT IT WRONG.
THE SNIPER IS MY CLIENT.
"AND HE INSISTS ON TAKING THE KILL SHOTS HIMSELF."
BLAMM

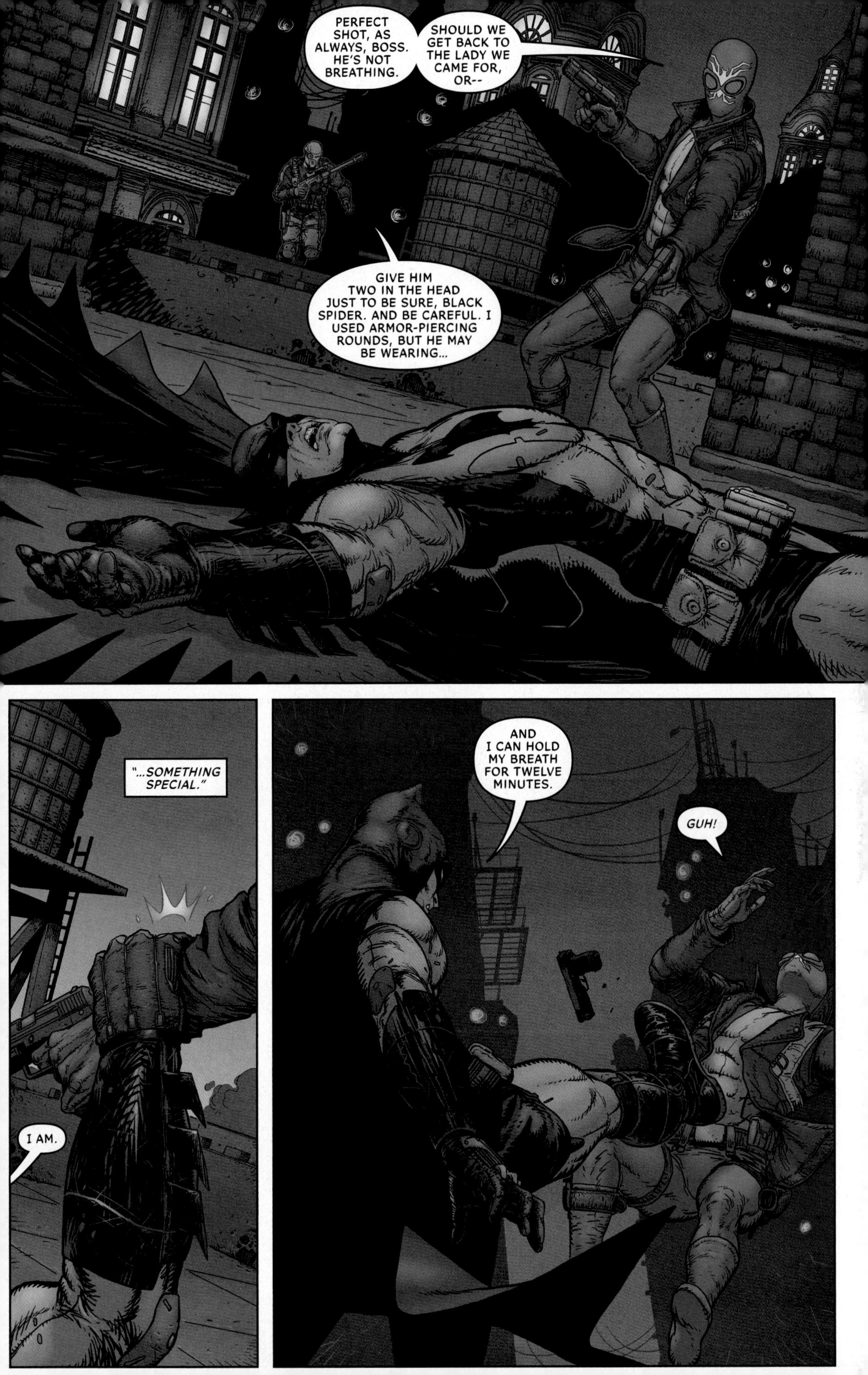
PERFECT SHOT, AS ALWAYS, BOSS. HE'S NOT BREATHING.
SHOULD WE GET BACK TO THE LADY WE CAME FOR, OR--
GIVE HIM TWO IN THE HEAD JUST TO BE SURE, BLACK SPIDER. AND BE CAREFUL. I USED ARMOR-PIERCING ROUNDS, BUT HE MAY BE WEARING...
"...SOMETHING SPECIAL."
I AM.
AND I CAN HOLD MY BREATH FOR TWELVE MINUTES.
GUH!

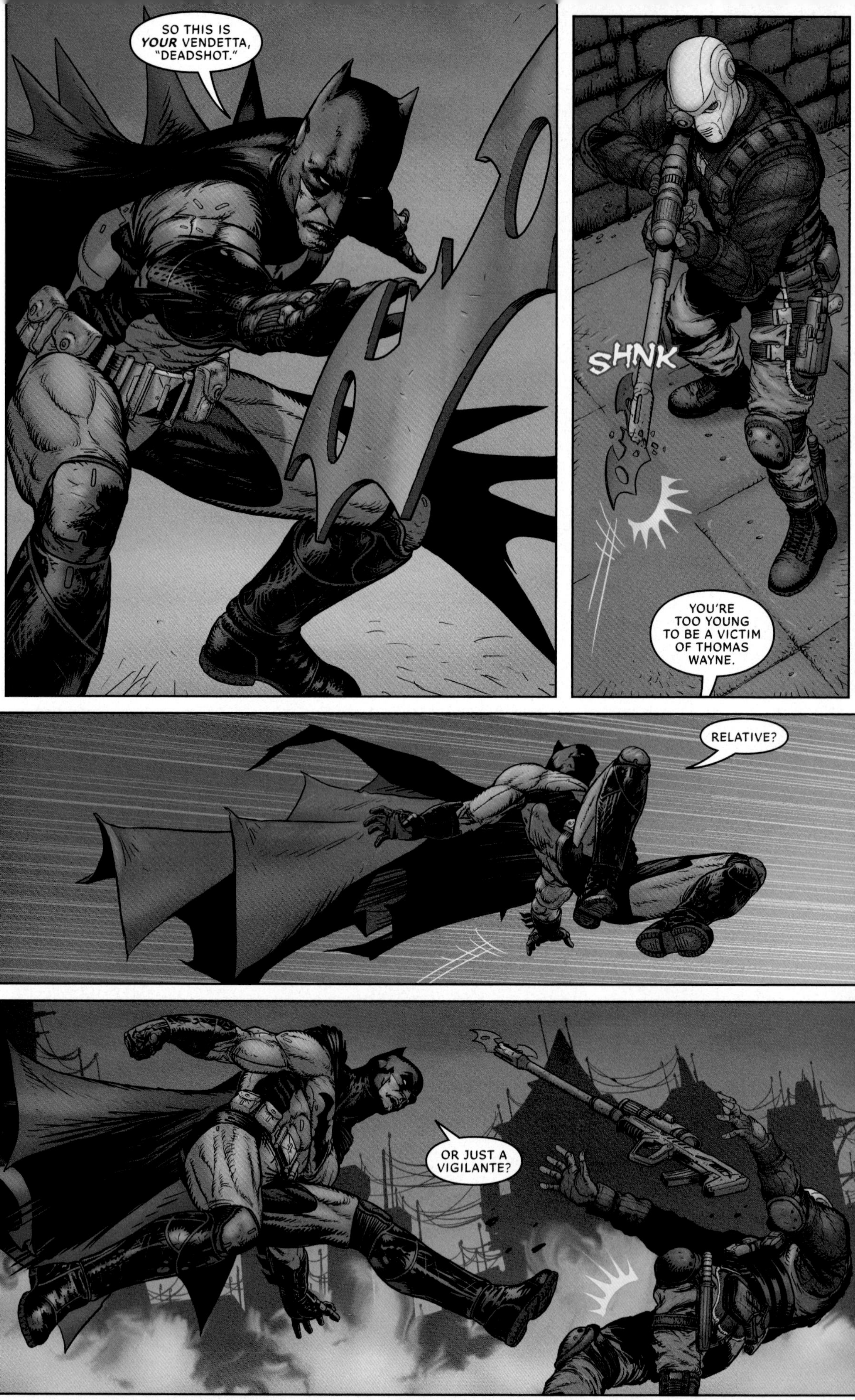
SO THIS IS *YOUR* VENDETTA, "DEADSHOT."
SHNK
YOU'RE TOO YOUNG TO BE A VICTIM OF THOMAS WAYNE.
RELATIVE?
OR JUST A VIGILANTE?

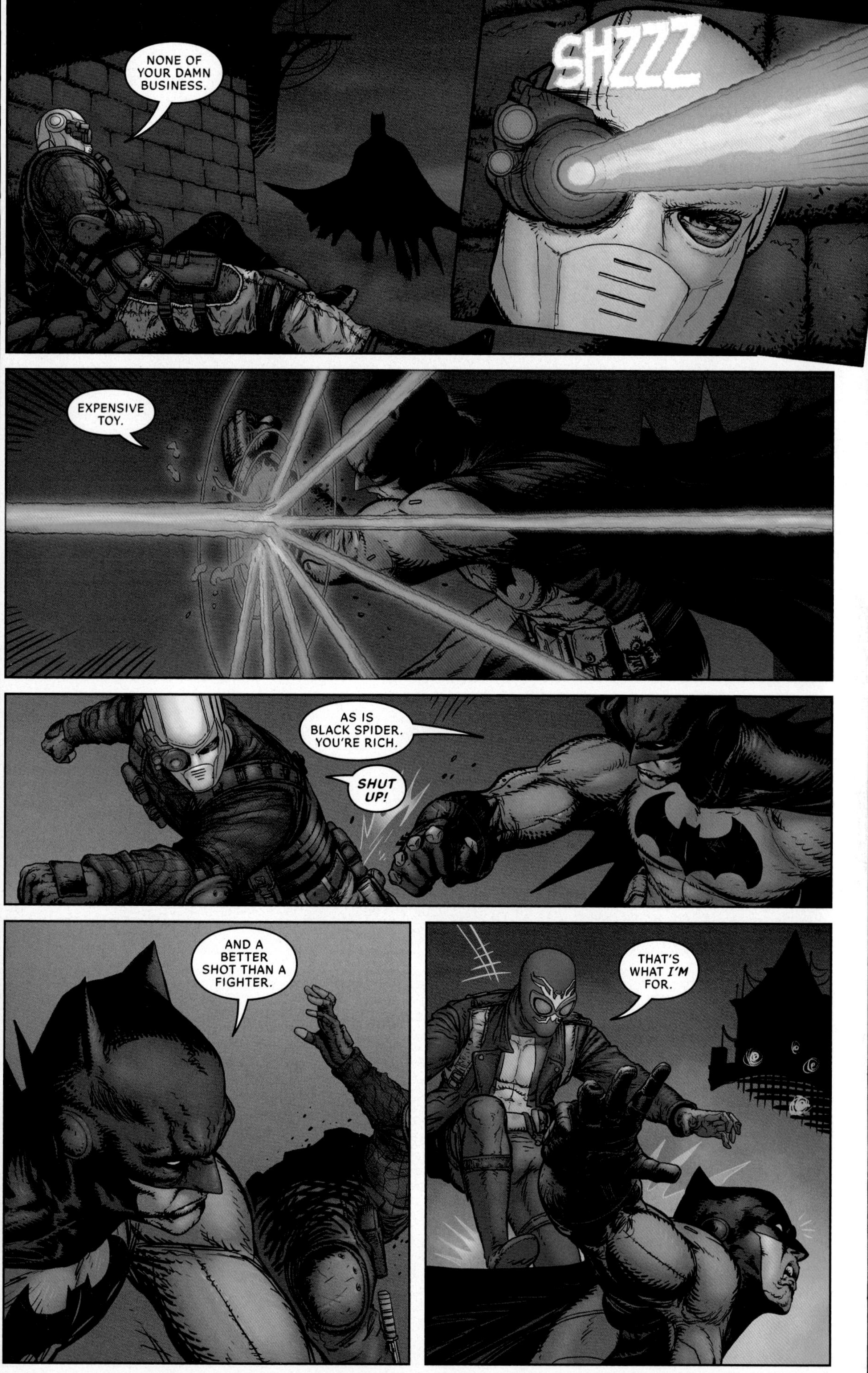
NONE OF YOUR DAMN BUSINESS.
SHZZZ
EXPENSIVE TOY.
AS IS BLACK SPIDER. YOU'RE RICH.
SHUT UP!
AND A BETTER SHOT THAN A FIGHTER.
THAT'S WHAT I'M FOR.

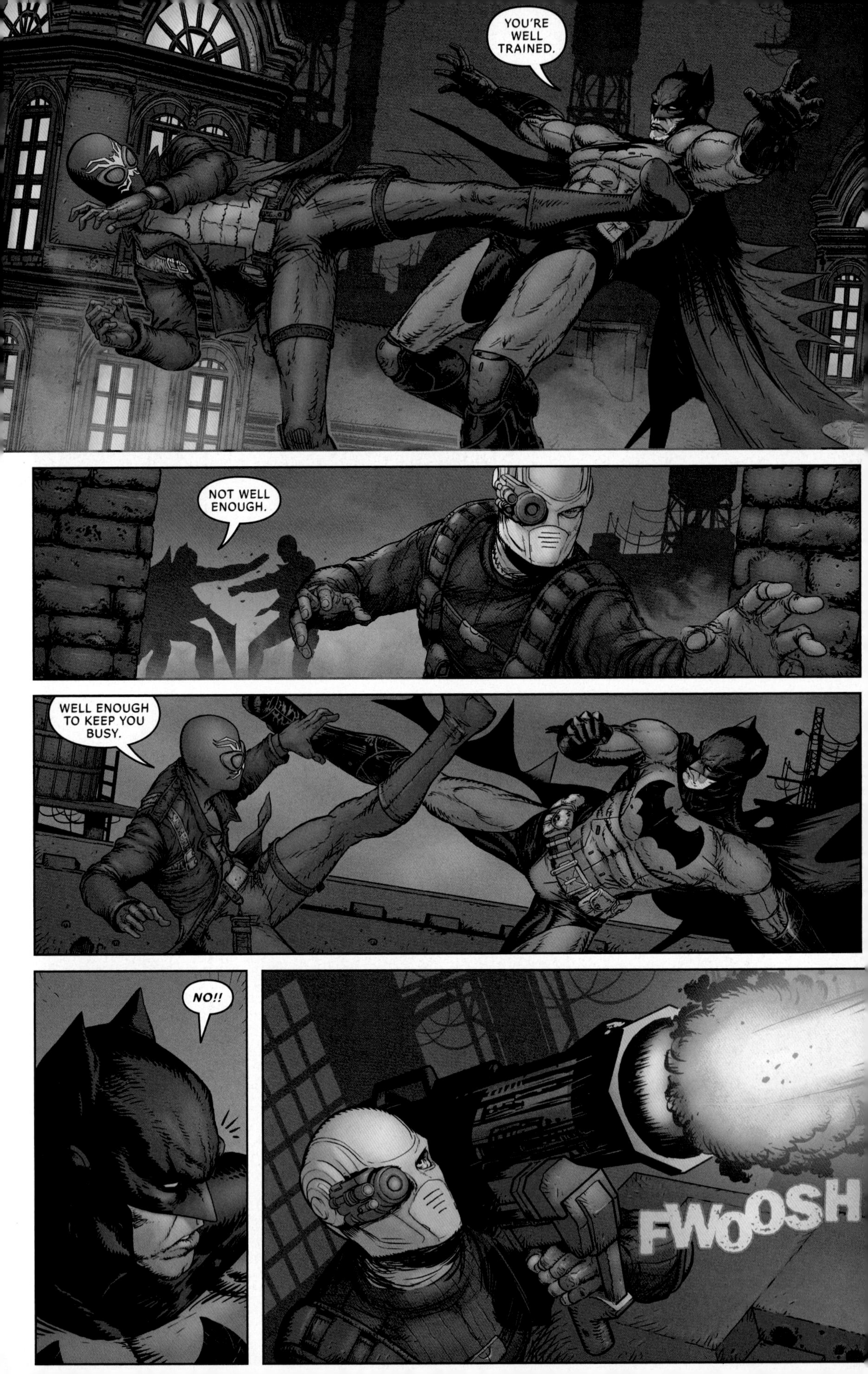
YOU'RE WELL TRAINED.
NOT WELL ENOUGH.
WELL ENOUGH TO KEEP YOU BUSY.
NO!!
FWOOSH

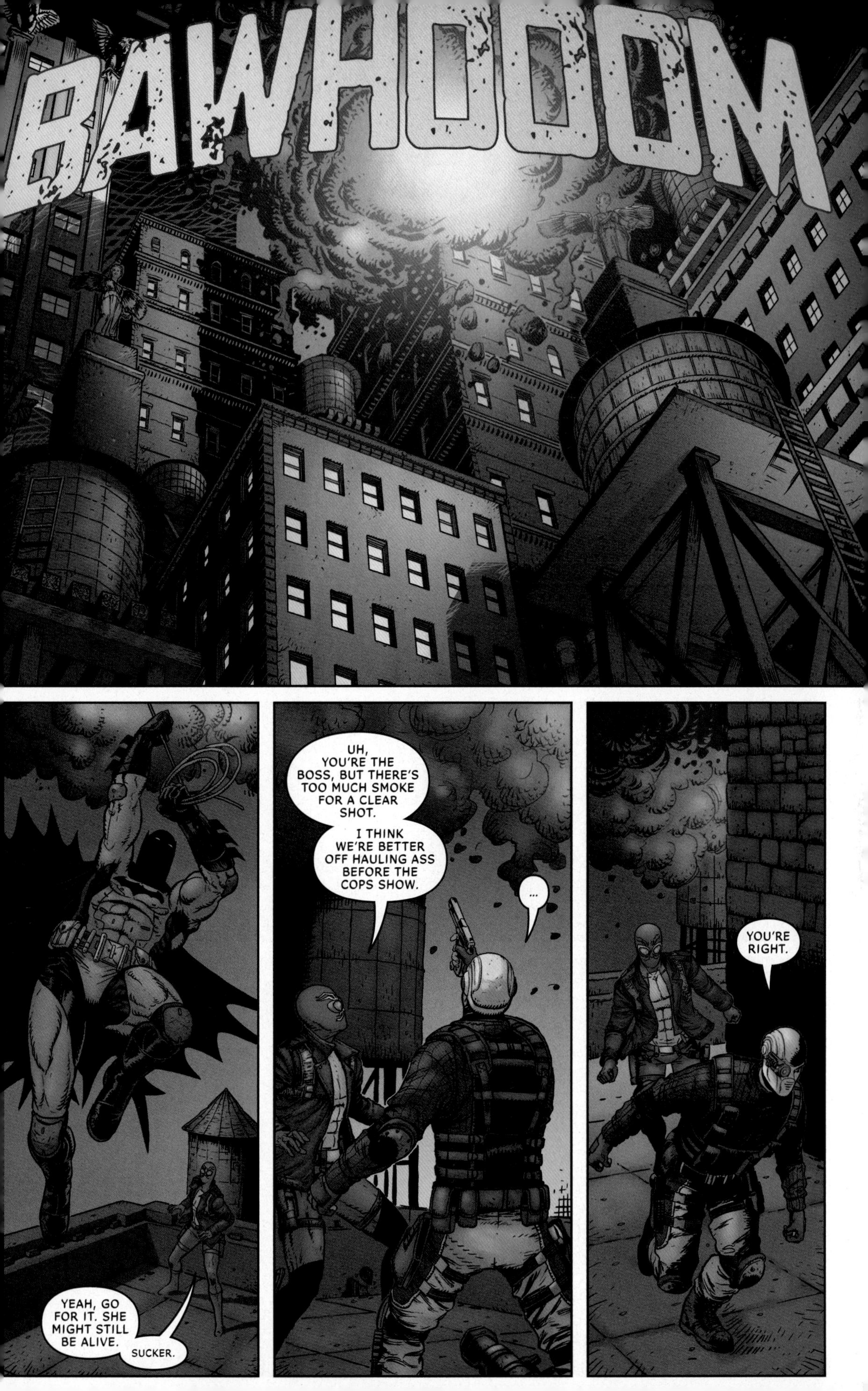
BAWHOOOM
UH, YOU'RE THE BOSS, BUT THERE'S TOO MUCH SMOKE FOR A CLEAR SHOT.
I THINK WE'RE BETTER OFF HAULING ASS BEFORE THE COPS SHOW.
...
YOU'RE RIGHT.
YEAH, GO FOR IT. SHE MIGHT STILL BE ALIVE.
SUCKER.

"WE'LL SEE HIM AGAIN."

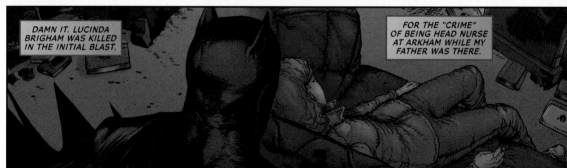

DAMN IT. LUCINDA BRIGHAM WAS KILLED IN THE INITIAL BLAST.

FOR THE "CRIME" OF BEING HEAD NURSE AT ARKHAM WHILE MY FATHER WAS THERE.

ALL I CAN DO NOW...

...IS MAKE SURE THE FIRE DOESN'T SPREAD PAST THIS APARTMENT.

FFSSSs

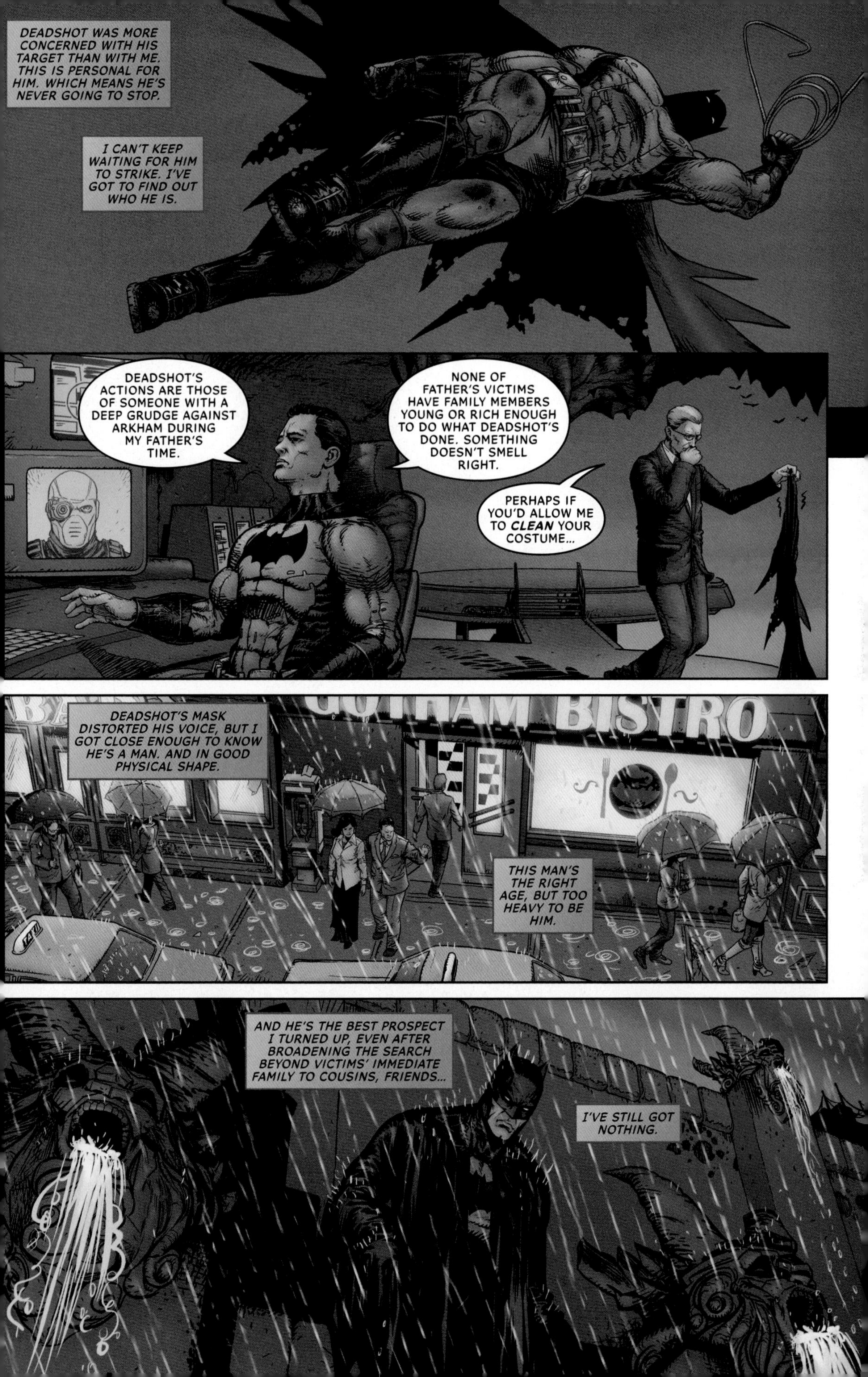
DEADSHOT WAS MORE CONCERNED WITH HIS TARGET THAN WITH ME. THIS IS PERSONAL FOR HIM. WHICH MEANS HE'S NEVER GOING TO STOP.
I CAN'T KEEP WAITING FOR HIM TO STRIKE. I'VE GOT TO FIND OUT WHO HE IS.
DEADSHOT'S ACTIONS ARE THOSE OF SOMEONE WITH A DEEP GRUDGE AGAINST ARKHAM DURING MY FATHER'S TIME.
NONE OF FATHER'S VICTIMS HAVE FAMILY MEMBERS YOUNG OR RICH ENOUGH TO DO WHAT DEADSHOT'S DONE. SOMETHING DOESN'T SMELL RIGHT.
PERHAPS IF YOU'D ALLOW ME TO *CLEAN* YOUR COSTUME...
GOTHAM BISTRO
DEADSHOT'S MASK DISTORTED HIS VOICE, BUT I GOT CLOSE ENOUGH TO KNOW HE'S A MAN. AND IN GOOD PHYSICAL SHAPE.
THIS MAN'S THE RIGHT AGE, BUT TOO HEAVY TO BE HIM.
AND HE'S THE BEST PROSPECT I TURNED UP, EVEN AFTER BROADENING THE SEARCH BEYOND VICTIMS' IMMEDIATE FAMILY TO COUSINS, FRIENDS...
I'VE STILL GOT NOTHING.

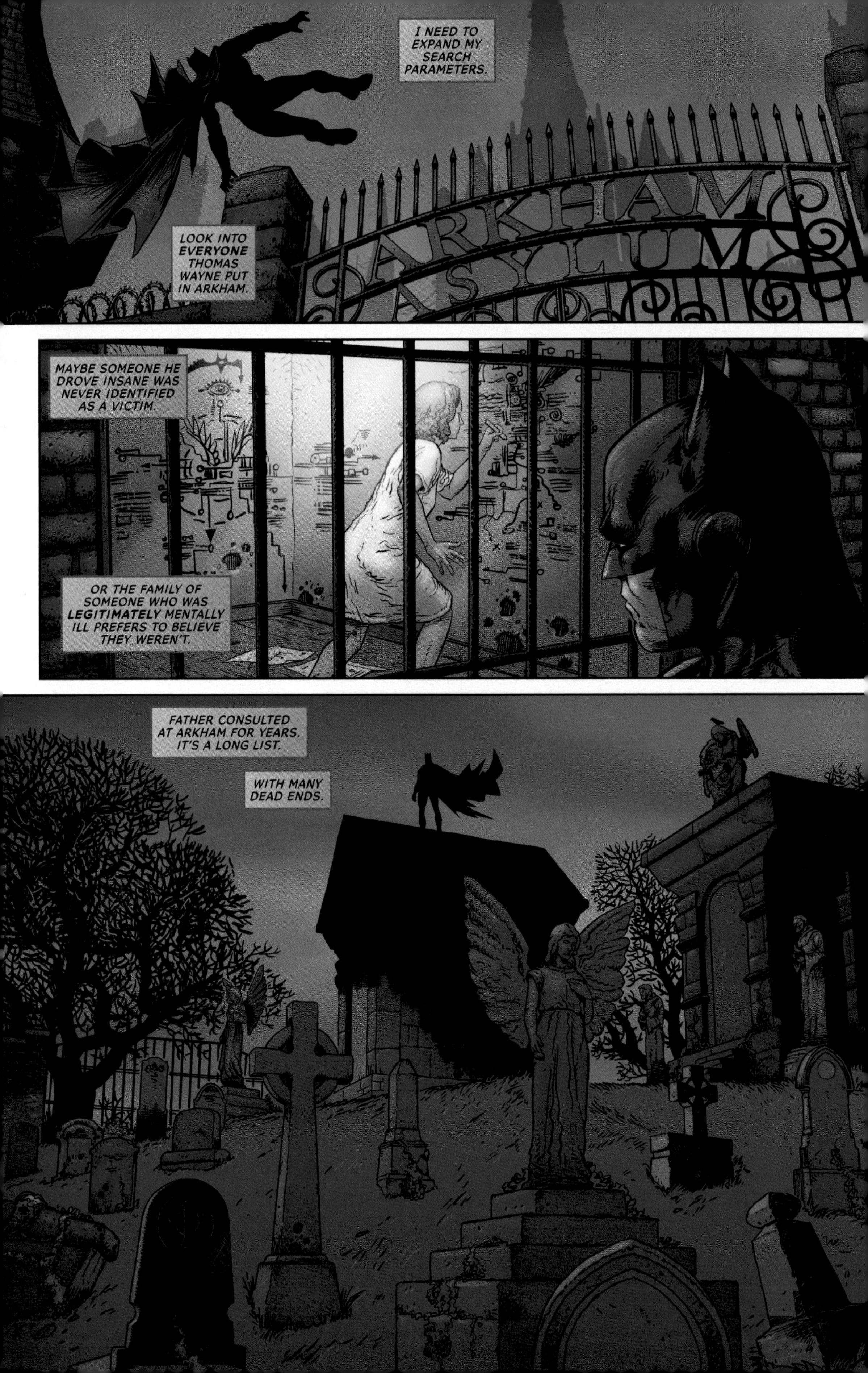

I NEED TO EXPAND MY SEARCH PARAMETERS.
ARKHAM ASYLUM
LOOK INTO EVERYONE THOMAS WAYNE PUT IN ARKHAM.
MAYBE SOMEONE HE DROVE INSANE WAS NEVER IDENTIFIED AS A VICTIM.
OR THE FAMILY OF SOMEONE WHO WAS LEGITIMATELY MENTALLY ILL PREFERS TO BELIEVE THEY WEREN'T.
FATHER CONSULTED AT ARKHAM FOR YEARS. IT'S A LONG LIST.
WITH MANY DEAD ENDS.

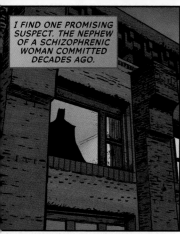

I FIND ONE PROMISING SUSPECT. THE NEPHEW OF A SCHIZOPHRENIC WOMAN COMMITTED DECADES AGO.

MILITARY EXPERIENCE. DISHONORABLE DISCHARGE, MEANING HE'S NOT ALLOWED TO OWN GUNS. AND HE'S GOT A DOZEN.

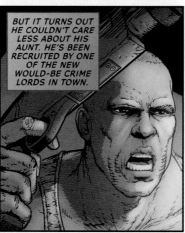

BUT IT TURNS OUT HE COULDN'T CARE LESS ABOUT HIS AUNT. HE'S BEEN RECRUITED BY ONE OF THE NEW WOULD-BE CRIME LORDS IN TOWN.

WHAT'S HIS NAME?

I--I DON'T KNOW WHO HE IS! IT'S ALL TEXTS ON A BURNER PHONE! DUDE LIKES TO MAKE A GAME OUT OF RECRUITING...GO HERE, DO THIS, SOLVE THAT PUZZLE.

WHAT HE'S PAYING, I DON'T MIND JUMPING THROUGH A FEW HOOPS...

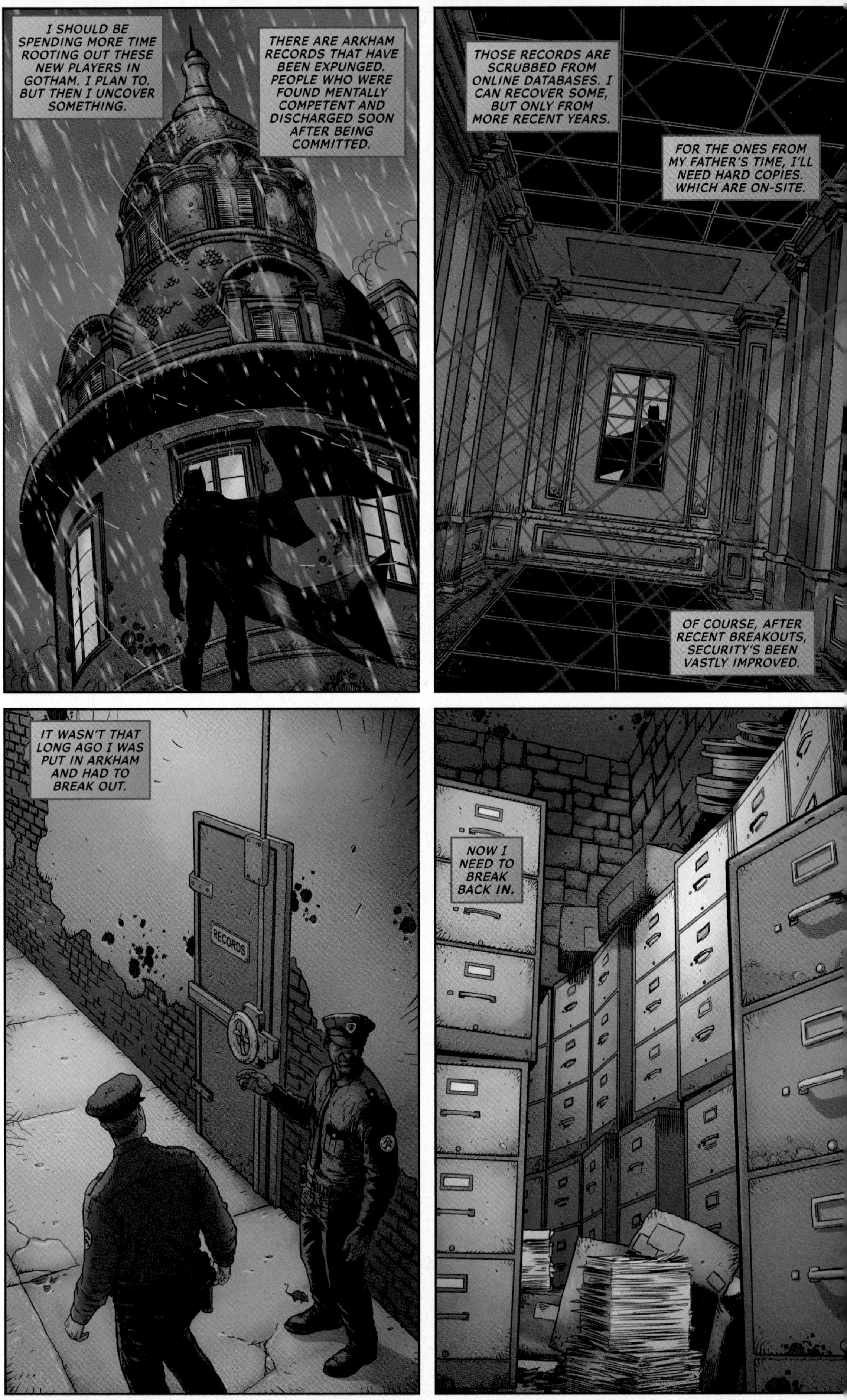
I SHOULD BE SPENDING MORE TIME ROOTING OUT THESE NEW PLAYERS IN GOTHAM. I PLAN TO. BUT THEN I UNCOVER SOMETHING.
THERE ARE ARKHAM RECORDS THAT HAVE BEEN EXPUNGED. PEOPLE WHO WERE FOUND MENTALLY COMPETENT AND DISCHARGED SOON AFTER BEING COMMITTED.
THOSE RECORDS ARE SCRUBBED FROM ONLINE DATABASES. I CAN RECOVER SOME, BUT ONLY FROM MORE RECENT YEARS.
FOR THE ONES FROM MY FATHER'S TIME, I'LL NEED HARD COPIES. WHICH ARE ON-SITE.
OF COURSE, AFTER RECENT BREAKOUTS, SECURITY'S BEEN VASTLY IMPROVED.
IT WASN'T THAT LONG AGO I WAS PUT IN ARKHAM AND HAD TO BREAK OUT.
RECORDS
NOW I NEED TO BREAK BACK IN.

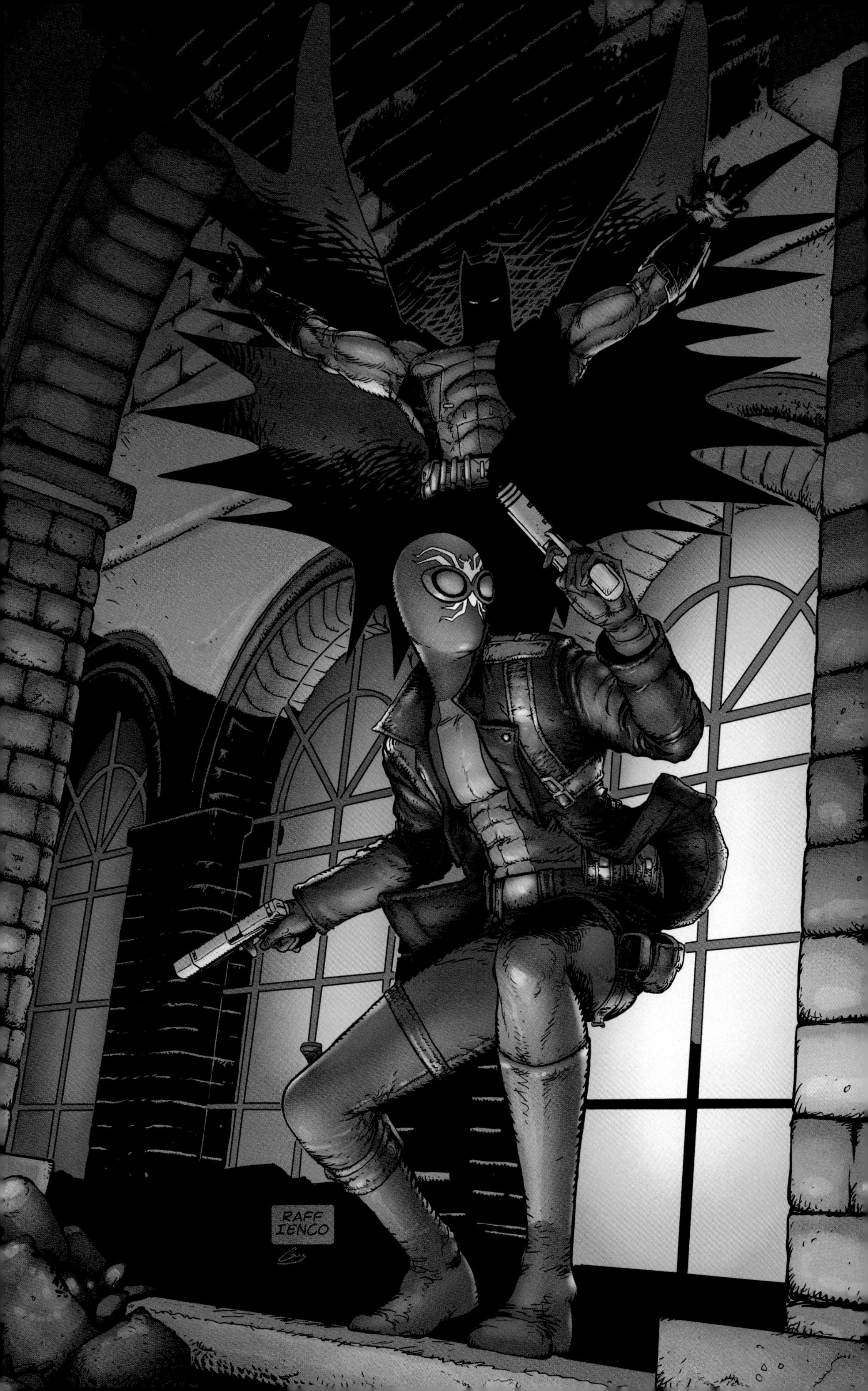
RAFF
IENCO

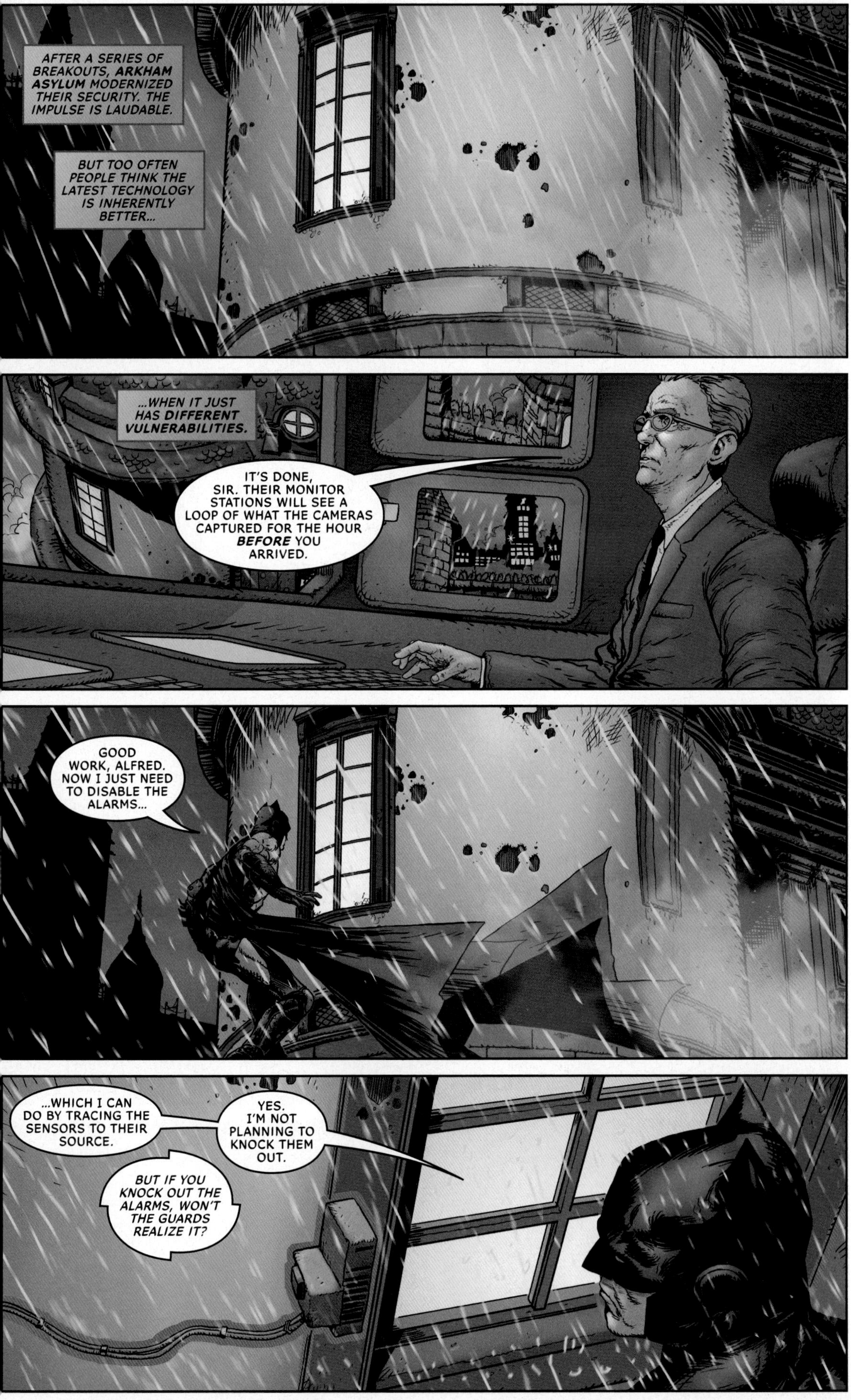
AFTER A SERIES OF BREAKOUTS, ARKHAM ASYLUM MODERNIZED THEIR SECURITY. THE IMPULSE IS LAUDABLE.
BUT TOO OFTEN PEOPLE THINK THE LATEST TECHNOLOGY IS INHERENTLY BETTER...
...WHEN IT JUST HAS DIFFERENT VULNERABILITIES.
IT'S DONE, SIR. THEIR MONITOR STATIONS WILL SEE A LOOP OF WHAT THE CAMERAS CAPTURED FOR THE HOUR BEFORE YOU ARRIVED.
GOOD WORK, ALFRED. NOW I JUST NEED TO DISABLE THE ALARMS...
...WHICH I CAN DO BY TRACING THE SENSORS TO THEIR SOURCE.
BUT IF YOU KNOCK OUT THE ALARMS, WON'T THE GUARDS REALIZE IT?
YES. I'M NOT PLANNING TO KNOCK THEM OUT.

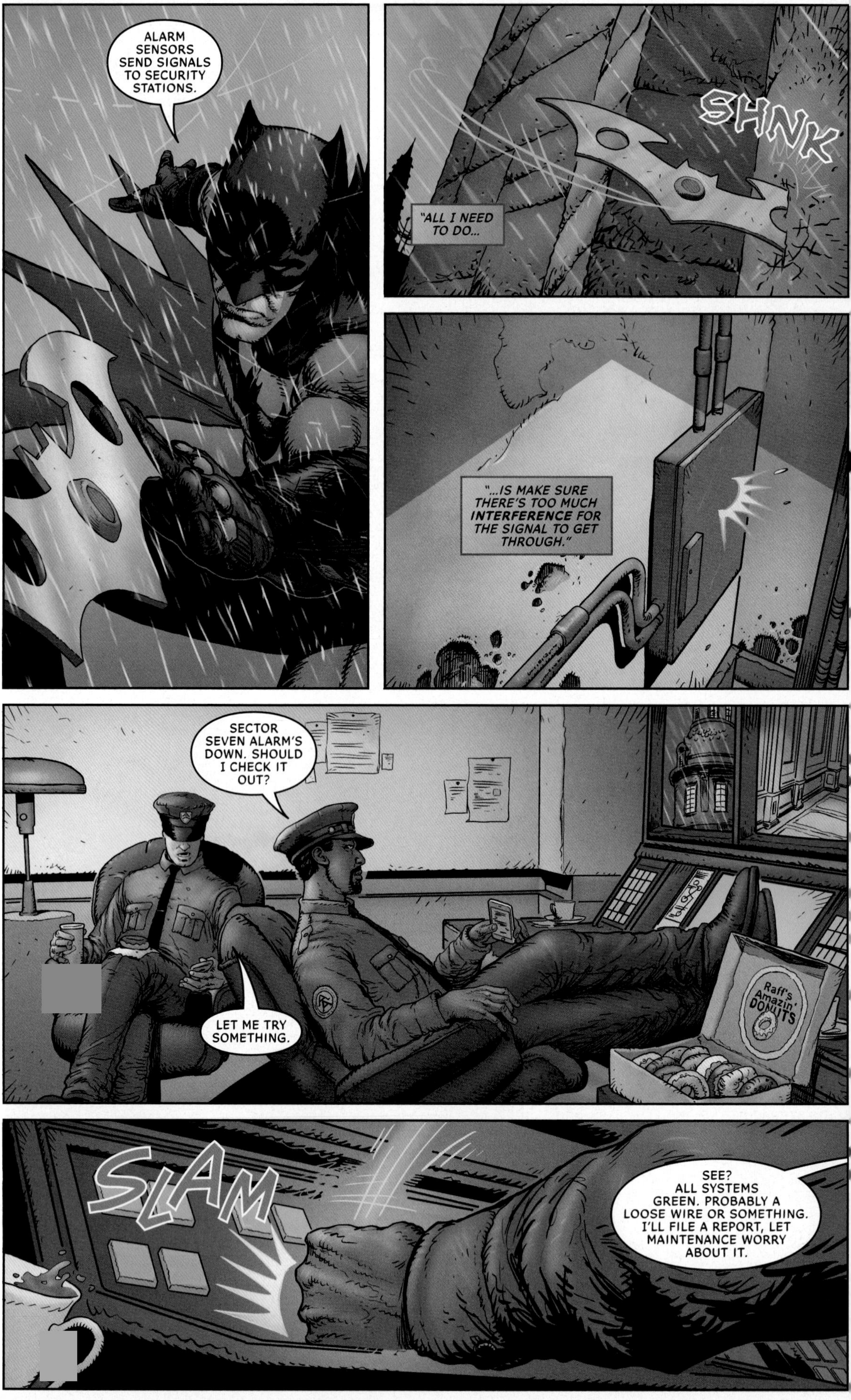
ALARM SENSORS SEND SIGNALS TO SECURITY STATIONS.
"ALL I NEED TO DO...
SHNK
"...IS MAKE SURE THERE'S TOO MUCH INTERFERENCE FOR THE SIGNAL TO GET THROUGH."
SECTOR SEVEN ALARM'S DOWN. SHOULD I CHECK IT OUT?
LET ME TRY SOMETHING.
Raff's Amazin' DONUTS
SLAM
SEE? ALL SYSTEMS GREEN. PROBABLY A LOOSE WIRE OR SOMETHING. I'LL FILE A REPORT, LET MAINTENANCE WORRY ABOUT IT.

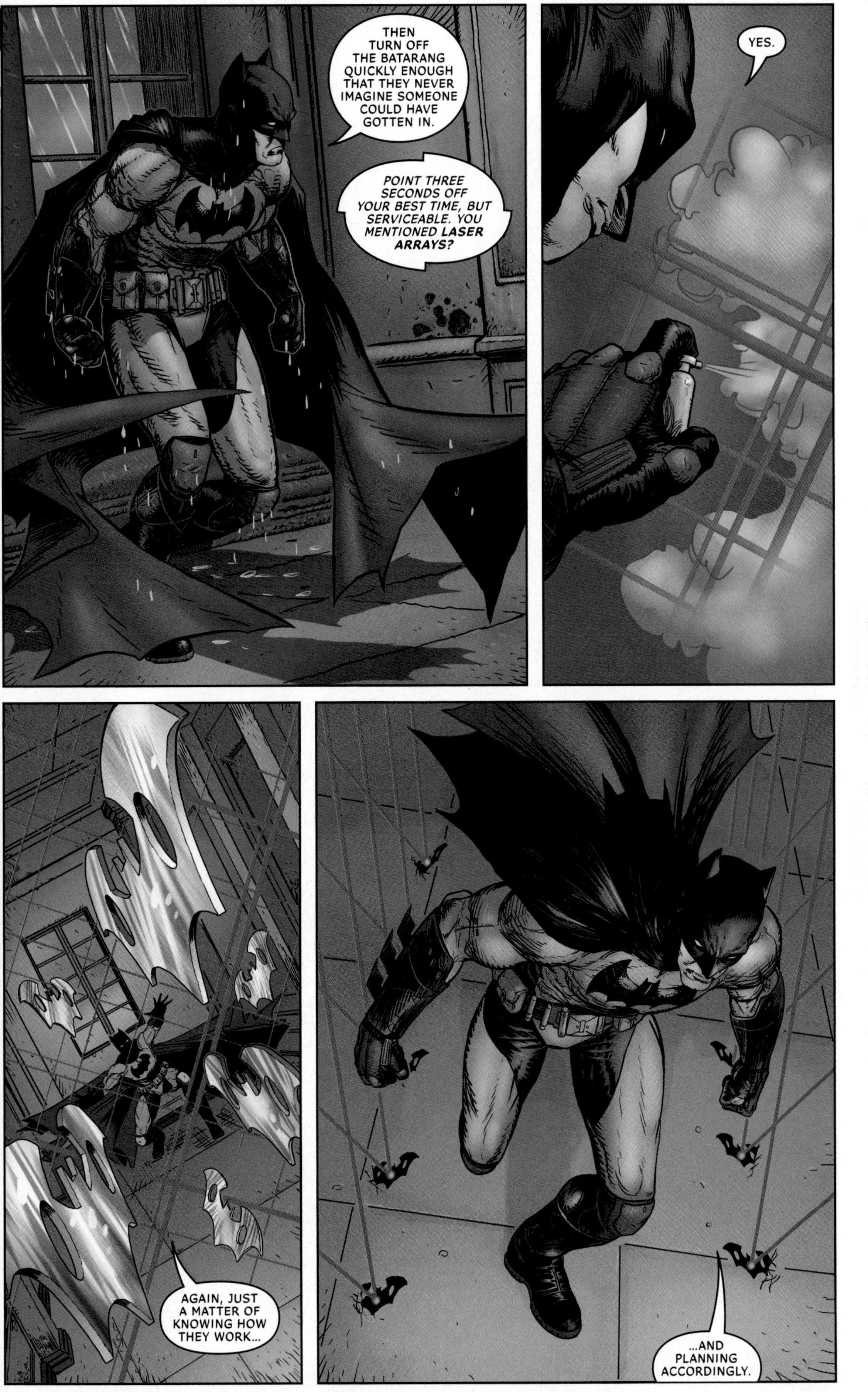
THEN TURN OFF THE BATARANG QUICKLY ENOUGH THAT THEY NEVER IMAGINE SOMEONE COULD HAVE GOTTEN IN.
*POINT THREE SECONDS OFF YOUR BEST TIME, BUT SERVICEABLE. YOU MENTIONED **LASER ARRAYS?***
YES.
AGAIN, JUST A MATTER OF KNOWING HOW THEY WORK...
...AND PLANNING ACCORDINGLY.

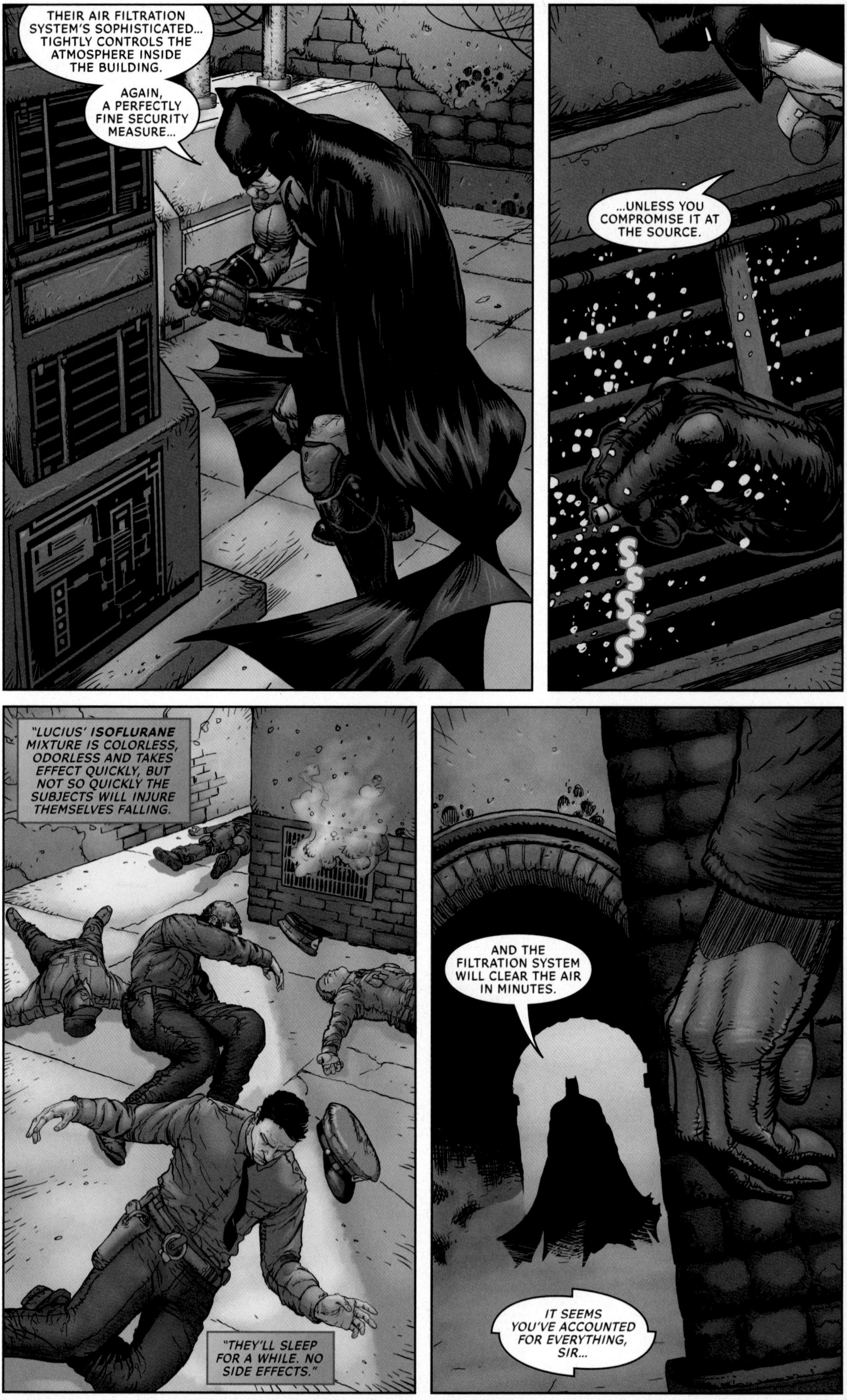
THEIR AIR FILTRATION SYSTEM'S SOPHISTICATED... TIGHTLY CONTROLS THE ATMOSPHERE INSIDE THE BUILDING.
AGAIN, A PERFECTLY FINE SECURITY MEASURE...
...UNLESS YOU COMPROMISE IT AT THE SOURCE.
SSSS
"LUCIUS' ISOFLURANE MIXTURE IS COLORLESS, ODORLESS AND TAKES EFFECT QUICKLY, BUT NOT SO QUICKLY THE SUBJECTS WILL INJURE THEMSELVES FALLING.
"THEY'LL SLEEP FOR A WHILE. NO SIDE EFFECTS."
AND THE FILTRATION SYSTEM WILL CLEAR THE AIR IN MINUTES.
IT SEEMS YOU'VE ACCOUNTED FOR EVERYTHING, SIR...

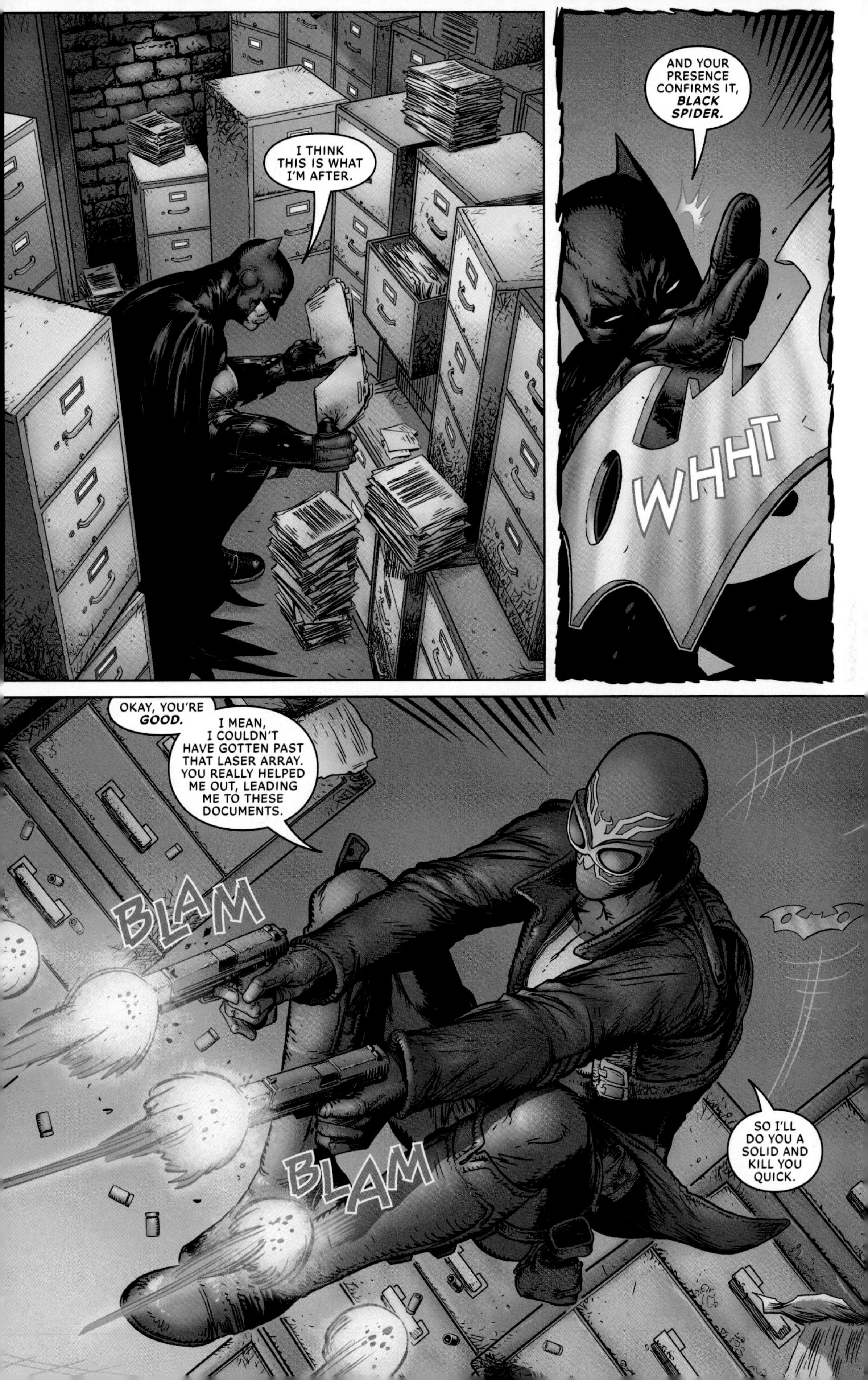
I THINK THIS IS WHAT I'M AFTER.
AND YOUR PRESENCE CONFIRMS IT, ***BLACK SPIDER.***
WHHT
OKAY, YOU'RE ***GOOD.***
I MEAN, I COULDN'T HAVE GOTTEN PAST THAT LASER ARRAY. YOU REALLY HELPED ME OUT, LEADING ME TO THESE DOCUMENTS.
BLAM
BLAM
SO I'LL DO YOU A SOLID AND KILL YOU QUICK.

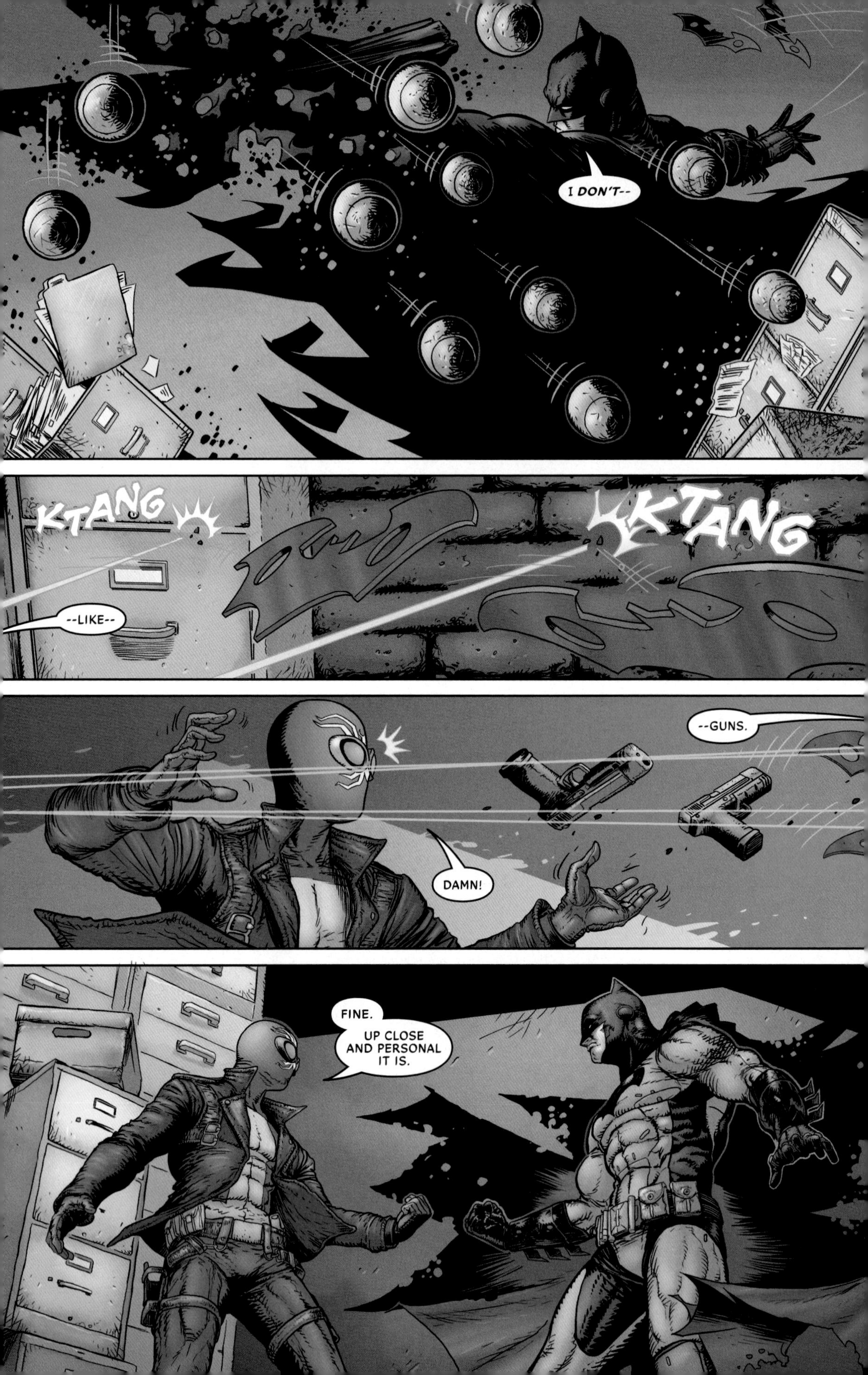
I DON'T--
KTANG
KTANG
--LIKE--
--GUNS.
DAMN!
FINE.
UP CLOSE AND PERSONAL IT IS.

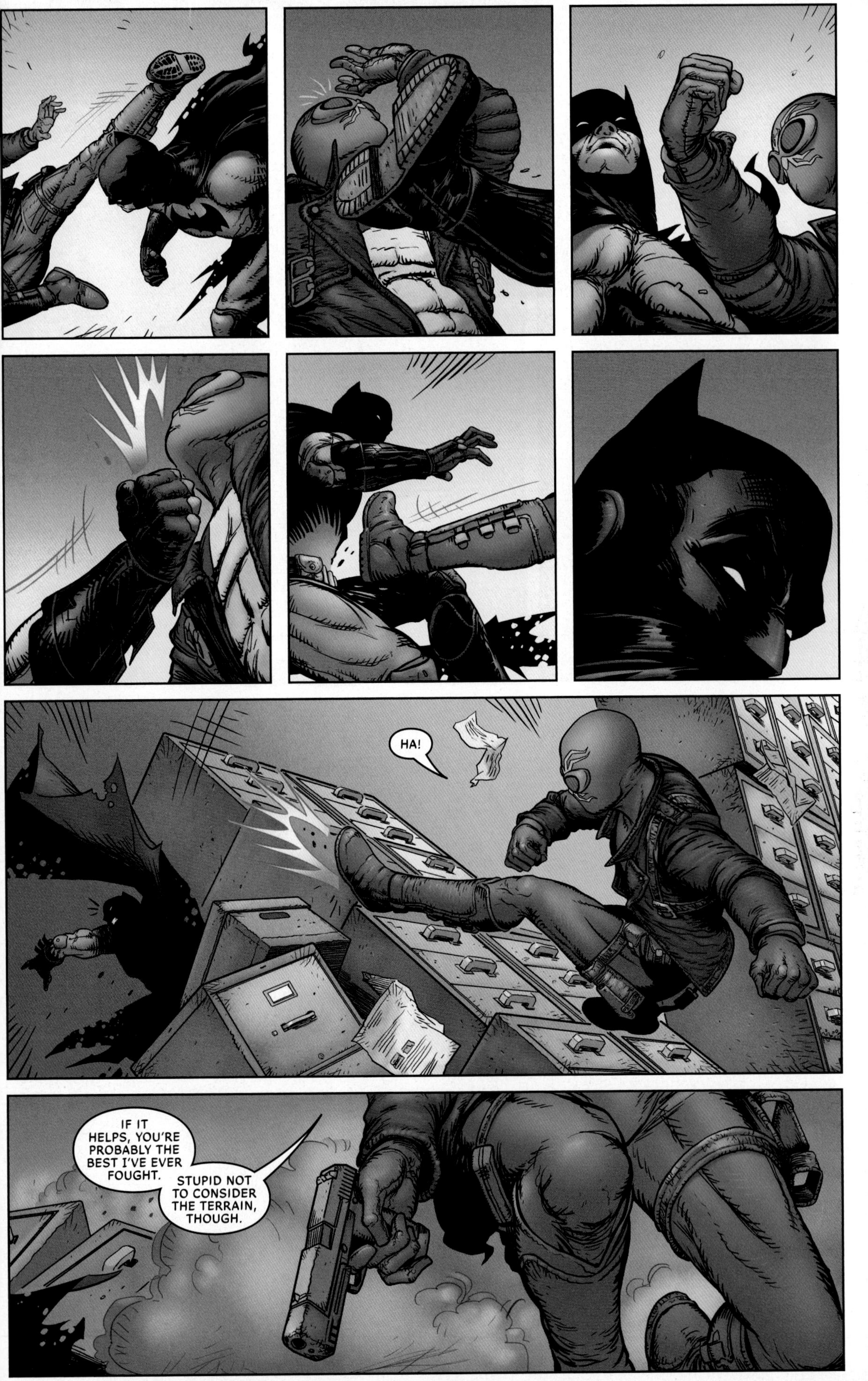
HA!
IF IT HELPS, YOU'RE PROBABLY THE BEST I'VE EVER FOUGHT.
STUPID NOT TO CONSIDER THE TERRAIN, THOUGH.

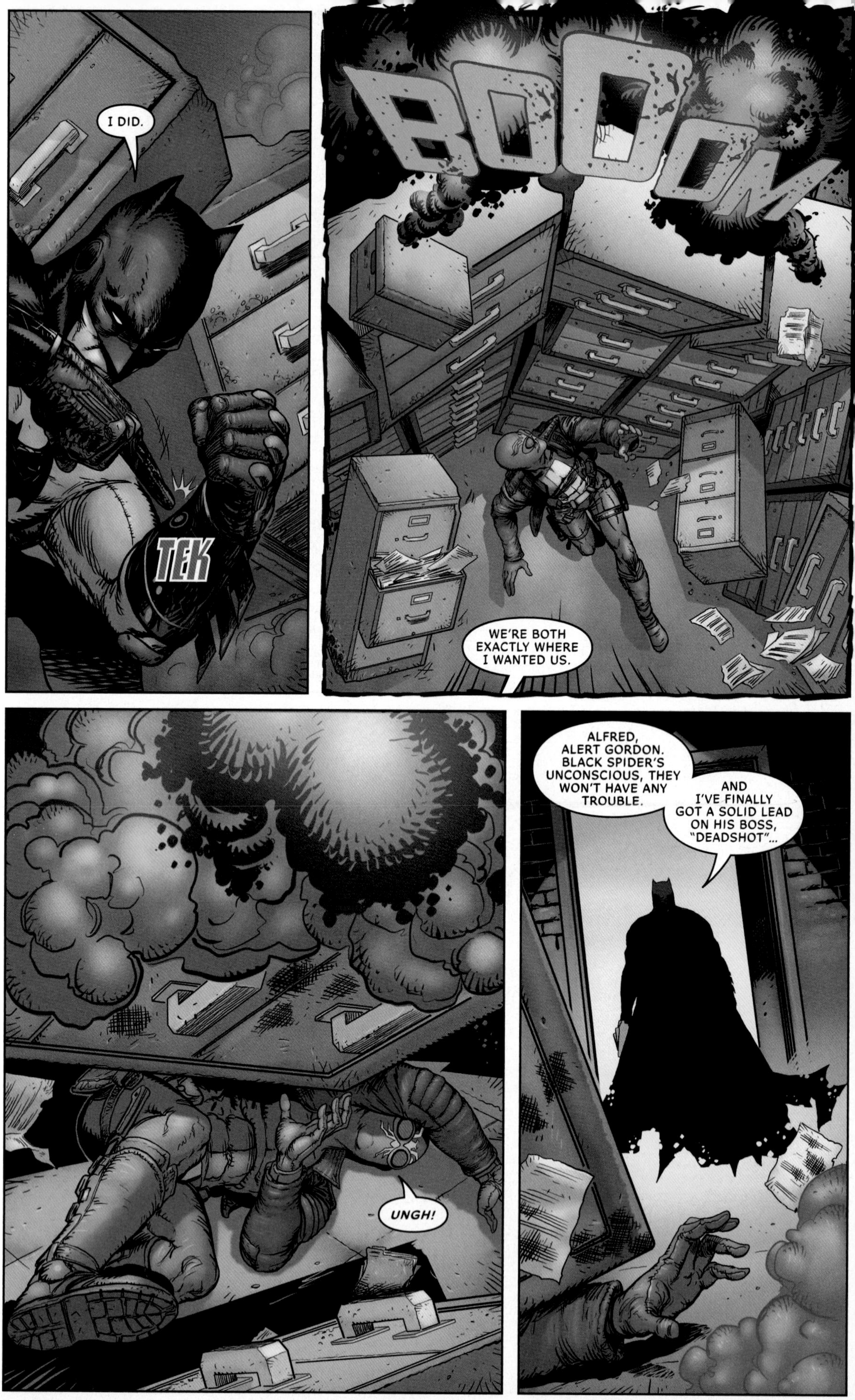
I DID.
TEK
BOOOM
WE'RE BOTH EXACTLY WHERE I WANTED US.
UNGH!
ALFRED, ALERT GORDON. BLACK SPIDER'S UNCONSCIOUS, THEY WON'T HAVE ANY TROUBLE.
AND I'VE FINALLY GOT A SOLID LEAD ON HIS BOSS, "DEADSHOT"...

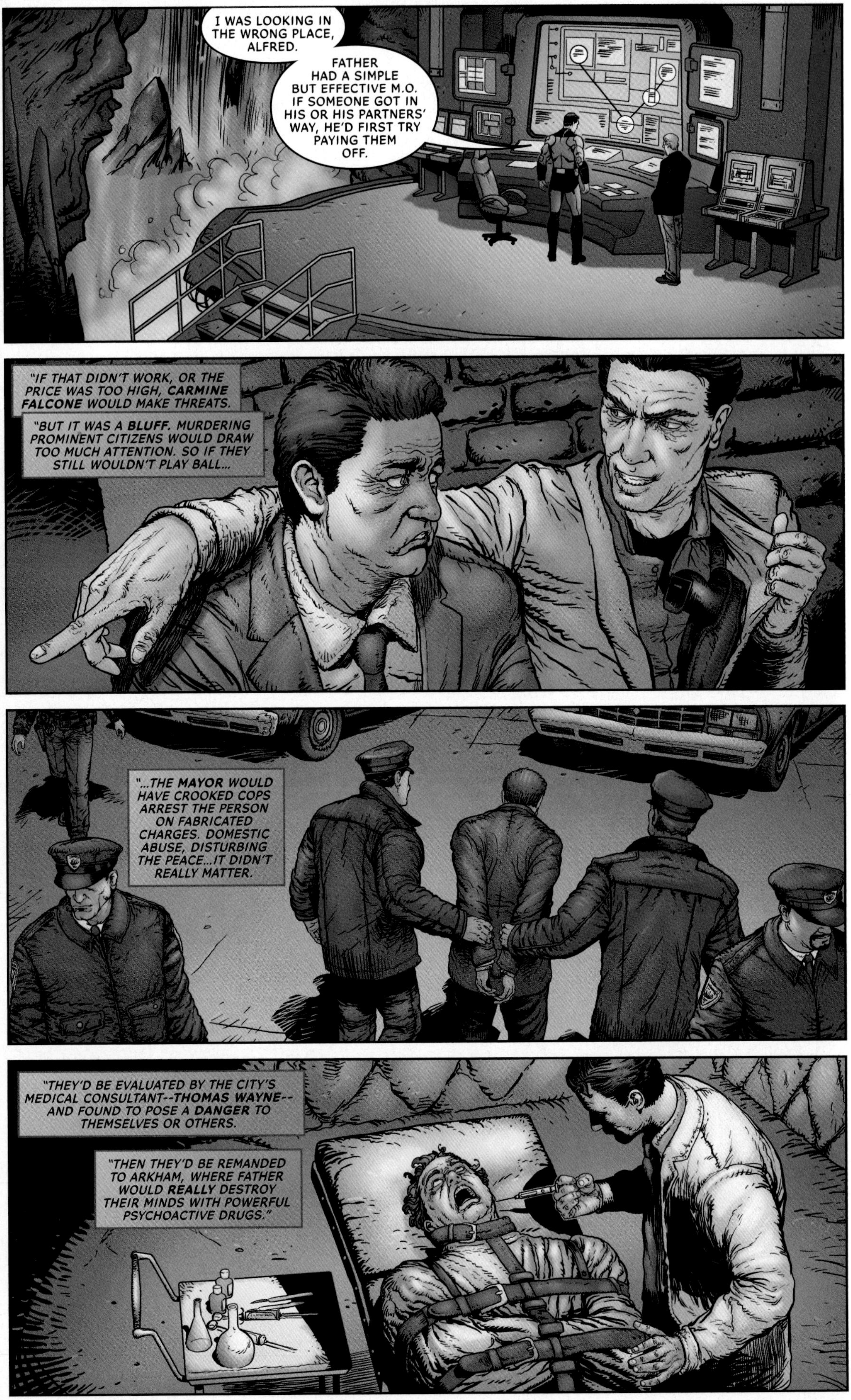
I WAS LOOKING IN THE WRONG PLACE, ALFRED.
FATHER HAD A SIMPLE BUT EFFECTIVE M.O. IF SOMEONE GOT IN HIS OR HIS PARTNERS' WAY, HE'D FIRST TRY PAYING THEM OFF.
"IF THAT DIDN'T WORK, OR THE PRICE WAS TOO HIGH, CARMINE FALCONE WOULD MAKE THREATS.
"BUT IT WAS A BLUFF. MURDERING PROMINENT CITIZENS WOULD DRAW TOO MUCH ATTENTION. SO IF THEY STILL WOULDN'T PLAY BALL...
"...THE MAYOR WOULD HAVE CROOKED COPS ARREST THE PERSON ON FABRICATED CHARGES. DOMESTIC ABUSE, DISTURBING THE PEACE...IT DIDN'T REALLY MATTER.
"THEY'D BE EVALUATED BY THE CITY'S MEDICAL CONSULTANT--THOMAS WAYNE--AND FOUND TO POSE A DANGER TO THEMSELVES OR OTHERS.
"THEN THEY'D BE REMANDED TO ARKHAM, WHERE FATHER WOULD REALLY DESTROY THEIR MINDS WITH POWERFUL PSYCHOACTIVE DRUGS."

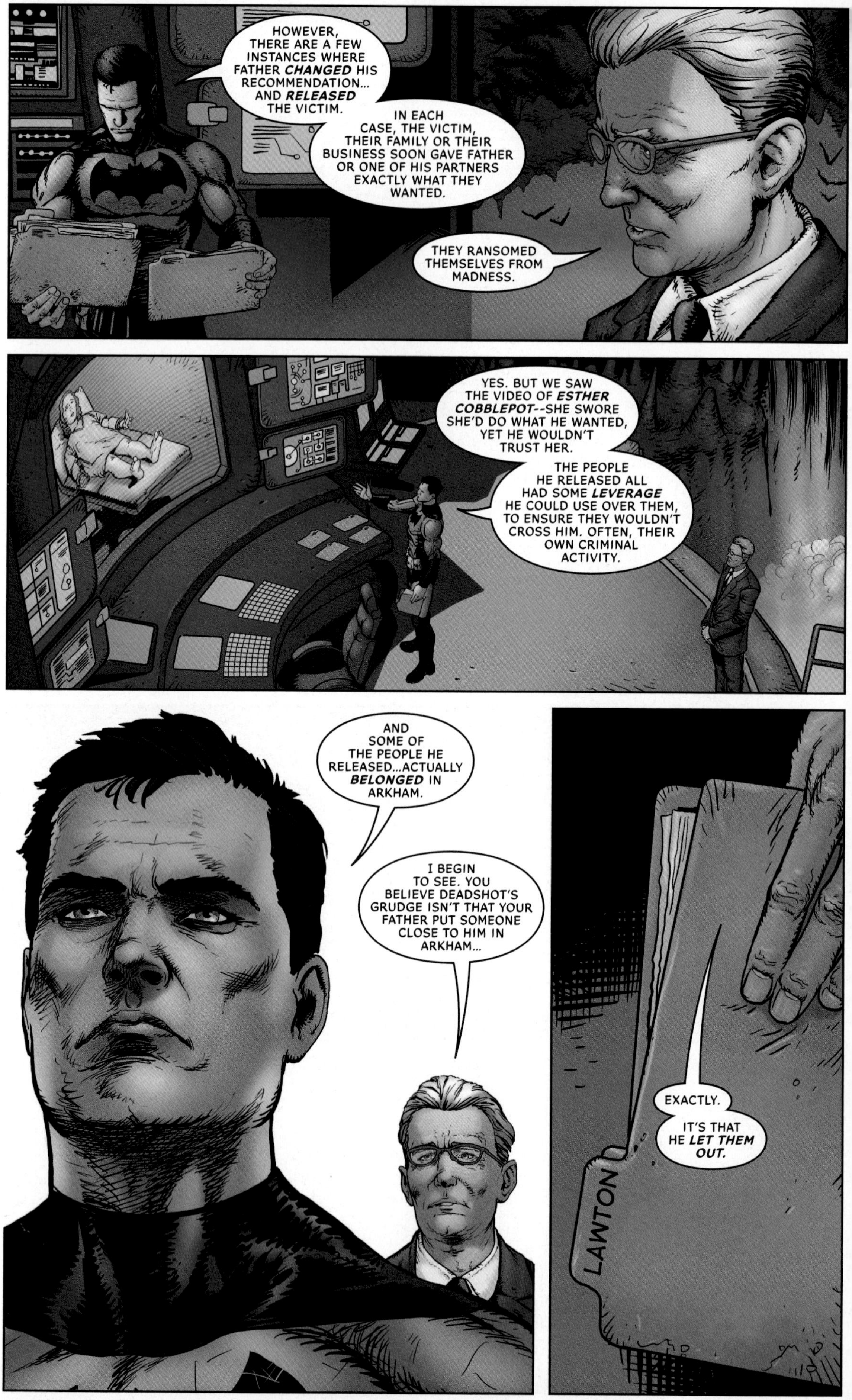
HOWEVER, THERE ARE A FEW INSTANCES WHERE FATHER CHANGED HIS RECOMMENDATION... AND RELEASED THE VICTIM.
IN EACH CASE, THE VICTIM, THEIR FAMILY OR THEIR BUSINESS SOON GAVE FATHER OR ONE OF HIS PARTNERS EXACTLY WHAT THEY WANTED.
THEY RANSOMED THEMSELVES FROM MADNESS.
YES. BUT WE SAW THE VIDEO OF ESTHER COBBLEPOT--SHE SWORE SHE'D DO WHAT HE WANTED, YET HE WOULDN'T TRUST HER.
THE PEOPLE HE RELEASED ALL HAD SOME LEVERAGE HE COULD USE OVER THEM, TO ENSURE THEY WOULDN'T CROSS HIM. OFTEN, THEIR OWN CRIMINAL ACTIVITY.
AND SOME OF THE PEOPLE HE RELEASED...ACTUALLY BELONGED IN ARKHAM.
I BEGIN TO SEE. YOU BELIEVE DEADSHOT'S GRUDGE ISN'T THAT YOUR FATHER PUT SOMEONE CLOSE TO HIM IN ARKHAM...
EXACTLY.
IT'S THAT HE LET THEM OUT.
LAWTON

GEORGE AND GENEVIEVE LAWTON. OLD MONEY ON BOTH SIDES OF THE FAMILY. TWO SONS: EDWARD AND FLOYD.

I REMEMBER. THEIR FORTUNE WAS BUILT ON REAL ESTATE. SOME OF THE MOST COVETED PROPERTIES IN GOTHAM.

AWFUL WHAT HAPPENED. AS I RECALL, THE OLDER BOY...

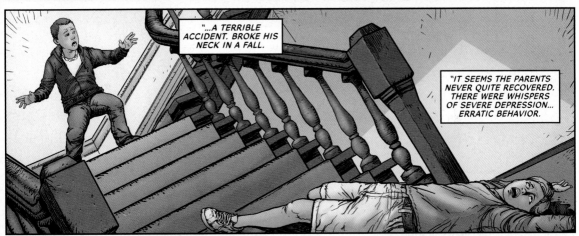

"...A TERRIBLE ACCIDENT. BROKE HIS NECK IN A FALL.

"IT SEEMS THE PARENTS NEVER QUITE RECOVERED. THERE WERE WHISPERS OF SEVERE DEPRESSION... ERRATIC BEHAVIOR.

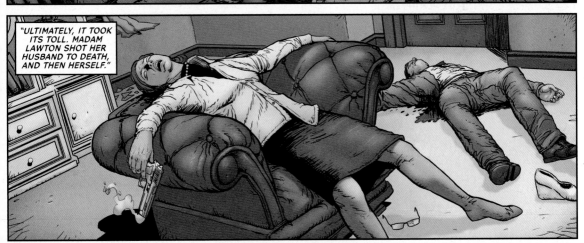

"ULTIMATELY, IT TOOK ITS TOLL. MADAM LAWTON SHOT HER HUSBAND TO DEATH, AND THEN HERSELF."

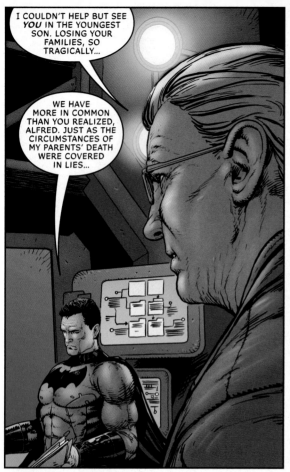

I COULDN'T HELP BUT SEE *YOU* IN THE YOUNGEST SON. LOSING YOUR FAMILIES, SO TRAGICALLY...

WE HAVE MORE IN COMMON THAN YOU REALIZED, ALFRED. JUST AS THE CIRCUMSTANCES OF MY PARENTS' DEATH WERE COVERED IN LIES...

...SO WERE THEIRS. JUST OVER A YEAR BEFORE EDDIE'S DEATH, THE LAWTONS WERE ARRESTED ON SUSPICION OF CHILD ABUSE.

THEY WERE PLACED IN *ARKHAM* FOR EVALUATION.

EVALUATION... BY THOMAS WAYNE?

YES. AND HE ULTIMATELY DEEMED THEM MODEL PARENTS. DOING THE BEST THEY COULD WITH AN EMOTIONALLY DISTURBED SON WHO SELF-HARMED AND BLAMED IT ON THEM.

THE LAWTONS WERE RELEASED. THREE MONTHS LATER, THEY SOLD THE BUILDING WE NOW KNOW AS *WAYNE TOWER* TO MY FATHER... FOR BELOW MARKET VALUE.

NINE MONTHS AFTER THAT, EDDIE WAS DEAD.

"FALLEN" DOWN THE STAIRS.

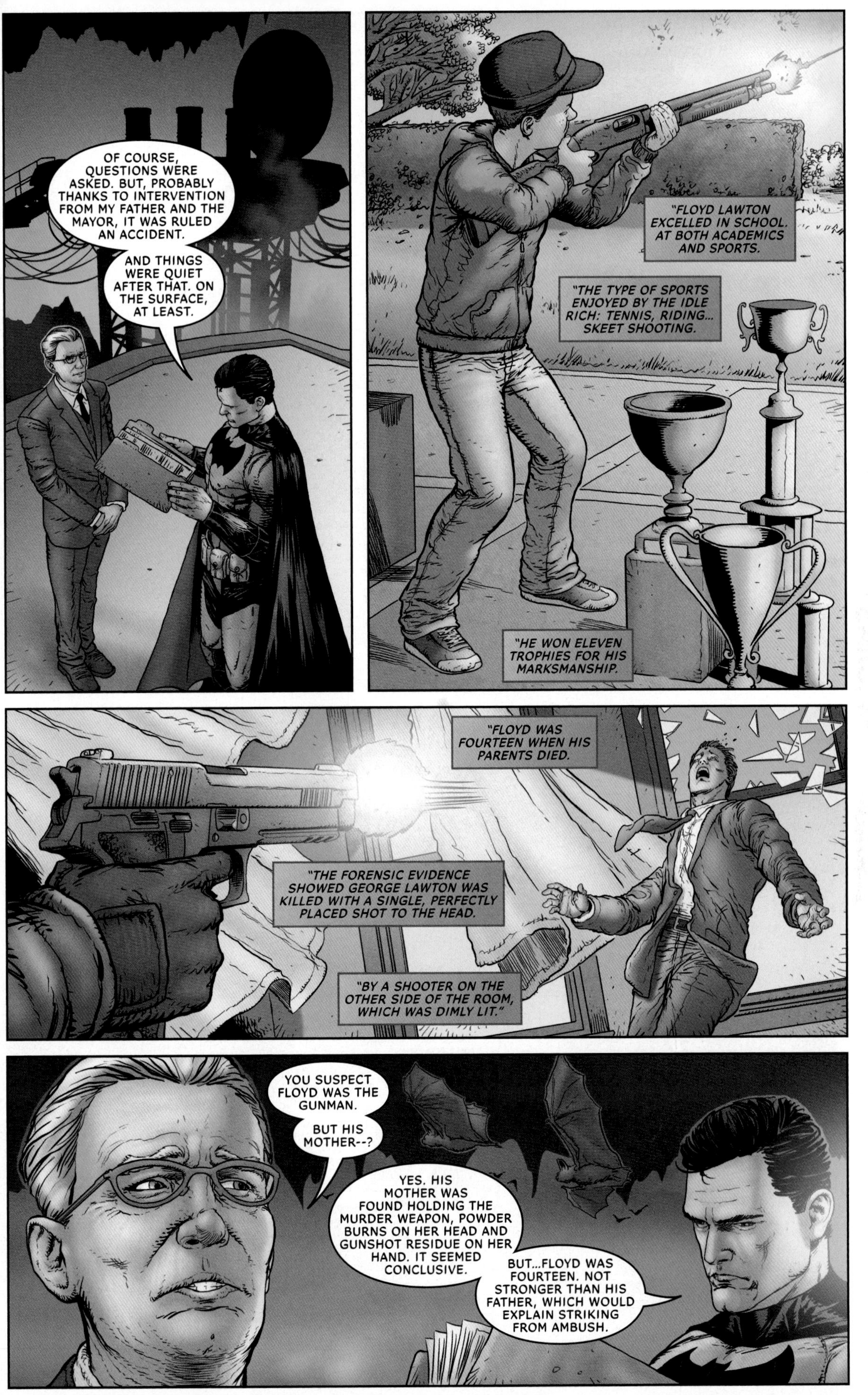
OF COURSE, QUESTIONS WERE ASKED. BUT, PROBABLY THANKS TO INTERVENTION FROM MY FATHER AND THE MAYOR, IT WAS RULED AN ACCIDENT.
AND THINGS WERE QUIET AFTER THAT. ON THE SURFACE, AT LEAST.
"FLOYD LAWTON EXCELLED IN SCHOOL. AT BOTH ACADEMICS AND SPORTS.
"THE TYPE OF SPORTS ENJOYED BY THE IDLE RICH: TENNIS, RIDING... SKEET SHOOTING.
"HE WON ELEVEN TROPHIES FOR HIS MARKSMANSHIP.
"FLOYD WAS FOURTEEN WHEN HIS PARENTS DIED.
"THE FORENSIC EVIDENCE SHOWED GEORGE LAWTON WAS KILLED WITH A SINGLE, PERFECTLY PLACED SHOT TO THE HEAD.
"BY A SHOOTER ON THE OTHER SIDE OF THE ROOM, WHICH WAS DIMLY LIT."
YOU SUSPECT FLOYD WAS THE GUNMAN.
BUT HIS MOTHER--?
YES. HIS MOTHER WAS FOUND HOLDING THE MURDER WEAPON, POWDER BURNS ON HER HEAD AND GUNSHOT RESIDUE ON HER HAND. IT SEEMED CONCLUSIVE.
BUT...FLOYD WAS FOURTEEN. NOT STRONGER THAN HIS FATHER, WHICH WOULD EXPLAIN STRIKING FROM AMBUSH.

"BUT HIS MOTHER WAS FRAIL. A SLIGHT WOMAN.

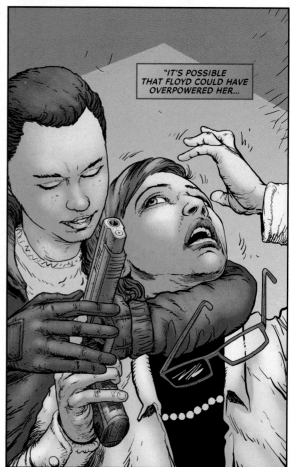

"IT'S POSSIBLE THAT FLOYD COULD HAVE OVERPOWERED HER...

"...WITH SUFFICIENT DETERMINATION."

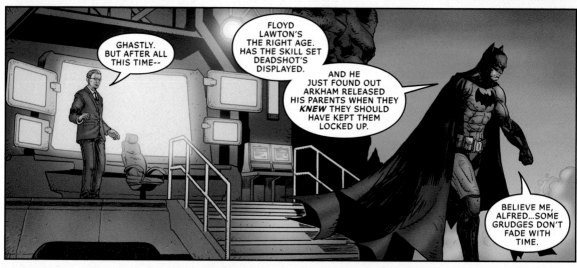

GHASTLY. BUT AFTER ALL THIS TIME--

FLOYD LAWTON'S THE RIGHT AGE. HAS THE SKILL SET DEADSHOT'S DISPLAYED.

AND HE JUST FOUND OUT ARKHAM RELEASED HIS PARENTS WHEN THEY *KNEW* THEY SHOULD HAVE KEPT THEM LOCKED UP.

BELIEVE ME, ALFRED...SOME GRUDGES DON'T FADE WITH TIME.

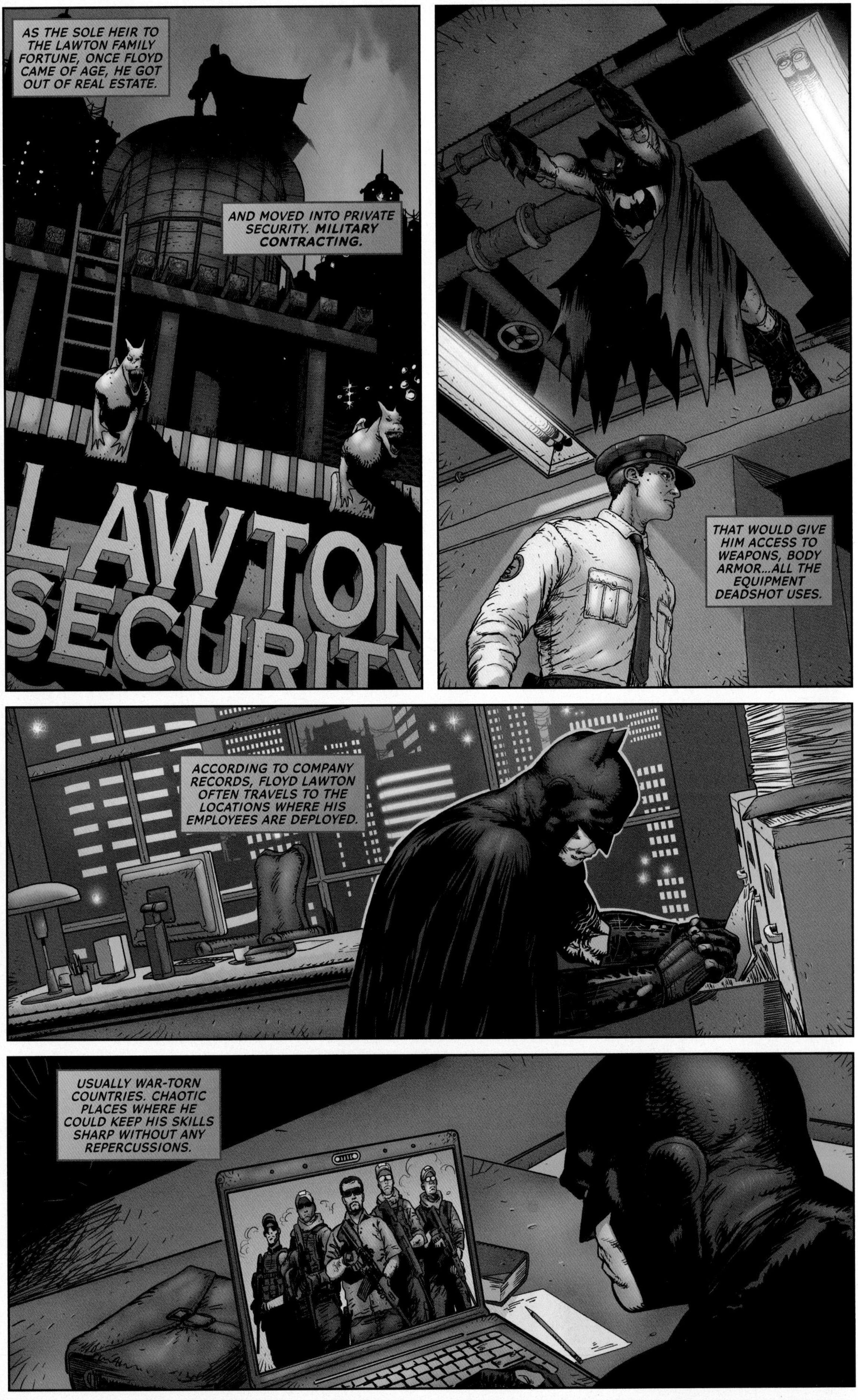
AS THE SOLE HEIR TO THE LAWTON FAMILY FORTUNE, ONCE FLOYD CAME OF AGE, HE GOT OUT OF REAL ESTATE.
AND MOVED INTO PRIVATE SECURITY. MILITARY CONTRACTING.
LAWTON SECURITY
THAT WOULD GIVE HIM ACCESS TO WEAPONS, BODY ARMOR...ALL THE EQUIPMENT DEADSHOT USES.
ACCORDING TO COMPANY RECORDS, FLOYD LAWTON OFTEN TRAVELS TO THE LOCATIONS WHERE HIS EMPLOYEES ARE DEPLOYED.
USUALLY WAR-TORN COUNTRIES. CHAOTIC PLACES WHERE HE COULD KEEP HIS SKILLS SHARP WITHOUT ANY REPERCUSSIONS.

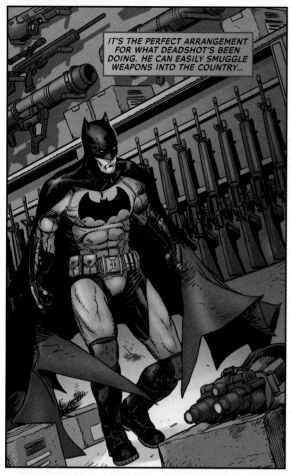

IT'S THE PERFECT ARRANGEMENT FOR WHAT DEADSHOT'S BEEN DOING. HE CAN EASILY SMUGGLE WEAPONS INTO THE COUNTRY...

...OR OUT. I'D IMAGINE ANY GUN HE'S USED IS NOW SEVERAL CONTINENTS AWAY.

FREEZE!

FOR LAWTON TO HAVE MAINTAINED HIS SKILLS, HIS ACCESS TO ARMAMENTS, LONG AFTER HE THOUGHT THE PEOPLE WHO HURT HIM WERE ALL DEAD, SUGGESTS SOMETHING DISTURBING.

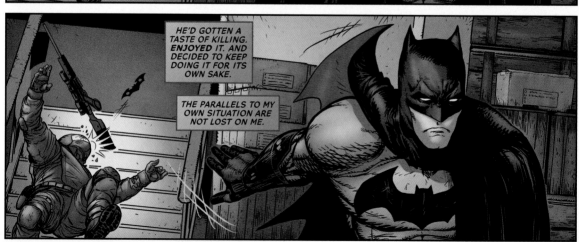

HE'D GOTTEN A TASTE OF KILLING. ENJOYED IT. AND DECIDED TO KEEP DOING IT FOR ITS OWN SAKE.

THE PARALLELS TO MY OWN SITUATION ARE NOT LOST ON ME.

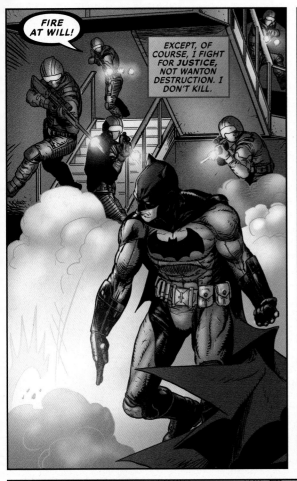

FIRE AT WILL!

EXCEPT, OF COURSE, I FIGHT FOR JUSTICE, NOT WANTON DESTRUCTION. I DON'T KILL.

AND WITH THESE MEN-- WHO ARE JUST DOING THEIR JOBS--I HAVE TO TAKE CARE TO NOT EVEN INJURE THEM.

BUT IT'S IMPORTANT THAT I BE SEEN. THAT WORD GETS BACK TO FLOYD LAWTON.

THAT HE KNOWS I'M ONTO HIM.

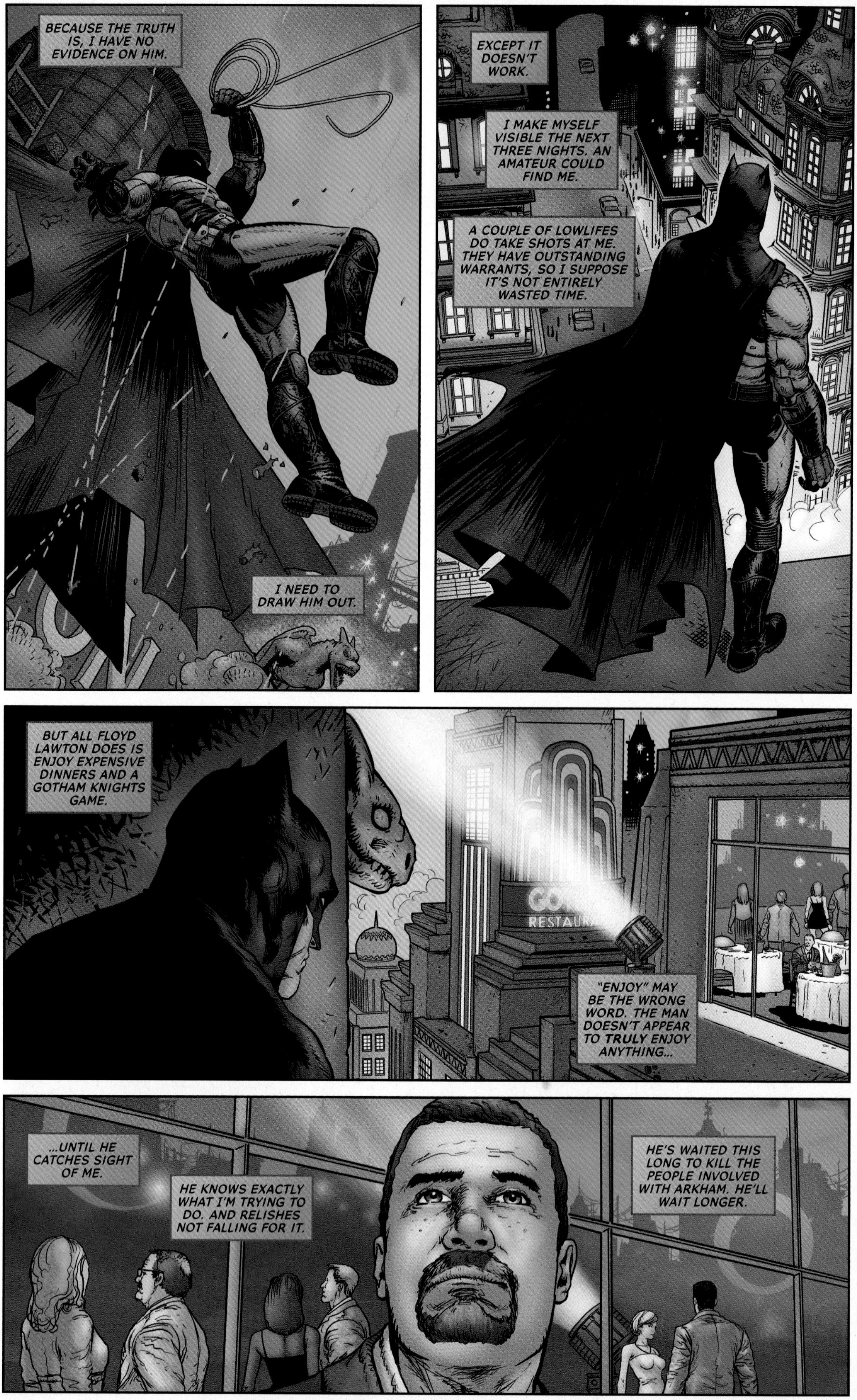
BECAUSE THE TRUTH IS, I HAVE NO EVIDENCE ON HIM.
I NEED TO DRAW HIM OUT.
EXCEPT IT DOESN'T WORK.
I MAKE MYSELF VISIBLE THE NEXT THREE NIGHTS. AN AMATEUR COULD FIND ME.
A COUPLE OF LOWLIFES DO TAKE SHOTS AT ME. THEY HAVE OUTSTANDING WARRANTS, SO I SUPPOSE IT'S NOT ENTIRELY WASTED TIME.
BUT ALL FLOYD LAWTON DOES IS ENJOY EXPENSIVE DINNERS AND A GOTHAM KNIGHTS GAME.
RESTAURA
"ENJOY" MAY BE THE WRONG WORD. THE MAN DOESN'T APPEAR TO **TRULY** ENJOY ANYTHING...
...UNTIL HE CATCHES SIGHT OF ME.
HE KNOWS EXACTLY WHAT I'M TRYING TO DO. AND RELISHES NOT FALLING FOR IT.
HE'S WAITED THIS LONG TO KILL THE PEOPLE INVOLVED WITH ARKHAM. HE'LL WAIT LONGER.

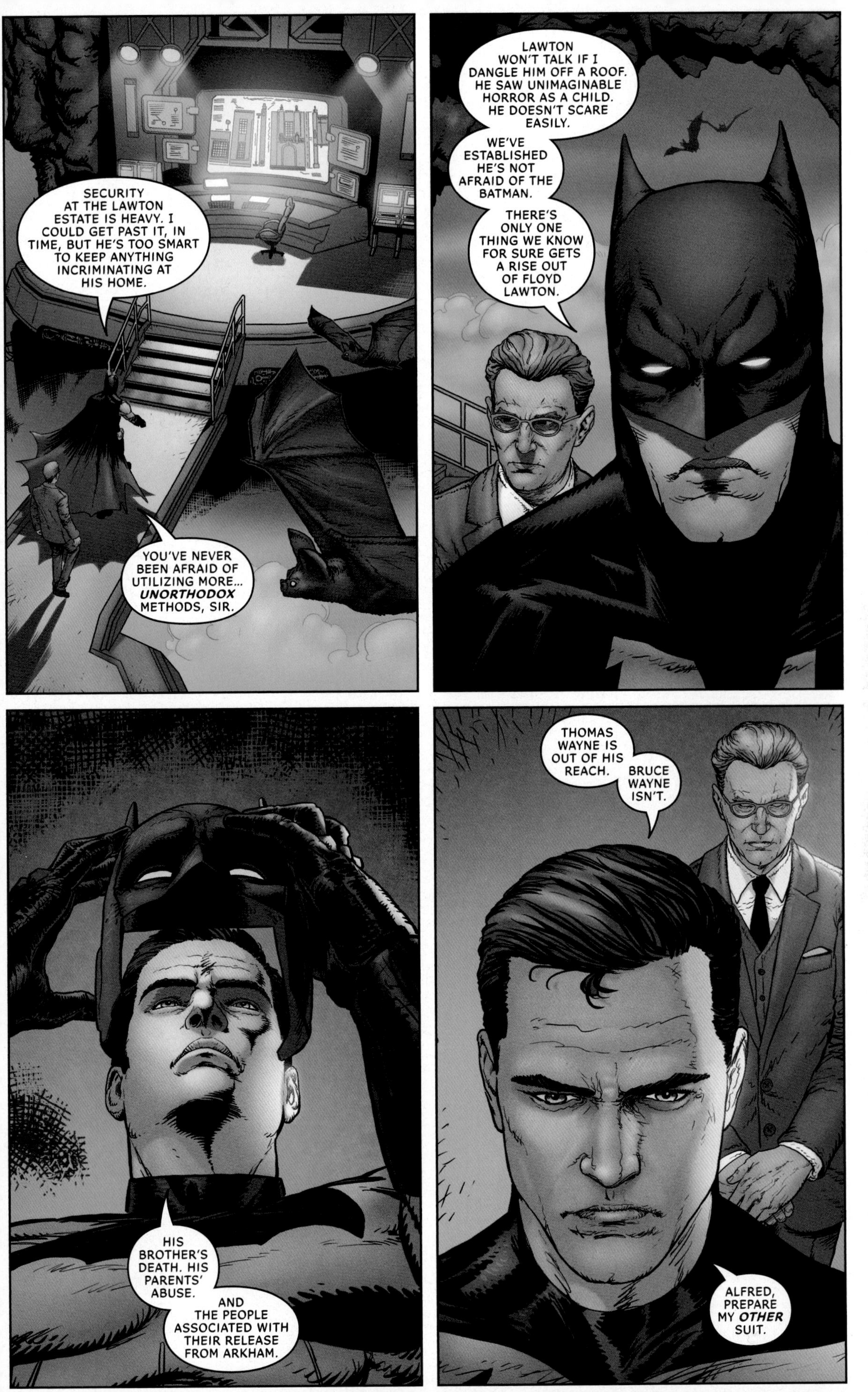
SECURITY AT THE LAWTON ESTATE IS HEAVY. I COULD GET PAST IT, IN TIME, BUT HE'S TOO SMART TO KEEP ANYTHING INCRIMINATING AT HIS HOME.
YOU'VE NEVER BEEN AFRAID OF UTILIZING MORE... *UNORTHODOX* METHODS, SIR.
LAWTON WON'T TALK IF I DANGLE HIM OFF A ROOF. HE SAW UNIMAGINABLE HORROR AS A CHILD. HE DOESN'T SCARE EASILY.
WE'VE ESTABLISHED HE'S NOT AFRAID OF THE BATMAN.
THERE'S ONLY ONE THING WE KNOW FOR SURE GETS A RISE OUT OF FLOYD LAWTON.
HIS BROTHER'S DEATH. HIS PARENTS' ABUSE.
AND THE PEOPLE ASSOCIATED WITH THEIR RELEASE FROM ARKHAM.
THOMAS WAYNE IS OUT OF HIS REACH.
BRUCE WAYNE ISN'T.
ALFRED, PREPARE MY *OTHER* SUIT.

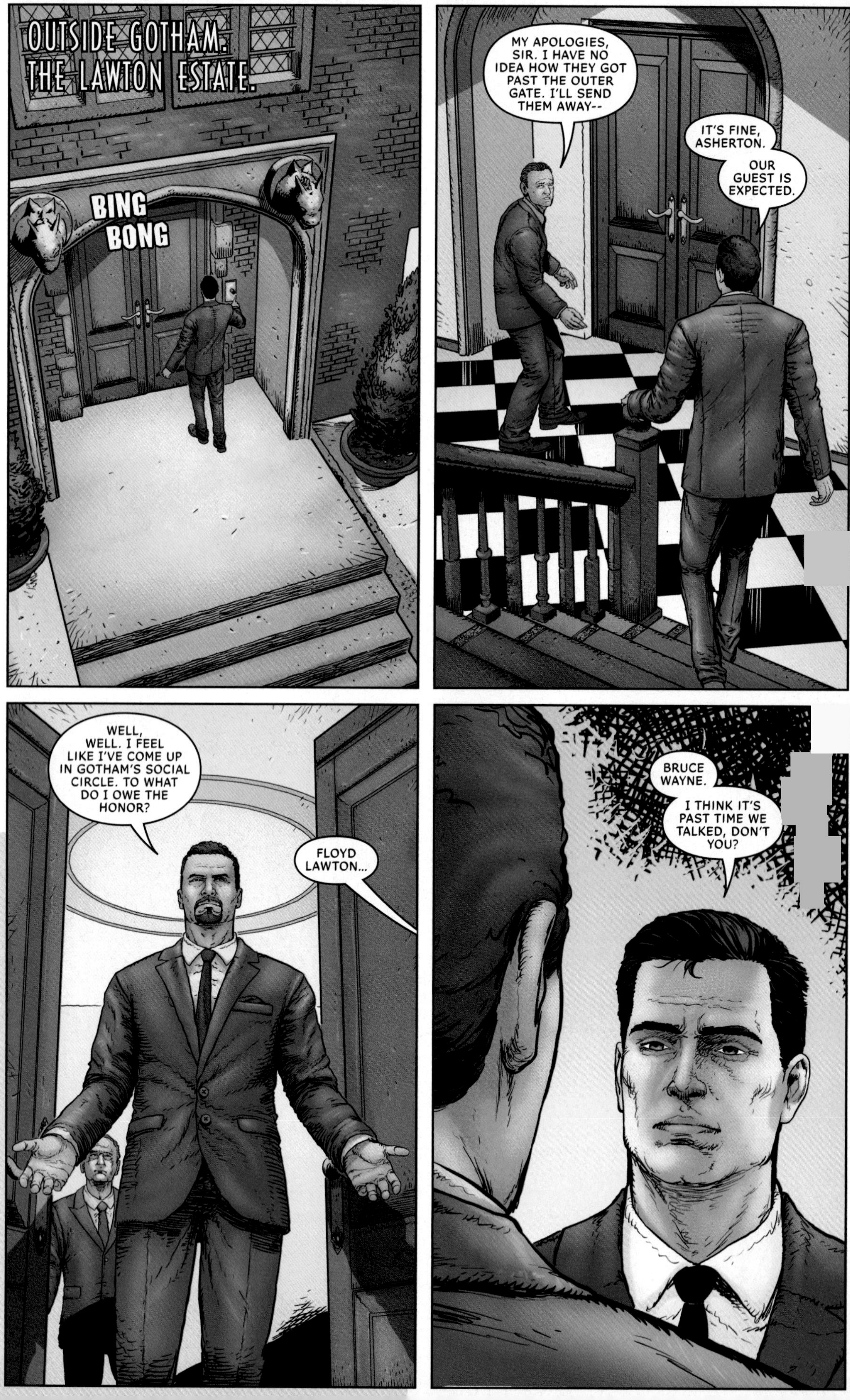
OUTSIDE GOTHAM. THE LAWTON ESTATE.
BING BONG
MY APOLOGIES, SIR. I HAVE NO IDEA HOW THEY GOT PAST THE OUTER GATE. I'LL SEND THEM AWAY--
IT'S FINE, ASHERTON.
OUR GUEST IS EXPECTED.
WELL, WELL. I FEEL LIKE I'VE COME UP IN GOTHAM'S SOCIAL CIRCLE. TO WHAT DO I OWE THE HONOR?
FLOYD LAWTON...
BRUCE WAYNE.
I THINK IT'S PAST TIME WE TALKED, DON'T YOU?

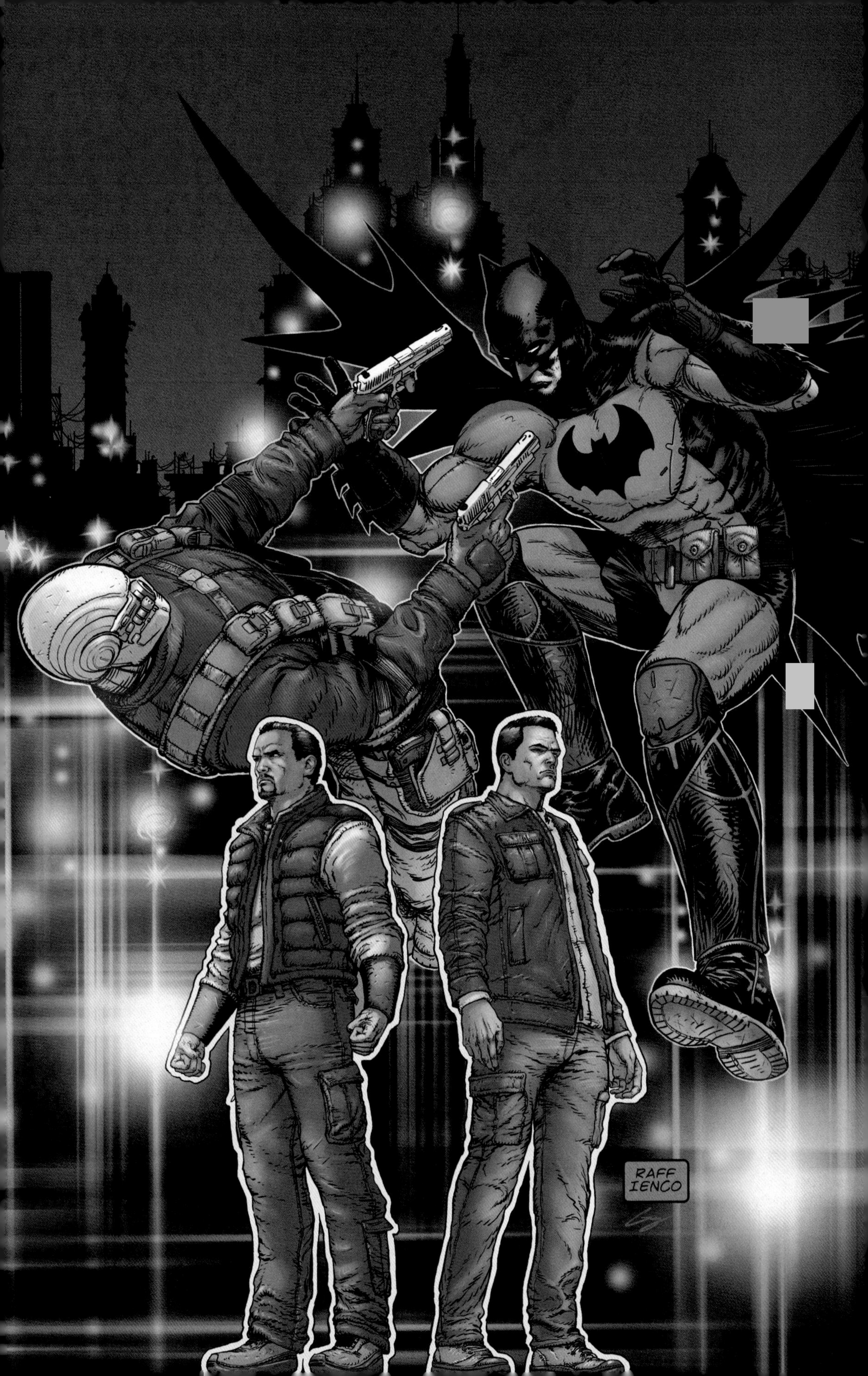
RAFF
IENCO

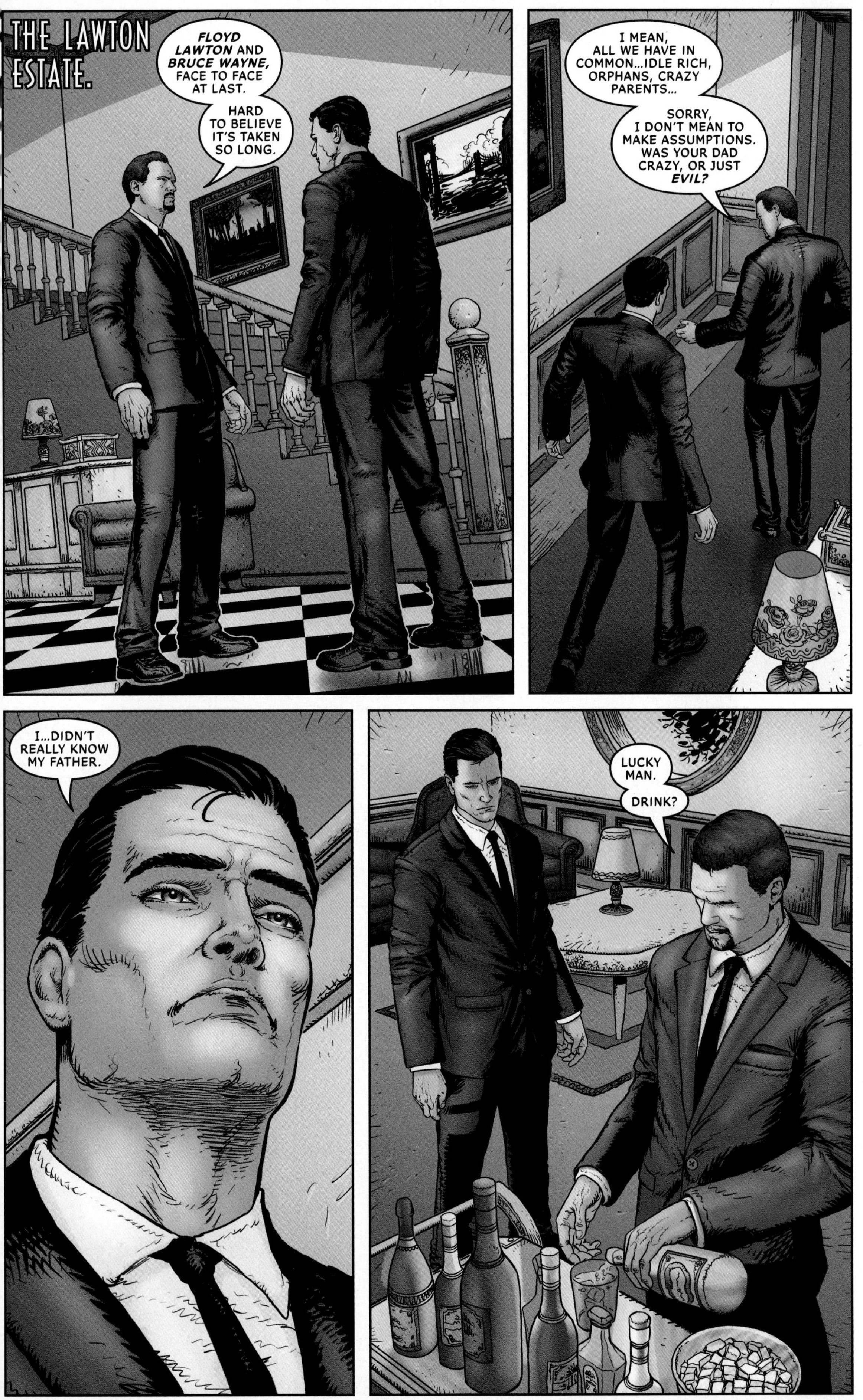
THE LAWTON ESTATE.
FLOYD LAWTON AND BRUCE WAYNE, FACE TO FACE AT LAST.
HARD TO BELIEVE IT'S TAKEN SO LONG.
I MEAN, ALL WE HAVE IN COMMON...IDLE RICH, ORPHANS, CRAZY PARENTS...
SORRY, I DON'T MEAN TO MAKE ASSUMPTIONS. WAS YOUR DAD CRAZY, OR JUST EVIL?
I...DIDN'T REALLY KNOW MY FATHER.
LUCKY MAN.
DRINK?

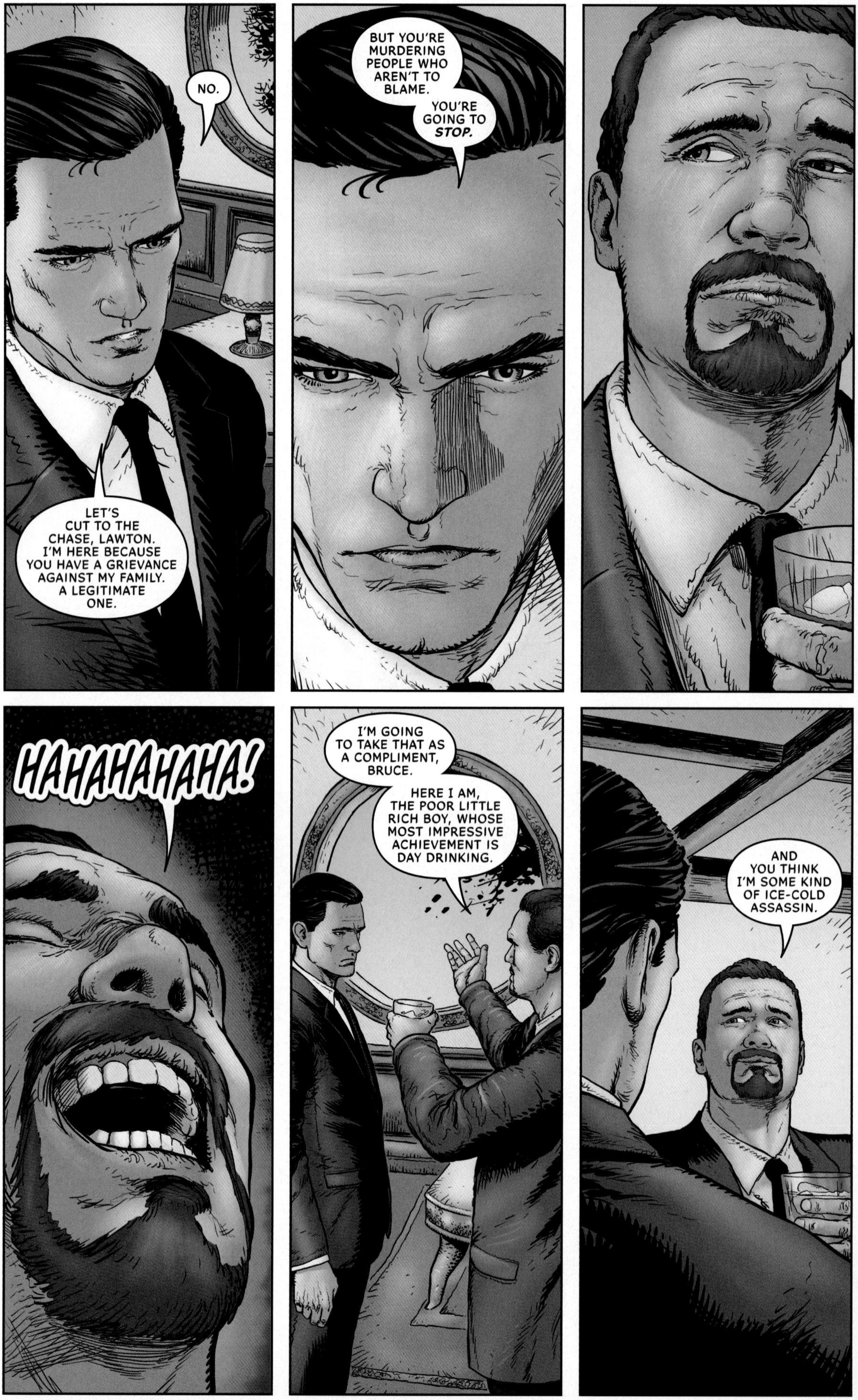
NO.
LET'S CUT TO THE CHASE, LAWTON. I'M HERE BECAUSE YOU HAVE A GRIEVANCE AGAINST MY FAMILY. A LEGITIMATE ONE.
BUT YOU'RE MURDERING PEOPLE WHO AREN'T TO BLAME.
YOU'RE GOING TO *STOP.*
HAHAHAHAHAHA!
I'M GOING TO TAKE THAT AS A COMPLIMENT, BRUCE.
HERE I AM, THE POOR LITTLE RICH BOY, WHOSE MOST IMPRESSIVE ACHIEVEMENT IS DAY DRINKING.
AND YOU THINK I'M SOME KIND OF ICE-COLD ASSASSIN.

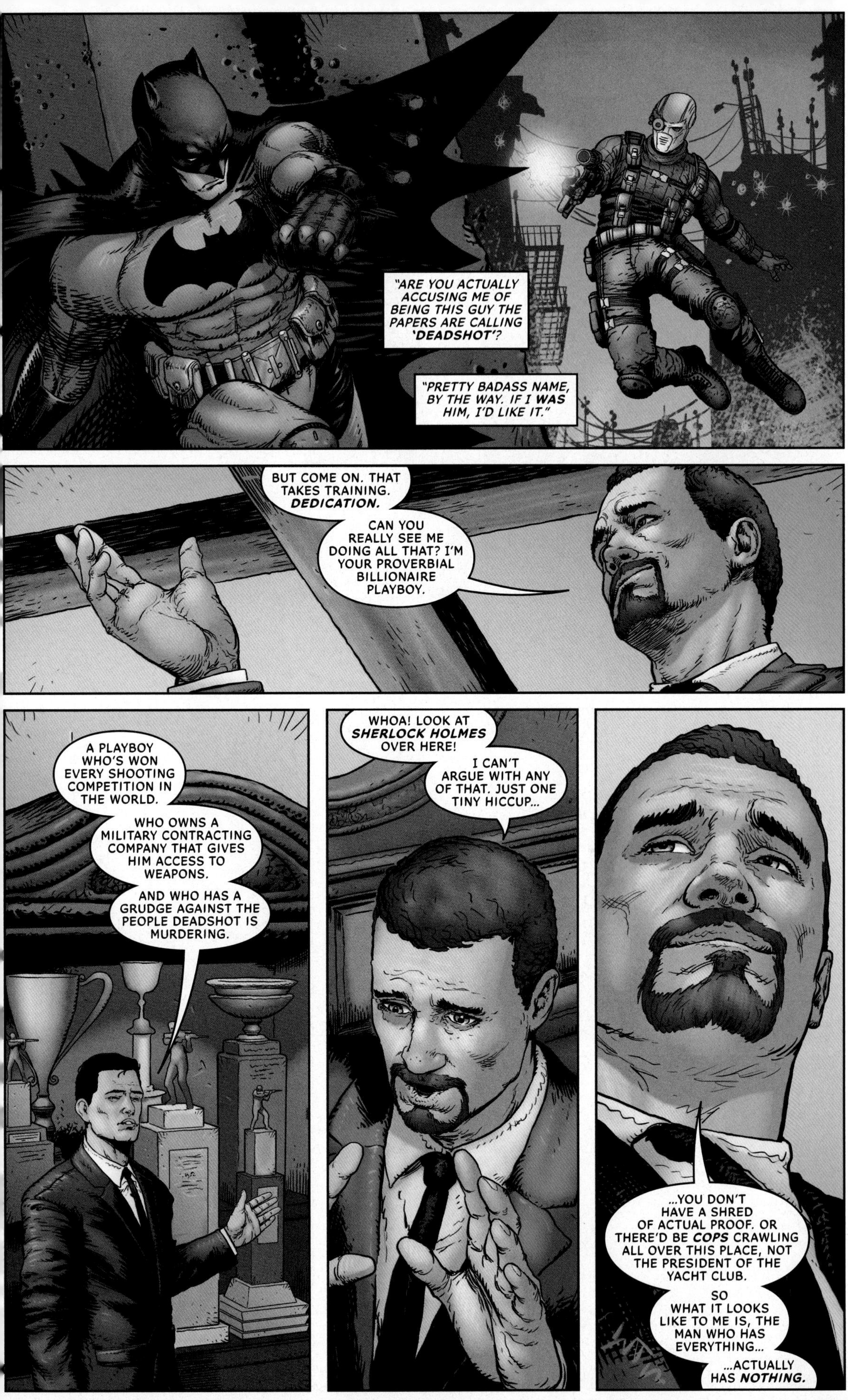

"ARE YOU ACTUALLY ACCUSING ME OF BEING THIS GUY THE PAPERS ARE CALLING *'DEADSHOT'*?
"PRETTY BADASS NAME, BY THE WAY. IF I *WAS* HIM, I'D LIKE IT."
BUT COME ON. THAT TAKES TRAINING. *DEDICATION.*
CAN YOU REALLY SEE ME DOING ALL THAT? I'M YOUR PROVERBIAL BILLIONAIRE PLAYBOY.
A PLAYBOY WHO'S WON EVERY SHOOTING COMPETITION IN THE WORLD.
WHO OWNS A MILITARY CONTRACTING COMPANY THAT GIVES HIM ACCESS TO WEAPONS.
AND WHO HAS A GRUDGE AGAINST THE PEOPLE DEADSHOT IS MURDERING.
WHOA! LOOK AT *SHERLOCK HOLMES* OVER HERE!
I CAN'T ARGUE WITH ANY OF THAT. JUST ONE TINY HICCUP...
...YOU DON'T HAVE A SHRED OF ACTUAL PROOF. OR THERE'D BE *COPS* CRAWLING ALL OVER THIS PLACE, NOT THE PRESIDENT OF THE YACHT CLUB.
SO WHAT IT LOOKS LIKE TO ME IS, THE MAN WHO HAS EVERYTHING...
...ACTUALLY HAS *NOTHING.*

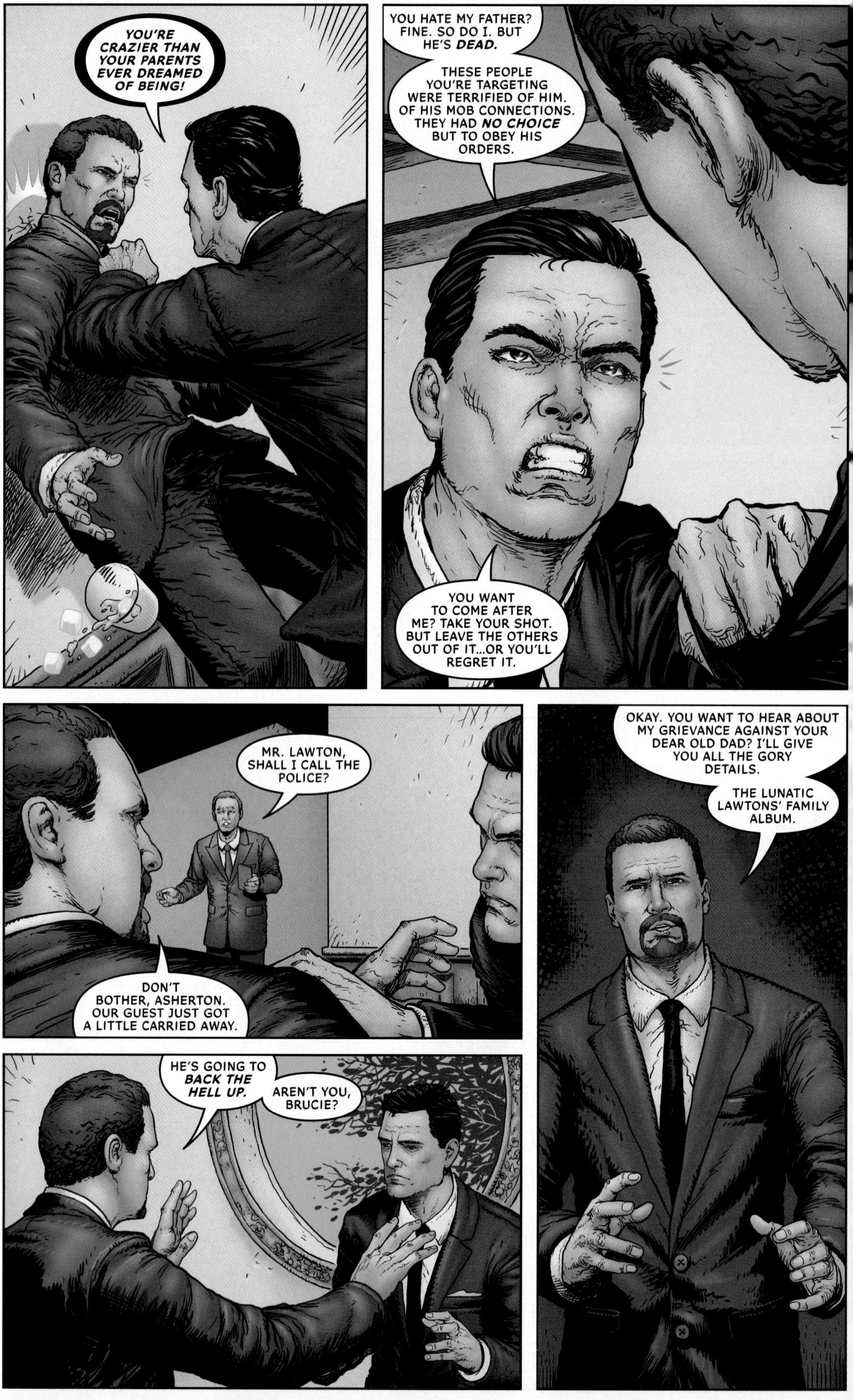
YOU'RE CRAZIER THAN YOUR PARENTS EVER DREAMED OF BEING!
YOU HATE MY FATHER? FINE. SO DO I. BUT HE'S DEAD.
THESE PEOPLE YOU'RE TARGETING WERE TERRIFIED OF HIM. OF HIS MOB CONNECTIONS. THEY HAD NO CHOICE BUT TO OBEY HIS ORDERS.
YOU WANT TO COME AFTER ME? TAKE YOUR SHOT. BUT LEAVE THE OTHERS OUT OF IT...OR YOU'LL REGRET IT.
MR. LAWTON, SHALL I CALL THE POLICE?
DON'T BOTHER, ASHERTON. OUR GUEST JUST GOT A LITTLE CARRIED AWAY.
HE'S GOING TO BACK THE HELL UP.
AREN'T YOU, BRUCIE?
OKAY. YOU WANT TO HEAR ABOUT MY GRIEVANCE AGAINST YOUR DEAR OLD DAD? I'LL GIVE YOU ALL THE GORY DETAILS.
THE LUNATIC LAWTONS' FAMILY ALBUM.

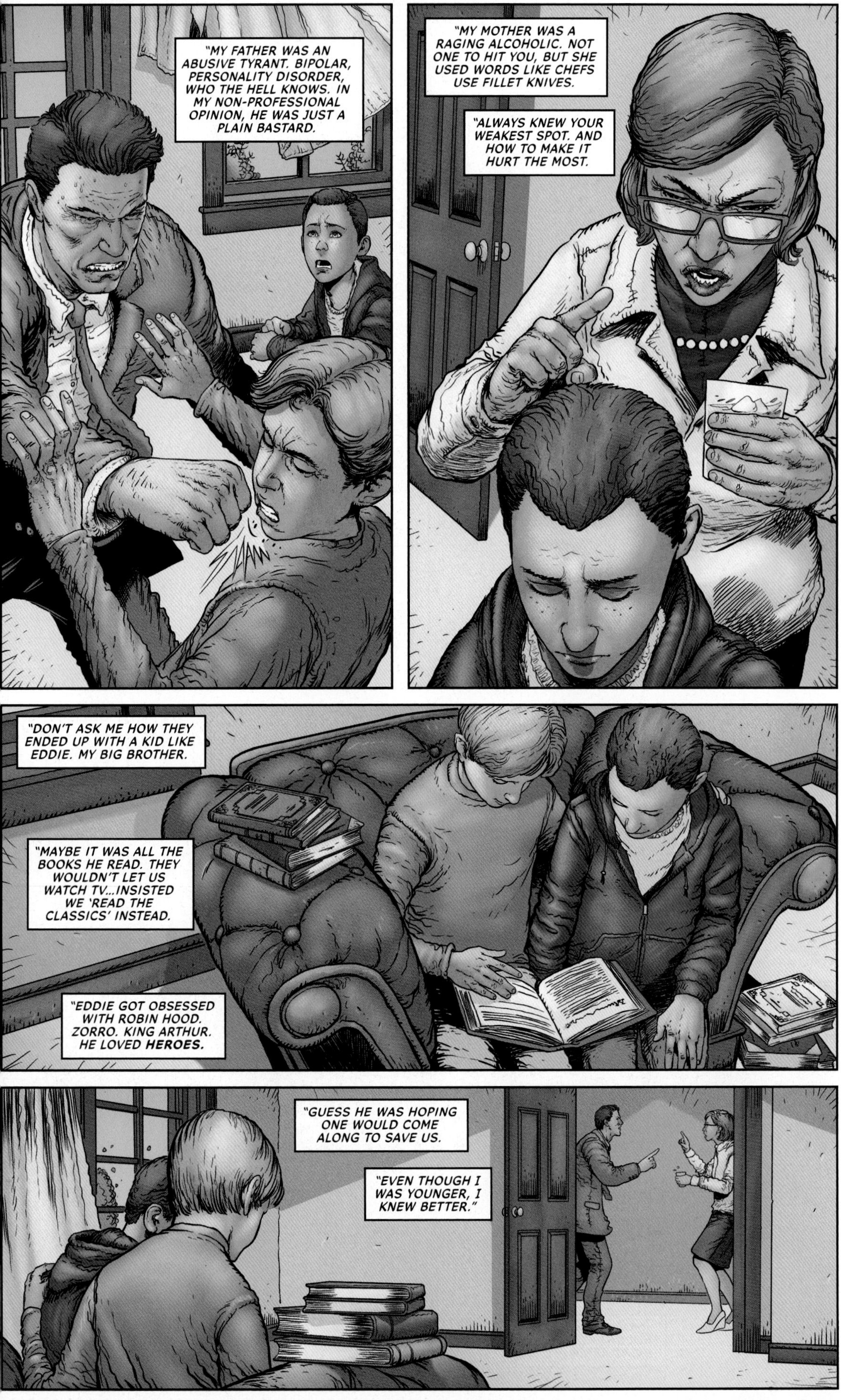
"MY FATHER WAS AN ABUSIVE TYRANT. BIPOLAR, PERSONALITY DISORDER, WHO THE HELL KNOWS. IN MY NON-PROFESSIONAL OPINION, HE WAS JUST A PLAIN BASTARD.
"MY MOTHER WAS A RAGING ALCOHOLIC. NOT ONE TO HIT YOU, BUT SHE USED WORDS LIKE CHEFS USE FILLET KNIVES.
"ALWAYS KNEW YOUR WEAKEST SPOT. AND HOW TO MAKE IT HURT THE MOST.
"DON'T ASK ME HOW THEY ENDED UP WITH A KID LIKE EDDIE. MY BIG BROTHER.
"MAYBE IT WAS ALL THE BOOKS HE READ. THEY WOULDN'T LET US WATCH TV...INSISTED WE 'READ THE CLASSICS' INSTEAD.
"EDDIE GOT OBSESSED WITH ROBIN HOOD. ZORRO. KING ARTHUR. HE LOVED **HEROES.**
"GUESS HE WAS HOPING ONE WOULD COME ALONG TO SAVE US.
"EVEN THOUGH I WAS YOUNGER, I KNEW BETTER."

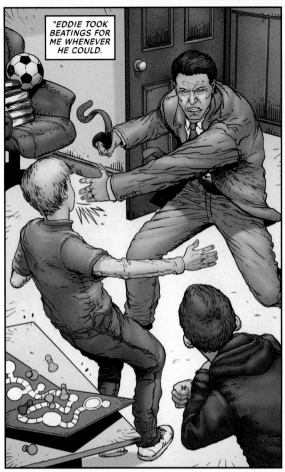

"EDDIE TOOK BEATINGS FOR ME WHENEVER HE COULD.

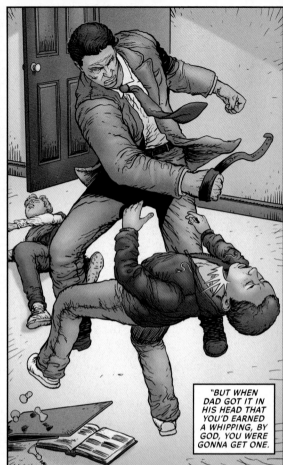

"BUT WHEN DAD GOT IT IN HIS HEAD THAT YOU'D EARNED A WHIPPING, BY GOD, YOU WERE GONNA GET ONE.

"FINALLY EDDIE SCREWED UP THE COURAGE TO REPORT OUR PARENTS.

"THE POLICE CAME AND GOT 'EM. TOOK THE BAD PEOPLE AWAY. JUST LIKE THE HEROES EDDIE LOOKED UP TO.

"FOR A MINUTE I THOUGHT HE'D BEEN RIGHT AFTER ALL."

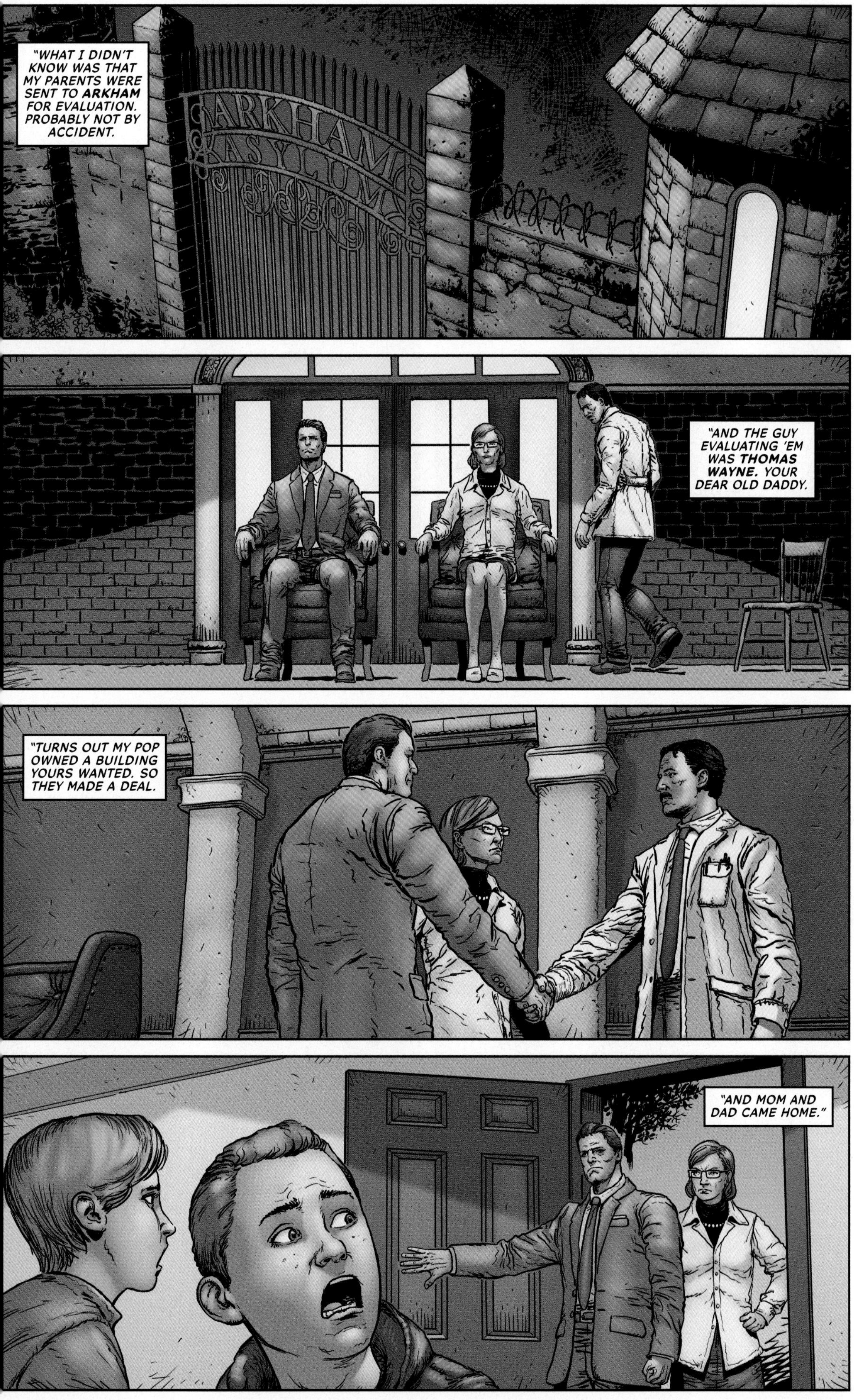
"WHAT I DIDN'T KNOW WAS THAT MY PARENTS WERE SENT TO ARKHAM FOR EVALUATION. PROBABLY NOT BY ACCIDENT.
ARKHAM ASYLUM
"AND THE GUY EVALUATING 'EM WAS THOMAS WAYNE. YOUR DEAR OLD DADDY.
"TURNS OUT MY POP OWNED A BUILDING YOURS WANTED. SO THEY MADE A DEAL.
"AND MOM AND DAD CAME HOME."

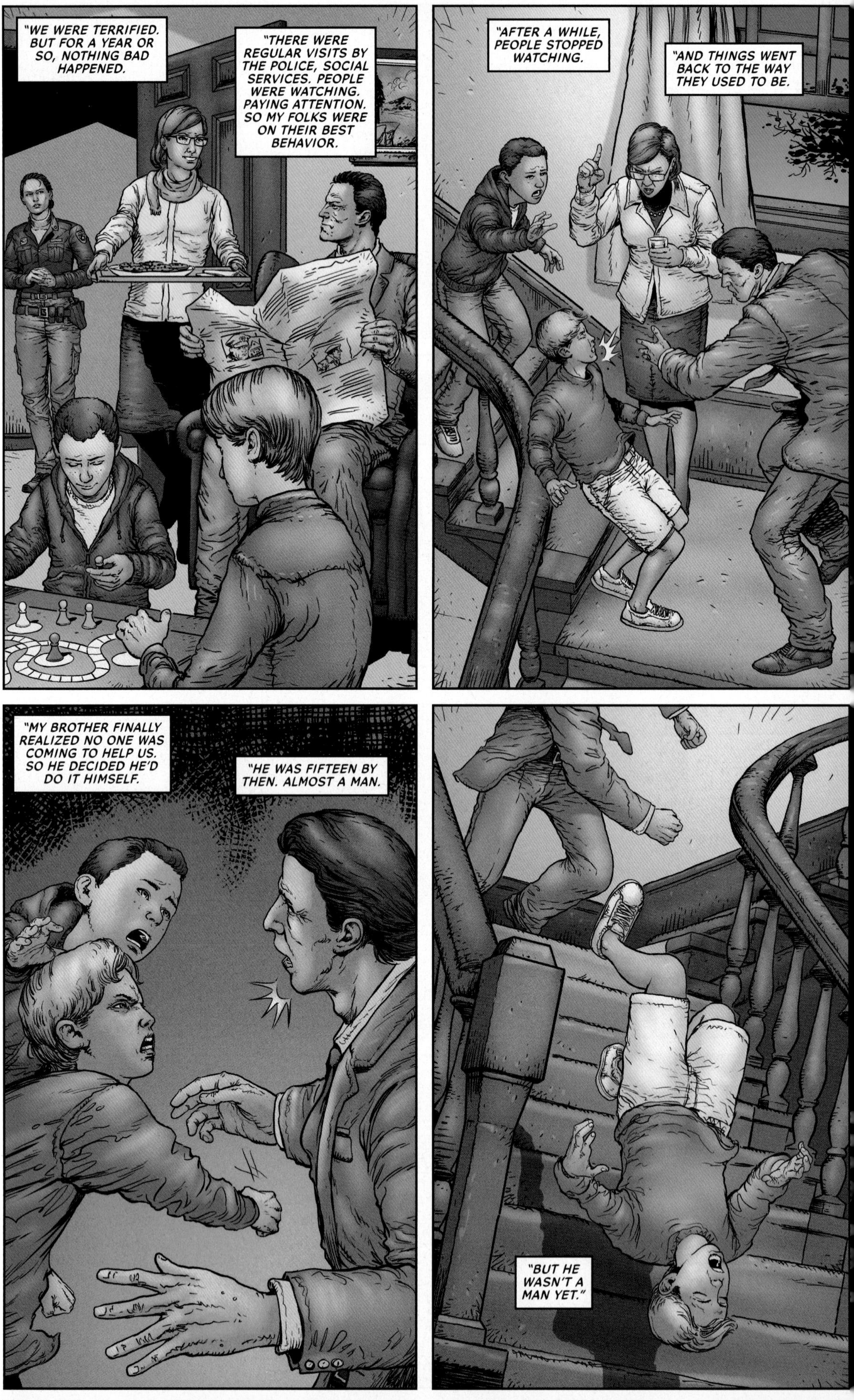
"WE WERE TERRIFIED. BUT FOR A YEAR OR SO, NOTHING BAD HAPPENED.
"THERE WERE REGULAR VISITS BY THE POLICE, SOCIAL SERVICES. PEOPLE WERE WATCHING. PAYING ATTENTION. SO MY FOLKS WERE ON THEIR BEST BEHAVIOR.
"AFTER A WHILE, PEOPLE STOPPED WATCHING.
"AND THINGS WENT BACK TO THE WAY THEY USED TO BE.
"MY BROTHER FINALLY REALIZED NO ONE WAS COMING TO HELP US. SO HE DECIDED HE'D DO IT HIMSELF.
"HE WAS FIFTEEN BY THEN. ALMOST A MAN.
"BUT HE WASN'T A MAN YET."

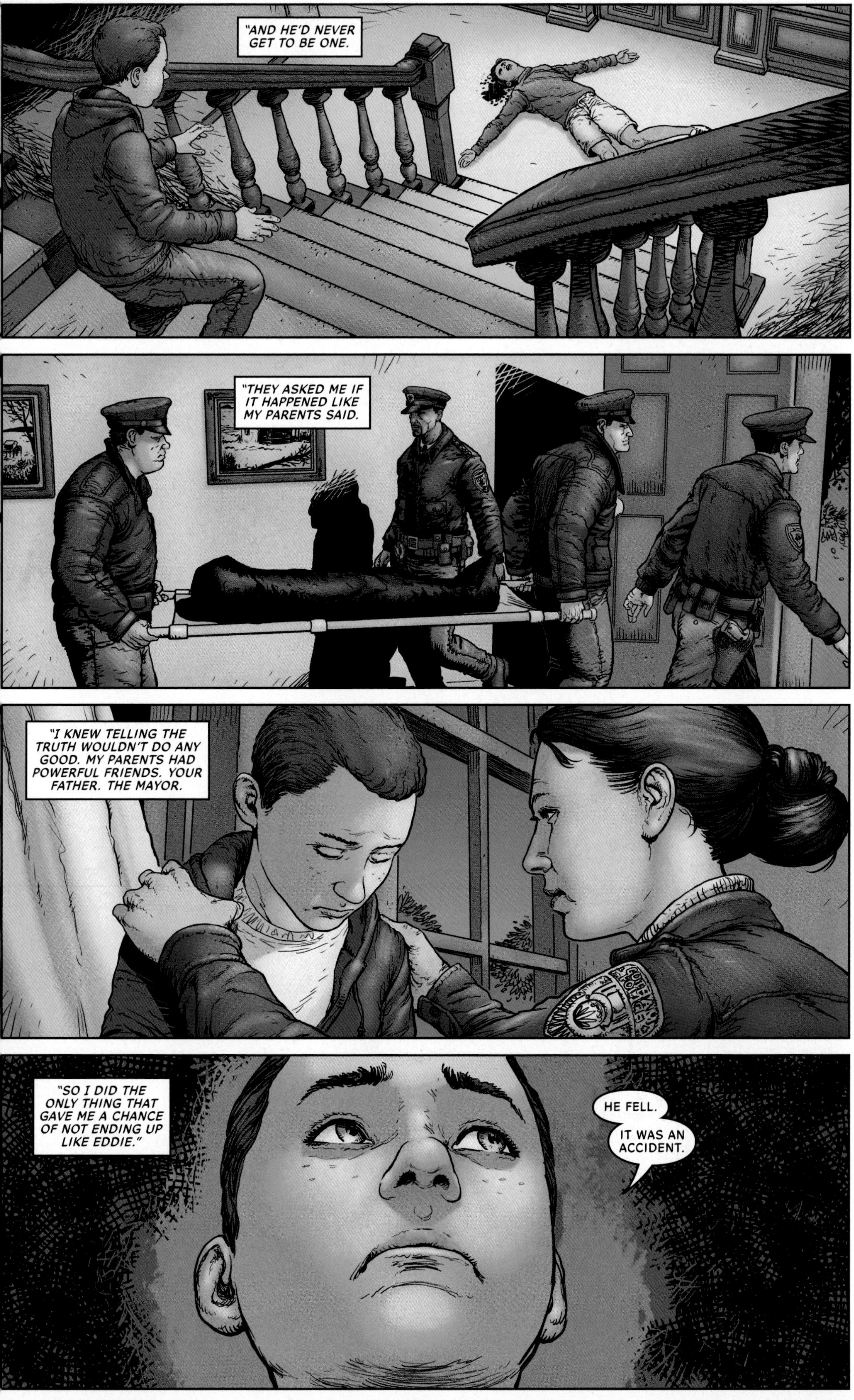
"AND HE'D NEVER GET TO BE ONE.
"THEY ASKED ME IF IT HAPPENED LIKE MY PARENTS SAID.
"I KNEW TELLING THE TRUTH WOULDN'T DO ANY GOOD. MY PARENTS HAD POWERFUL FRIENDS. YOUR FATHER. THE MAYOR.
"SO I DID THE ONLY THING THAT GAVE ME A CHANCE OF NOT ENDING UP LIKE EDDIE."
HE FELL.
IT WAS AN ACCIDENT.

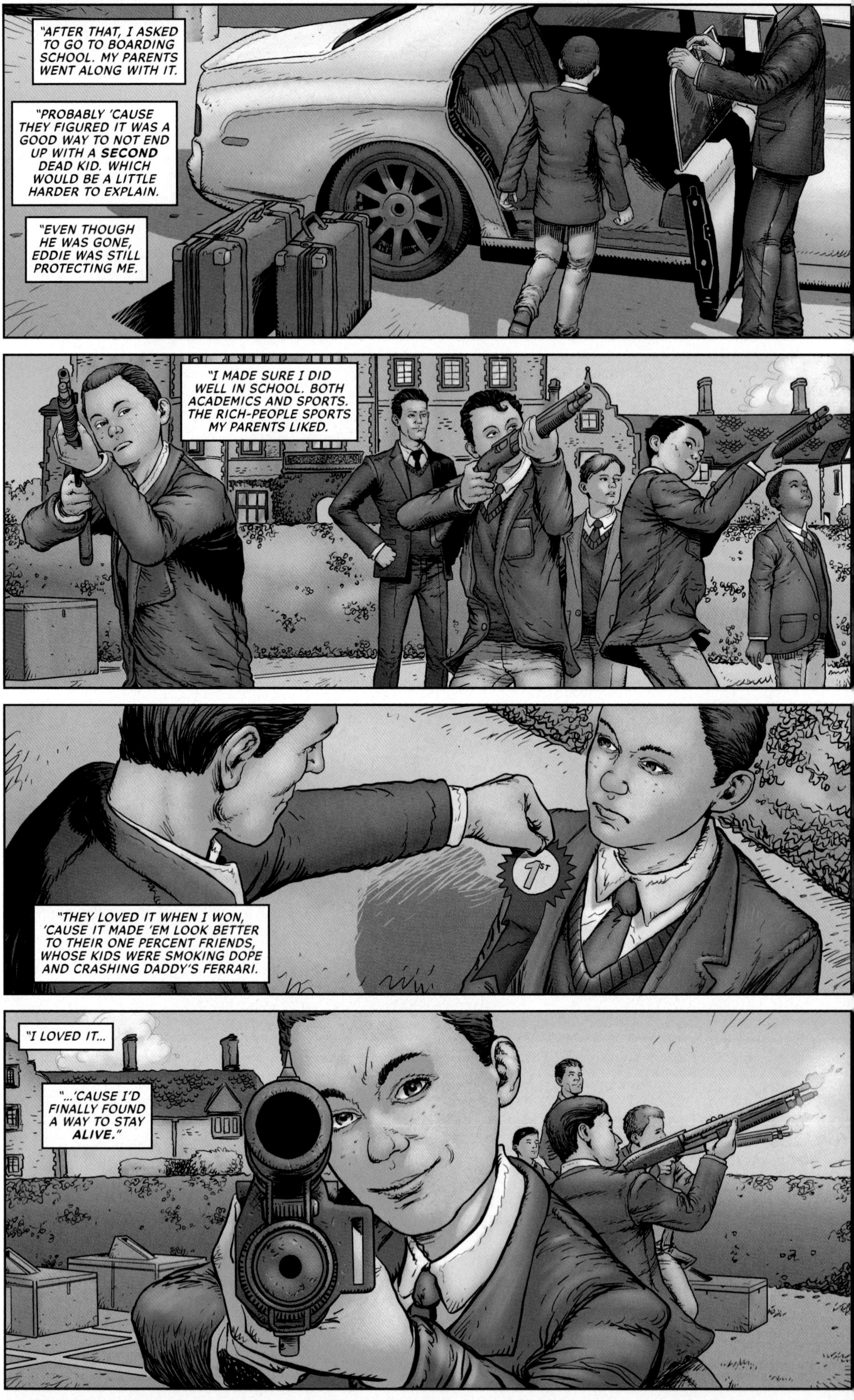
"AFTER THAT, I ASKED TO GO TO BOARDING SCHOOL. MY PARENTS WENT ALONG WITH IT.
"PROBABLY 'CAUSE THEY FIGURED IT WAS A GOOD WAY TO NOT END UP WITH A **SECOND** DEAD KID. WHICH WOULD BE A LITTLE HARDER TO EXPLAIN.
"EVEN THOUGH HE WAS GONE, EDDIE WAS STILL PROTECTING ME.
"I MADE SURE I DID WELL IN SCHOOL. BOTH ACADEMICS AND SPORTS. THE RICH-PEOPLE SPORTS MY PARENTS LIKED.
1ST
"THEY LOVED IT WHEN I WON, 'CAUSE IT MADE 'EM LOOK BETTER TO THEIR ONE PERCENT FRIENDS, WHOSE KIDS WERE SMOKING DOPE AND CRASHING DADDY'S FERRARI.
"I LOVED IT...
"...'CAUSE I'D FINALLY FOUND A WAY TO STAY **ALIVE.**"

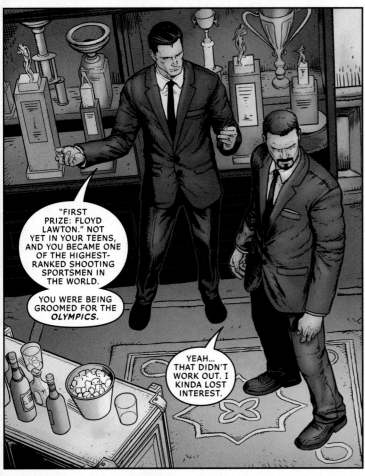

"FIRST PRIZE: FLOYD LAWTON." NOT YET IN YOUR TEENS, AND YOU BECAME ONE OF THE HIGHEST-RANKED SHOOTING SPORTSMEN IN THE WORLD.

YOU WERE BEING GROOMED FOR THE *OLYMPICS.*

YEAH... THAT DIDN'T WORK OUT. I KINDA LOST INTEREST.

AFTER YOUR PARENTS DIED.

"DIED." WHAT A POLITE WAY OF PUTTING IT. YOU DON'T HAVE TO PUSSYFOOT AROUND IT, WAYNE...

"...MY MOTHER *SHOT* MY FATHER, THEN HERSELF.

"GOOD RIDDANCE."

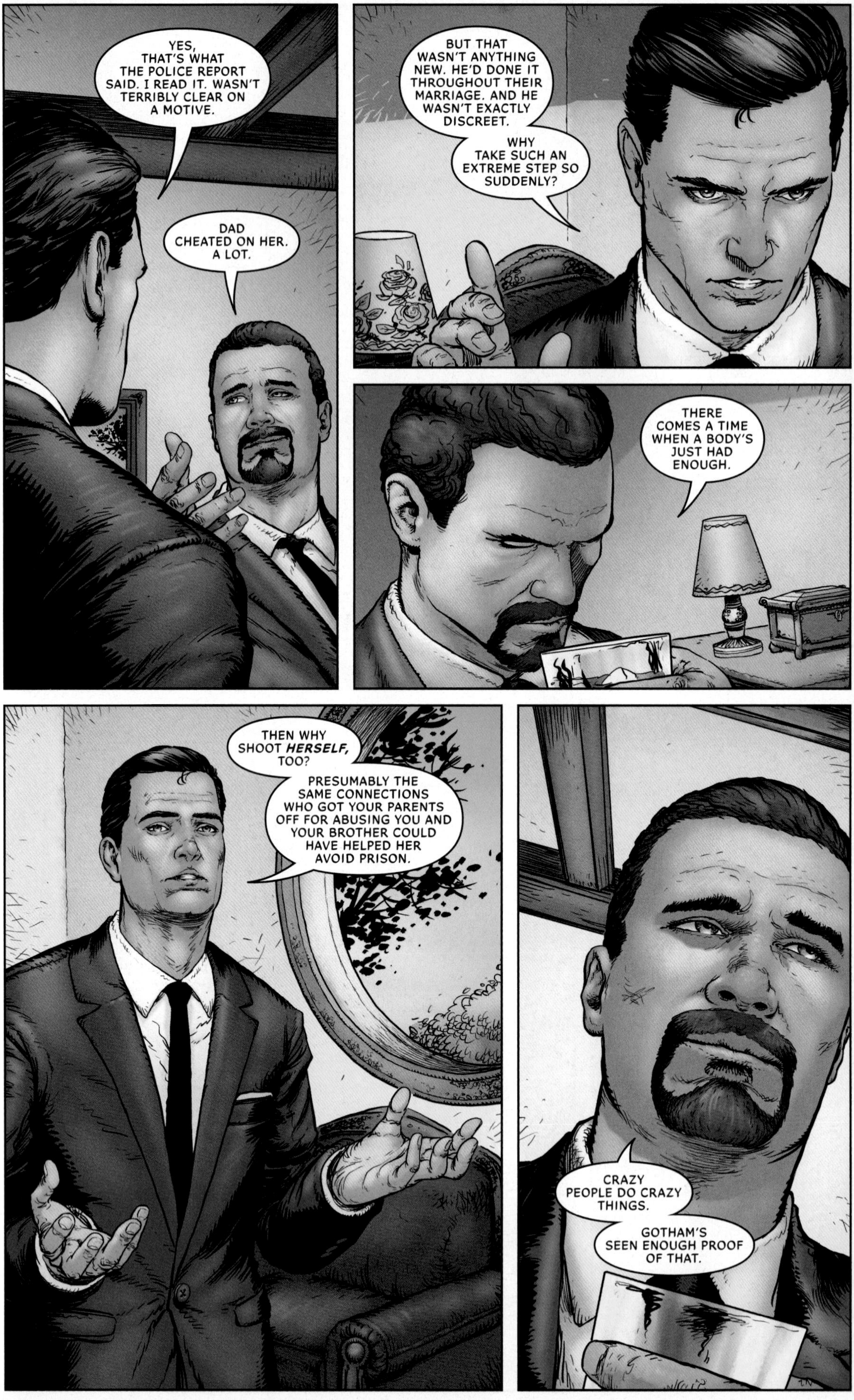
YES, THAT'S WHAT THE POLICE REPORT SAID. I READ IT. WASN'T TERRIBLY CLEAR ON A MOTIVE.
DAD CHEATED ON HER. A LOT.
BUT THAT WASN'T ANYTHING NEW. HE'D DONE IT THROUGHOUT THEIR MARRIAGE. AND HE WASN'T EXACTLY DISCREET.
WHY TAKE SUCH AN EXTREME STEP SO SUDDENLY?
THERE COMES A TIME WHEN A BODY'S JUST HAD ENOUGH.
THEN WHY SHOOT *HERSELF,* TOO?
PRESUMABLY THE SAME CONNECTIONS WHO GOT YOUR PARENTS OFF FOR ABUSING YOU AND YOUR BROTHER COULD HAVE HELPED HER AVOID PRISON.
CRAZY PEOPLE DO CRAZY THINGS.
GOTHAM'S SEEN ENOUGH PROOF OF THAT.

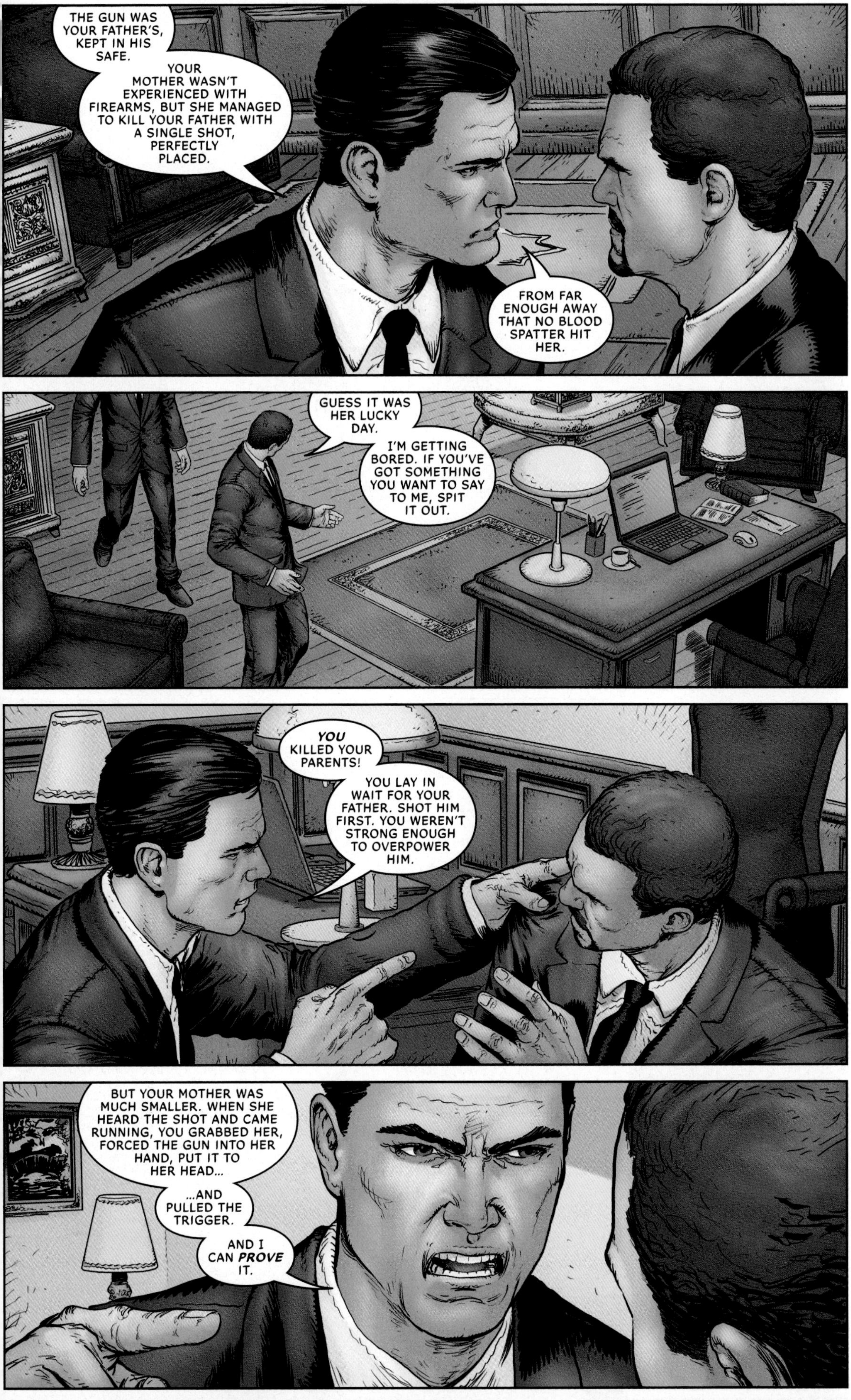
THE GUN WAS YOUR FATHER'S, KEPT IN HIS SAFE.
YOUR MOTHER WASN'T EXPERIENCED WITH FIREARMS, BUT SHE MANAGED TO KILL YOUR FATHER WITH A SINGLE SHOT, PERFECTLY PLACED.
FROM FAR ENOUGH AWAY THAT NO BLOOD SPATTER HIT HER.
GUESS IT WAS HER LUCKY DAY.
I'M GETTING BORED. IF YOU'VE GOT SOMETHING YOU WANT TO SAY TO ME, SPIT IT OUT.
YOU KILLED YOUR PARENTS!
YOU LAY IN WAIT FOR YOUR FATHER. SHOT HIM FIRST. YOU WEREN'T STRONG ENOUGH TO OVERPOWER HIM.
BUT YOUR MOTHER WAS MUCH SMALLER. WHEN SHE HEARD THE SHOT AND CAME RUNNING, YOU GRABBED HER, FORCED THE GUN INTO HER HAND, PUT IT TO HER HEAD...
...AND PULLED THE TRIGGER.
AND I CAN *PROVE* IT.

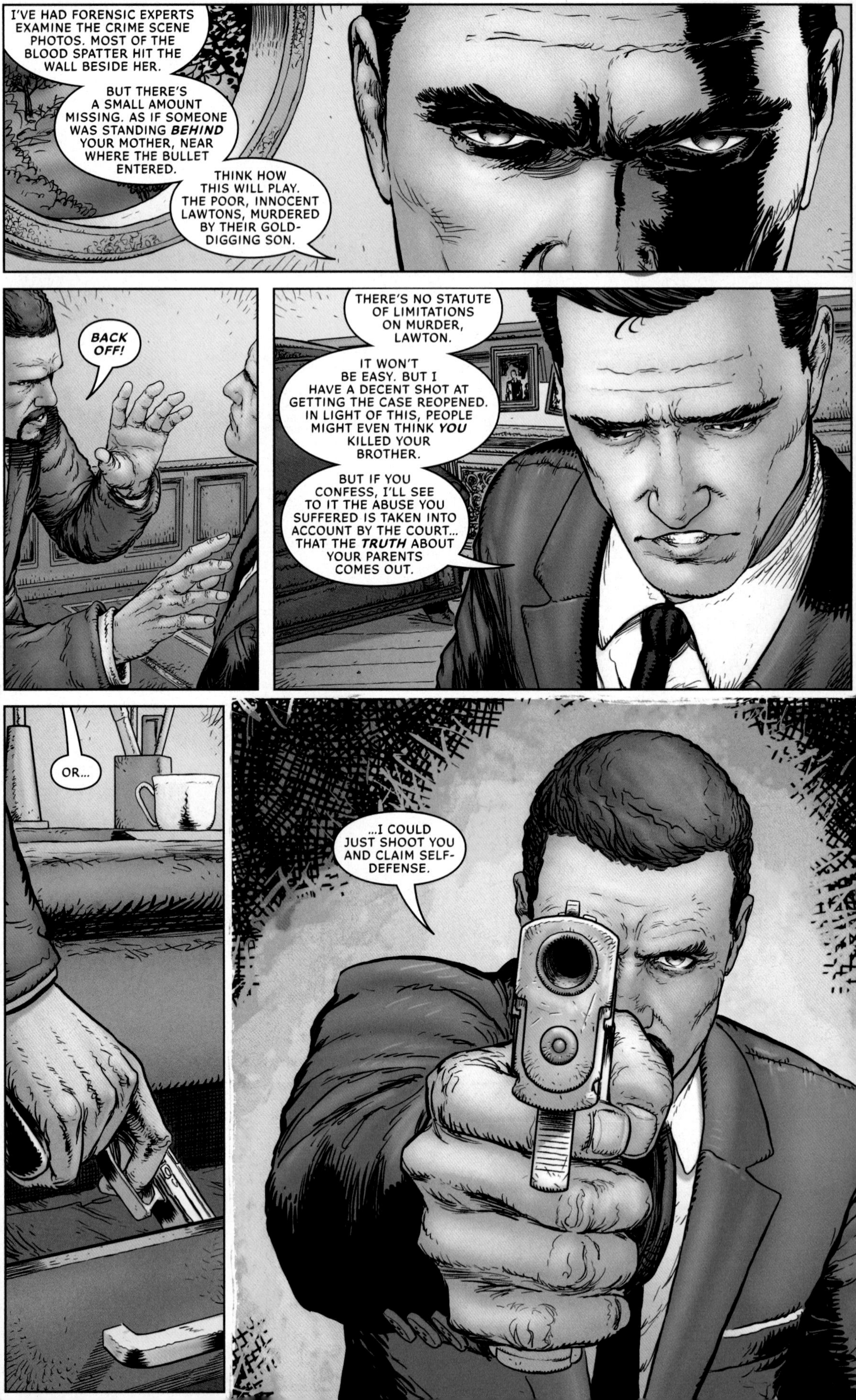
I'VE HAD FORENSIC EXPERTS EXAMINE THE CRIME SCENE PHOTOS. MOST OF THE BLOOD SPATTER HIT THE WALL BESIDE HER.
BUT THERE'S A SMALL AMOUNT MISSING. AS IF SOMEONE WAS STANDING BEHIND YOUR MOTHER, NEAR WHERE THE BULLET ENTERED.
THINK HOW THIS WILL PLAY. THE POOR, INNOCENT LAWTONS, MURDERED BY THEIR GOLD-DIGGING SON.
BACK OFF!
THERE'S NO STATUTE OF LIMITATIONS ON MURDER, LAWTON.
IT WON'T BE EASY. BUT I HAVE A DECENT SHOT AT GETTING THE CASE REOPENED. IN LIGHT OF THIS, PEOPLE MIGHT EVEN THINK YOU KILLED YOUR BROTHER.
BUT IF YOU CONFESS, I'LL SEE TO IT THE ABUSE YOU SUFFERED IS TAKEN INTO ACCOUNT BY THE COURT... THAT THE TRUTH ABOUT YOUR PARENTS COMES OUT.
OR...
...I COULD JUST SHOOT YOU AND CLAIM SELF-DEFENSE.

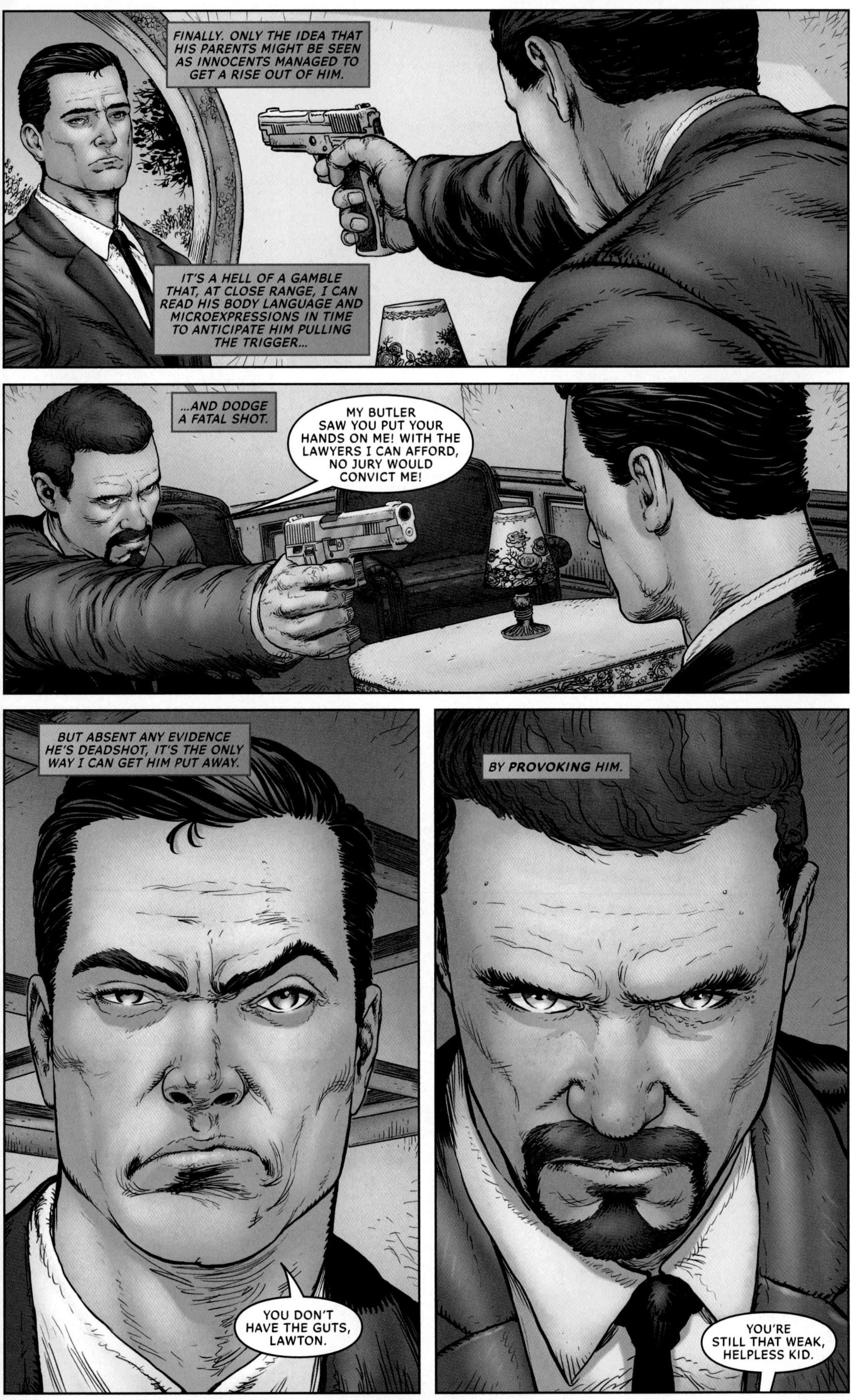
FINALLY. ONLY THE IDEA THAT HIS PARENTS MIGHT BE SEEN AS INNOCENTS MANAGED TO GET A RISE OUT OF HIM.
IT'S A HELL OF A GAMBLE THAT, AT CLOSE RANGE, I CAN READ HIS BODY LANGUAGE AND MICROEXPRESSIONS IN TIME TO ANTICIPATE HIM PULLING THE TRIGGER...
...AND DODGE A FATAL SHOT.
MY BUTLER SAW YOU PUT YOUR HANDS ON ME! WITH THE LAWYERS I CAN AFFORD, NO JURY WOULD CONVICT ME!
BUT ABSENT ANY EVIDENCE HE'S DEADSHOT, IT'S THE ONLY WAY I CAN GET HIM PUT AWAY.
YOU DON'T HAVE THE GUTS, LAWTON.
BY PROVOKING HIM.
YOU'RE STILL THAT WEAK, HELPLESS KID.

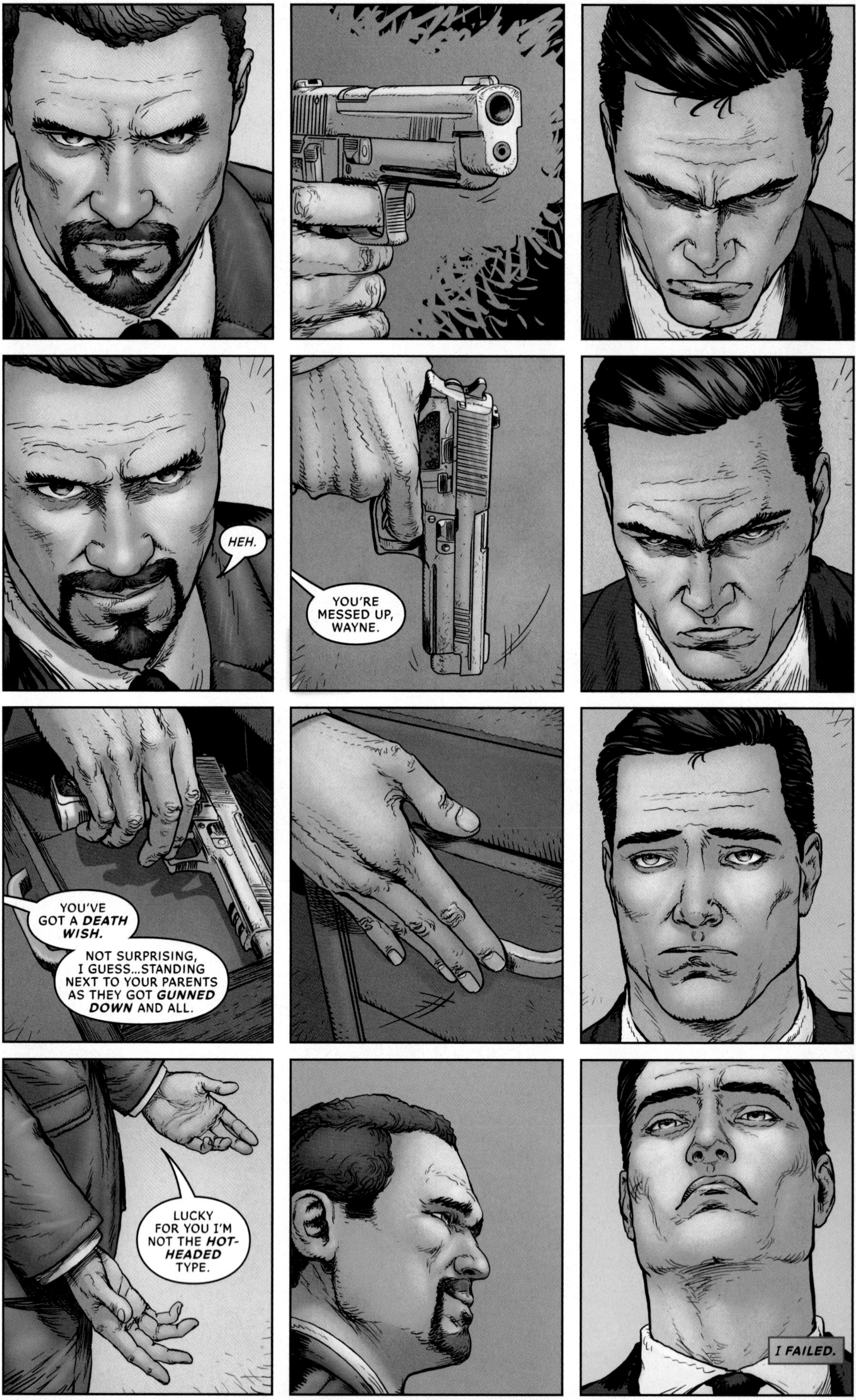
HEH.
YOU'RE MESSED UP, WAYNE.
YOU'VE GOT A DEATH WISH.
NOT SURPRISING, I GUESS...STANDING NEXT TO YOUR PARENTS AS THEY GOT GUNNED DOWN AND ALL.
LUCKY FOR YOU I'M NOT THE HOT-HEADED TYPE.
I FAILED.

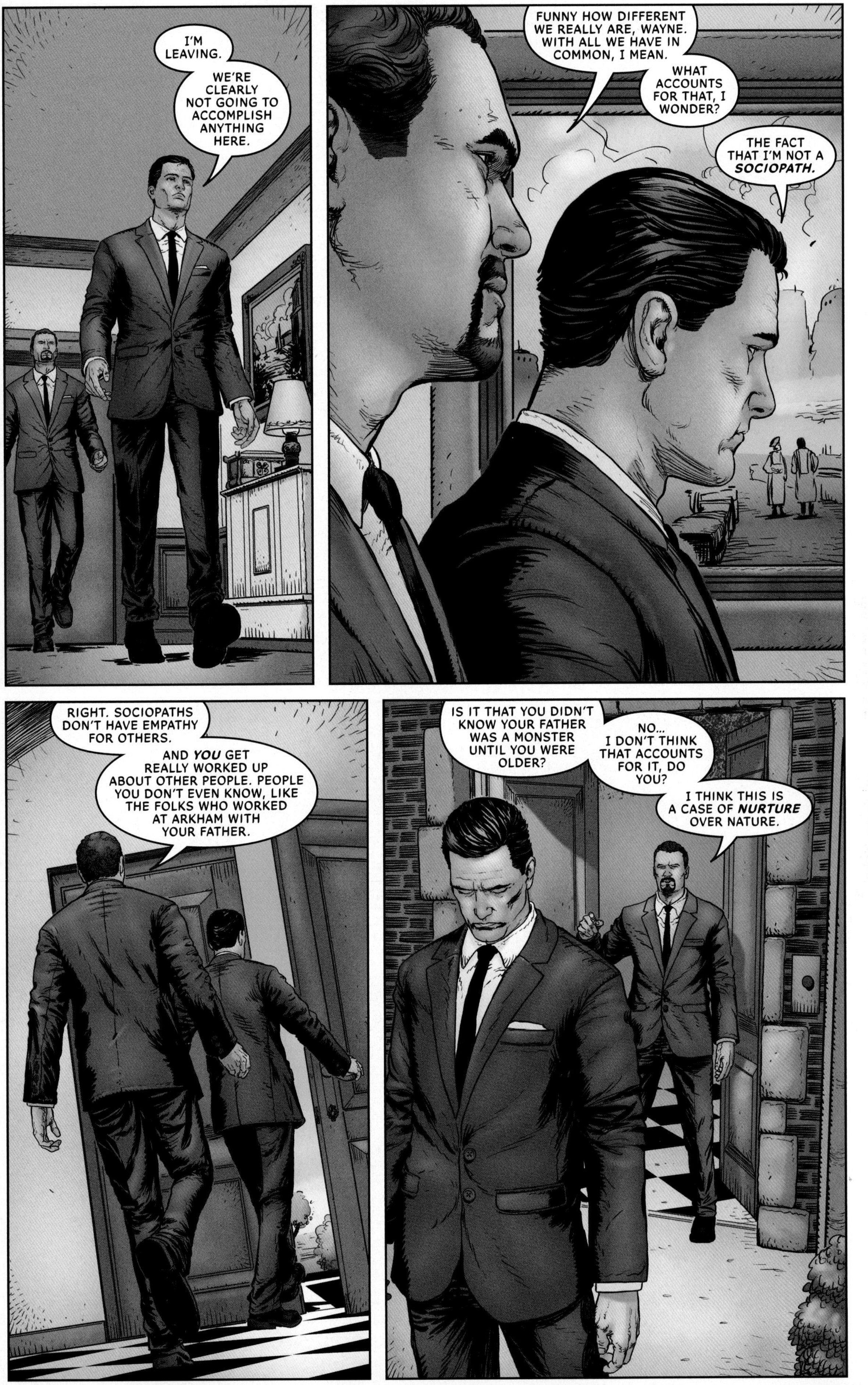
I'M LEAVING.
WE'RE CLEARLY NOT GOING TO ACCOMPLISH ANYTHING HERE.
FUNNY HOW DIFFERENT WE REALLY ARE, WAYNE. WITH ALL WE HAVE IN COMMON, I MEAN.
WHAT ACCOUNTS FOR THAT, I WONDER?
THE FACT THAT I'M NOT A ***SOCIOPATH.***
RIGHT. SOCIOPATHS DON'T HAVE EMPATHY FOR OTHERS.
AND ***YOU*** GET REALLY WORKED UP ABOUT OTHER PEOPLE. PEOPLE YOU DON'T EVEN KNOW, LIKE THE FOLKS WHO WORKED AT ARKHAM WITH YOUR FATHER.
IS IT THAT YOU DIDN'T KNOW YOUR FATHER WAS A MONSTER UNTIL YOU WERE OLDER?
NO... I DON'T THINK THAT ACCOUNTS FOR IT, DO YOU?
I THINK THIS IS A CASE OF ***NURTURE*** OVER NATURE.

WHAT DOES THAT MEAN?

WELL, WHEN MY FOLKS DIED, ALL I ENDED UP WITH WAS THIS. I MEAN, A FORTUNE...I'M NOT COMPLAINING.

BUT NO FAMILY. NO GUARDIANS. NOT EVEN ANY FRIENDS, REALLY.

JUST A TRUST THAT PAID FOR MY SCHOOL AND A DISTANT UNCLE WHO SIPHONED OFF WHAT HE COULD WHILE HE DRANK HIMSELF TO DEATH.

BUT YOU...YOU HAD THINGS TO HOLD ON TO. THE FAMILY BUSINESS, THE CHARITABLE FOUNDATION. AND *PEOPLE.*

PEOPLE WHO CARED ABOUT YOU, AND WHO YOU CARED ABOUT.

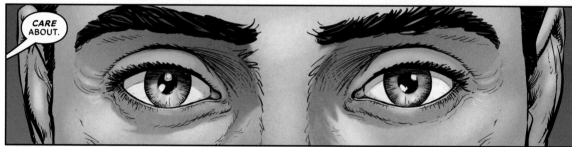

CARE ABOUT.

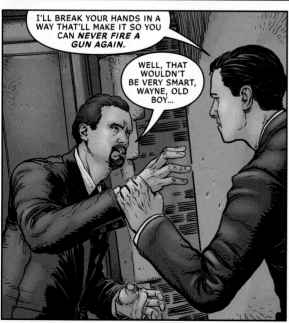

I'LL BREAK YOUR HANDS IN A WAY THAT'LL MAKE IT SO YOU CAN *NEVER FIRE A GUN AGAIN.*

WELL, THAT WOULDN'T BE VERY SMART, WAYNE, OLD BOY...

...WITH ALL THESE *WITNESSES* AROUND.

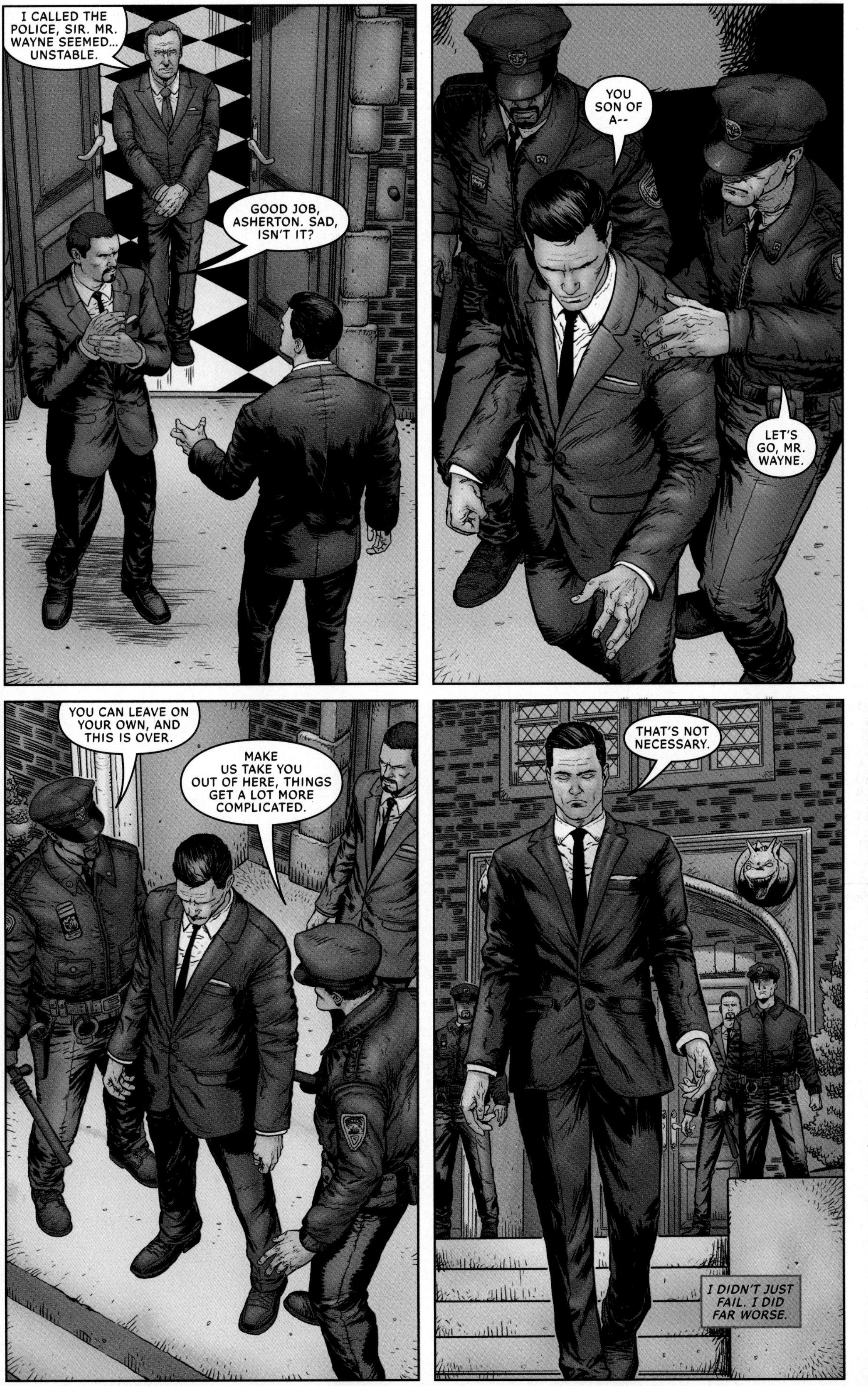
I CALLED THE POLICE, SIR. MR. WAYNE SEEMED... UNSTABLE.
GOOD JOB, ASHERTON. SAD, ISN'T IT?
YOU SON OF A--
LET'S GO, MR. WAYNE.
YOU CAN LEAVE ON YOUR OWN, AND THIS IS OVER.
MAKE US TAKE YOU OUT OF HERE, THINGS GET A LOT MORE COMPLICATED.
THAT'S NOT NECESSARY.
I DIDN'T JUST FAIL. I DID FAR WORSE.

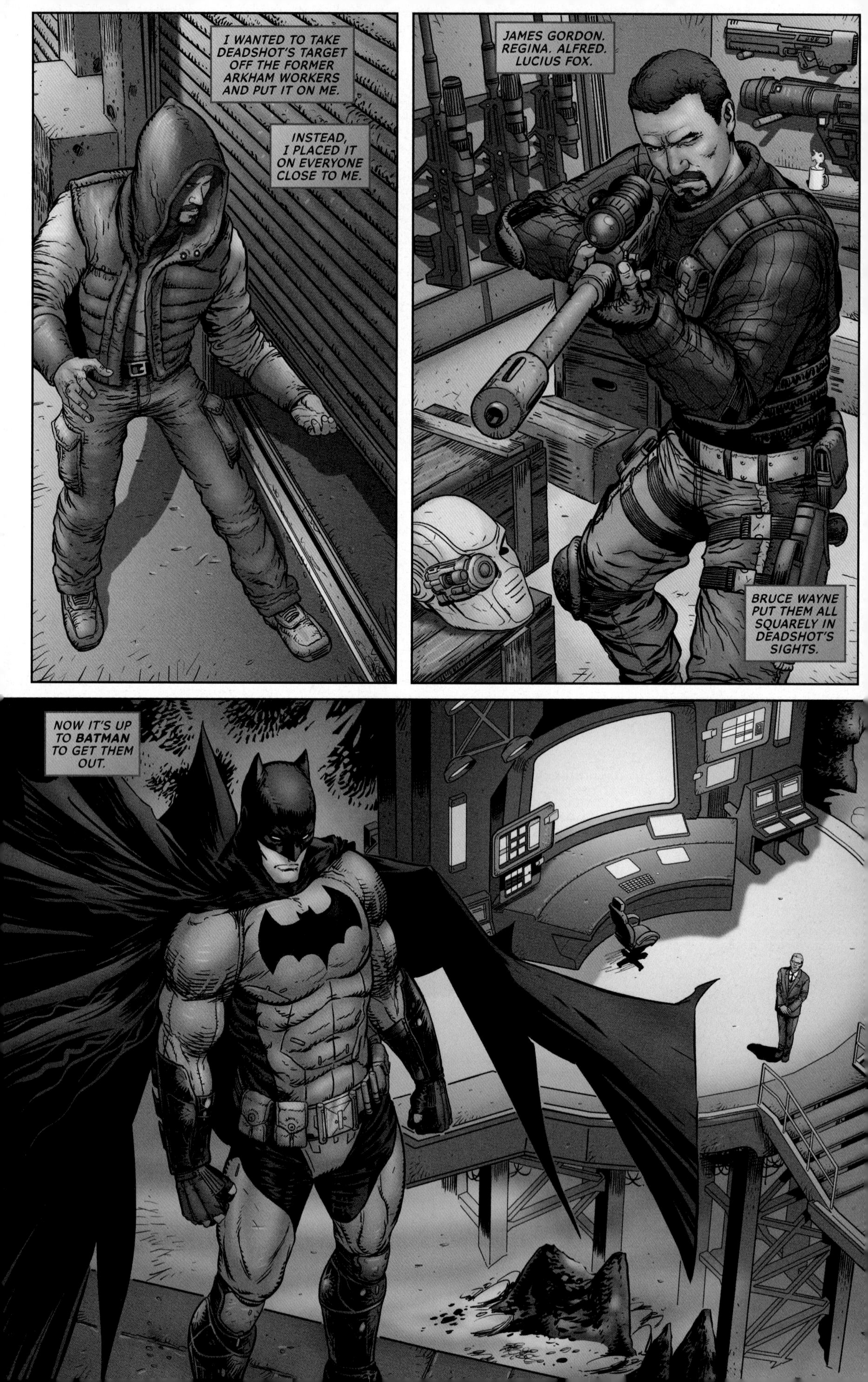
I WANTED TO TAKE DEADSHOT'S TARGET OFF THE FORMER ARKHAM WORKERS AND PUT IT ON ME.
INSTEAD, I PLACED IT ON EVERYONE CLOSE TO ME.
JAMES GORDON. REGINA. ALFRED. LUCIUS FOX.
BRUCE WAYNE PUT THEM ALL SQUARELY IN DEADSHOT'S SIGHTS.
NOW IT'S UP TO **BATMAN** TO GET THEM OUT.

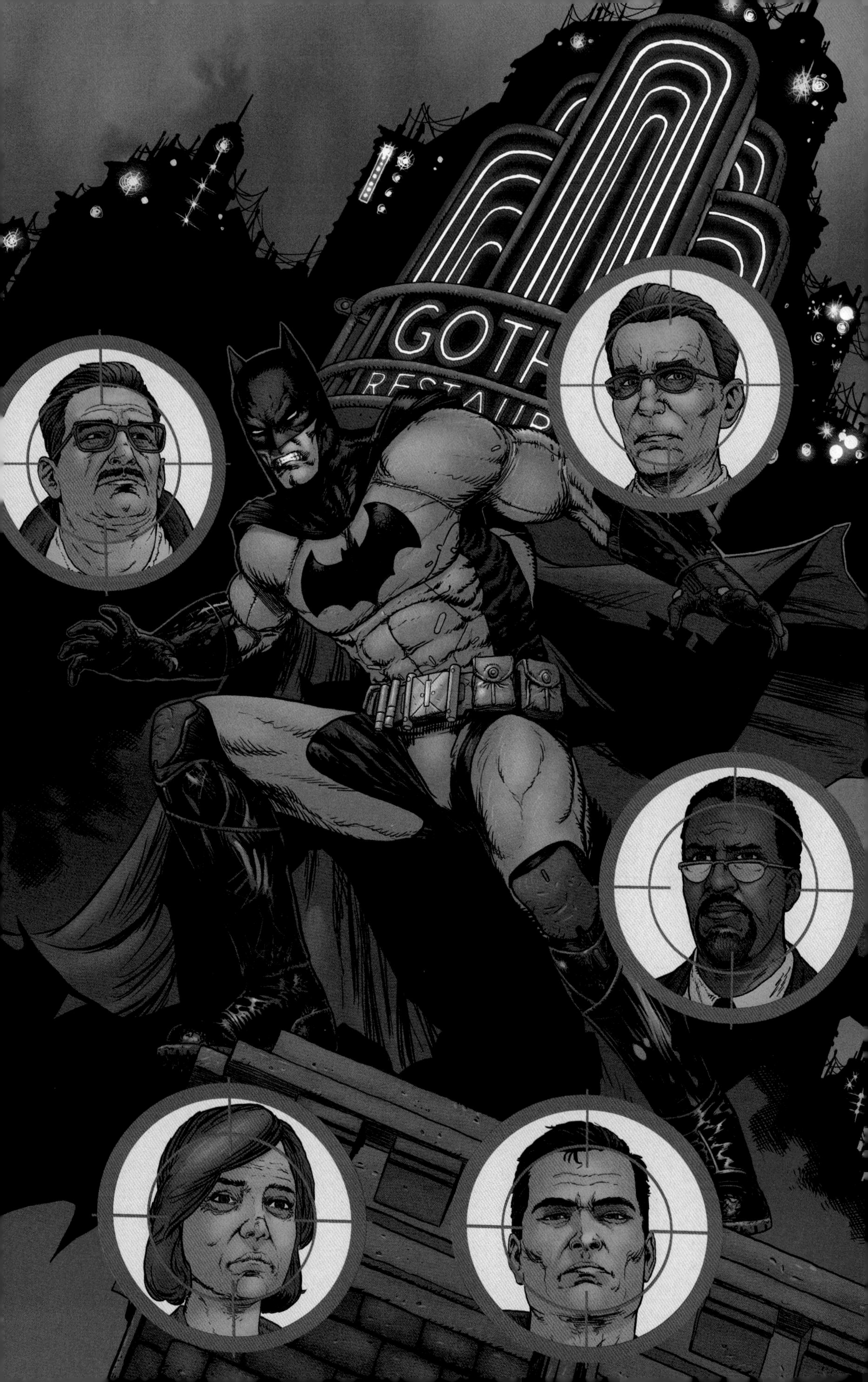
GOTH
RESTAUR

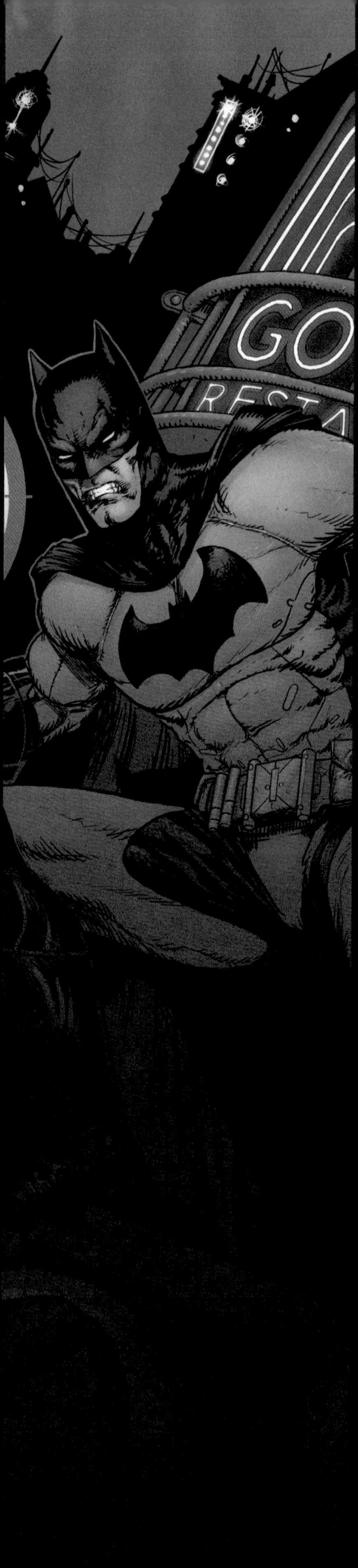
GO
RESTA

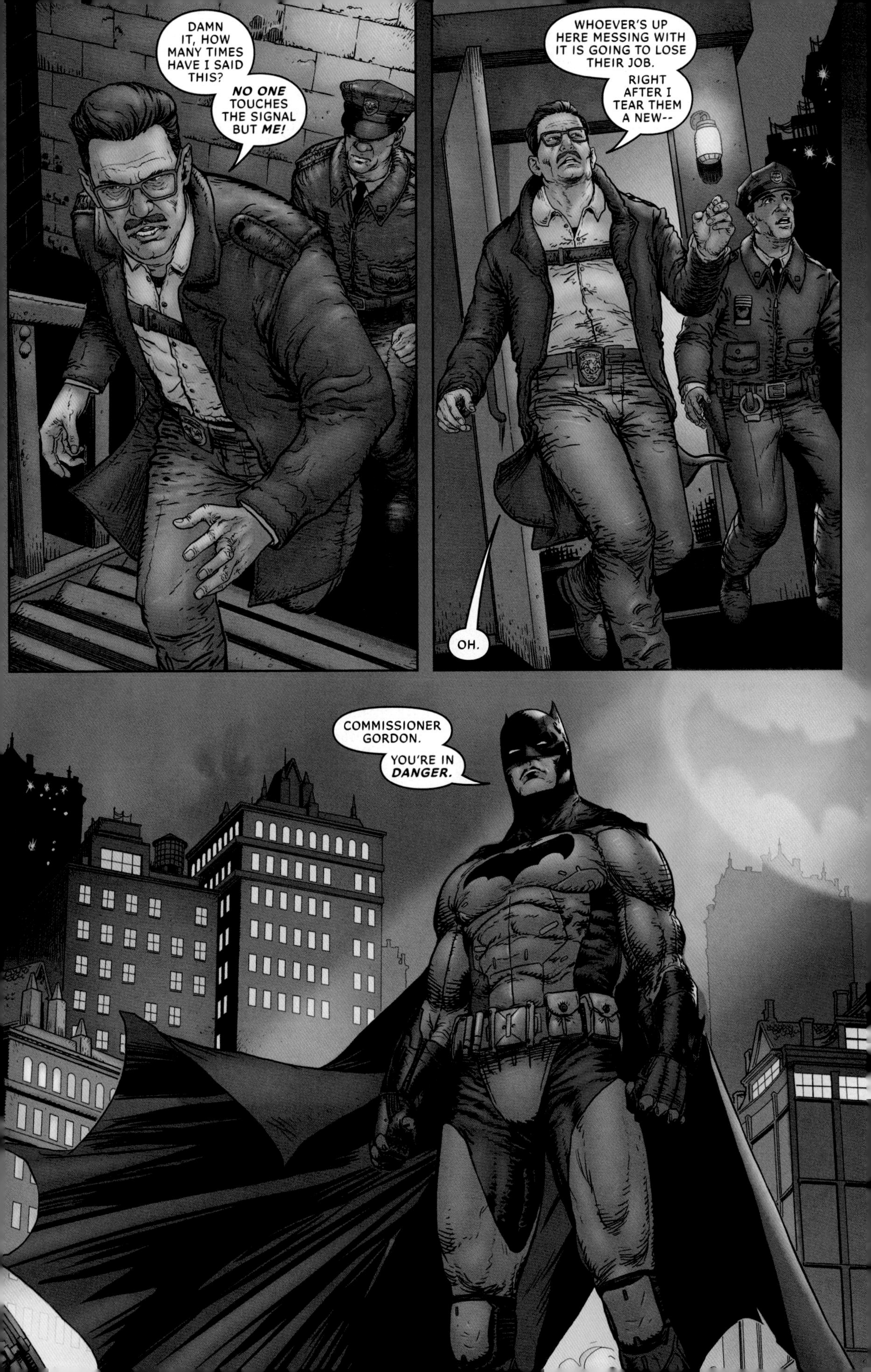
DAMN IT, HOW MANY TIMES HAVE I SAID THIS?
NO ONE TOUCHES THE SIGNAL BUT ME!
WHOEVER'S UP HERE MESSING WITH IT IS GOING TO LOSE THEIR JOB.
RIGHT AFTER I TEAR THEM A NEW--
OH.
COMMISSIONER GORDON.
YOU'RE IN DANGER.

GIVE US THE ROOF, WILL YOU, ROBBINS?

I'M A COP, BATMAN. BEING IN DANGER COMES WITH THE JOB.

I'M TALKING ABOUT *DEADSHOT.* I HAVE REASON TO BELIEVE HE'S TARGETING PEOPLE HE PERCEIVES AS...CLOSE... TO ME.

IT'S PUBLICLY KNOWN I'M WORKING WITH YOU.

I'M THE LEAST OF YOUR WORRIES. I AVOID BEING IN A CLEAR LINE OF FIRE AS A MATTER OF COURSE.

THIS IS THE MOST EXPOSED I'VE BEEN ALL WEEK.

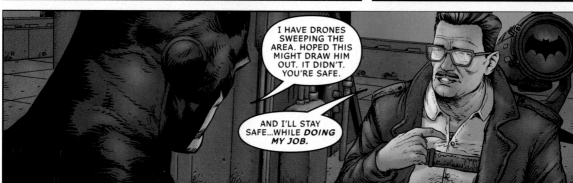

I HAVE DRONES SWEEPING THE AREA. HOPED THIS MIGHT DRAW HIM OUT. IT DIDN'T. YOU'RE SAFE.

AND I'LL STAY SAFE...WHILE *DOING MY JOB.*

YOU'LL WANT TO TALK TO BRUCE WAYNE. EVERYONE KNOWS HE'S FINANCING OUR...EXPERIMENT WITH WORKING TOGETHER.

ALREADY DONE. THERE ARE OTHERS I NEED TO SEE. BE CAREFUL, GORDON.

I'M TOUCHED. THIS MEAN WERE FRIENDS?

I NEED TO GET MORE CONSIDERATE FRIENDS.

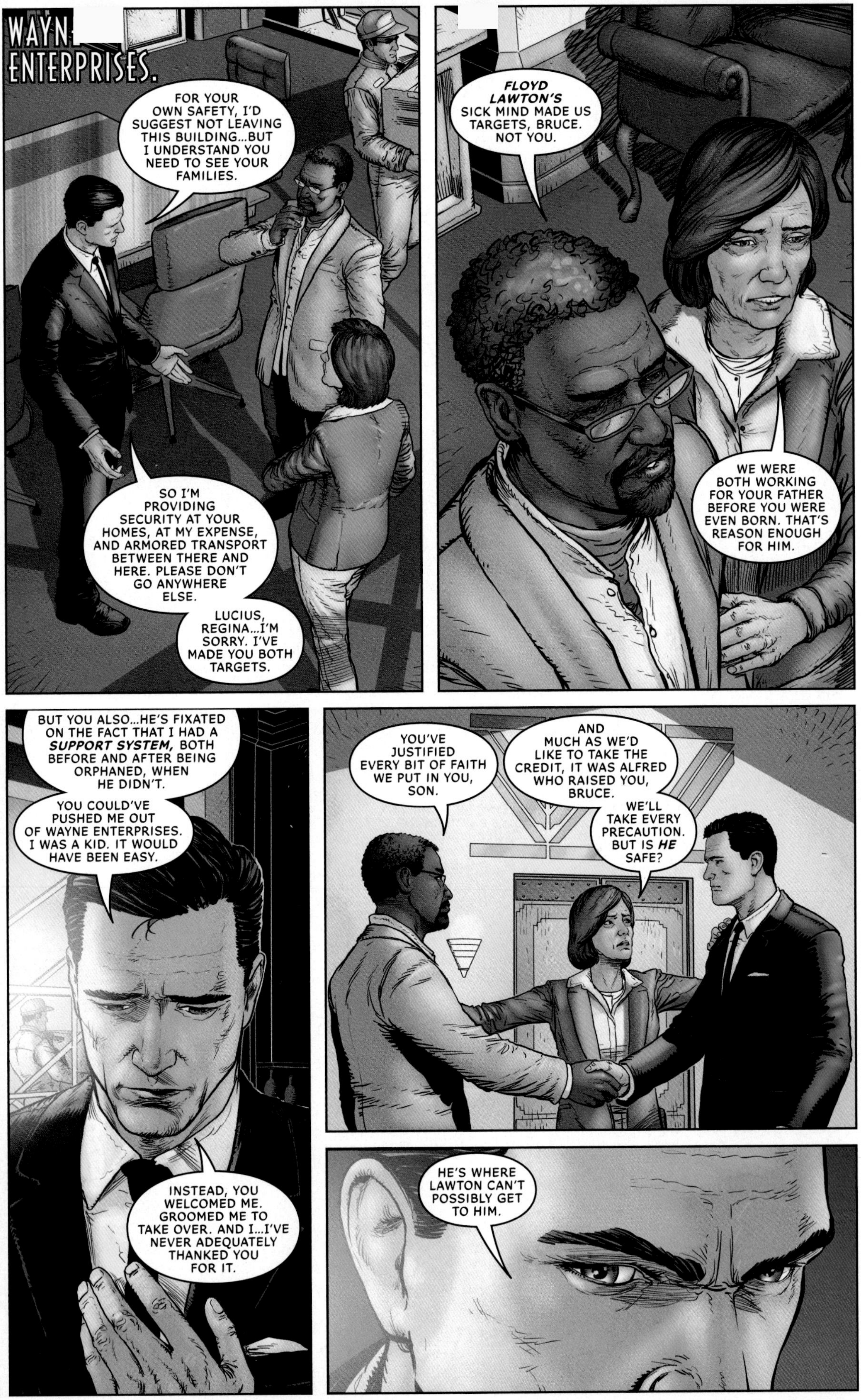
WAYN-
ENTERPRISES.
FOR YOUR OWN SAFETY, I'D SUGGEST NOT LEAVING THIS BUILDING...BUT I UNDERSTAND YOU NEED TO SEE YOUR FAMILIES.
SO I'M PROVIDING SECURITY AT YOUR HOMES, AT MY EXPENSE, AND ARMORED TRANSPORT BETWEEN THERE AND HERE. PLEASE DON'T GO ANYWHERE ELSE.
LUCIUS, REGINA...I'M SORRY. I'VE MADE YOU BOTH TARGETS.
FLOYD LAWTON'S SICK MIND MADE US TARGETS, BRUCE. NOT YOU.
WE WERE BOTH WORKING FOR YOUR FATHER BEFORE YOU WERE EVEN BORN. THAT'S REASON ENOUGH FOR HIM.
BUT YOU ALSO...HE'S FIXATED ON THE FACT THAT I HAD A SUPPORT SYSTEM, BOTH BEFORE AND AFTER BEING ORPHANED, WHEN HE DIDN'T.
YOU COULD'VE PUSHED ME OUT OF WAYNE ENTERPRISES. I WAS A KID. IT WOULD HAVE BEEN EASY.
INSTEAD, YOU WELCOMED ME. GROOMED ME TO TAKE OVER. AND I...I'VE NEVER ADEQUATELY THANKED YOU FOR IT.
YOU'VE JUSTIFIED EVERY BIT OF FAITH WE PUT IN YOU, SON.
AND MUCH AS WE'D LIKE TO TAKE THE CREDIT, IT WAS ALFRED WHO RAISED YOU, BRUCE.
WE'LL TAKE EVERY PRECAUTION. BUT IS HE SAFE?
HE'S WHERE LAWTON CAN'T POSSIBLY GET TO HIM.

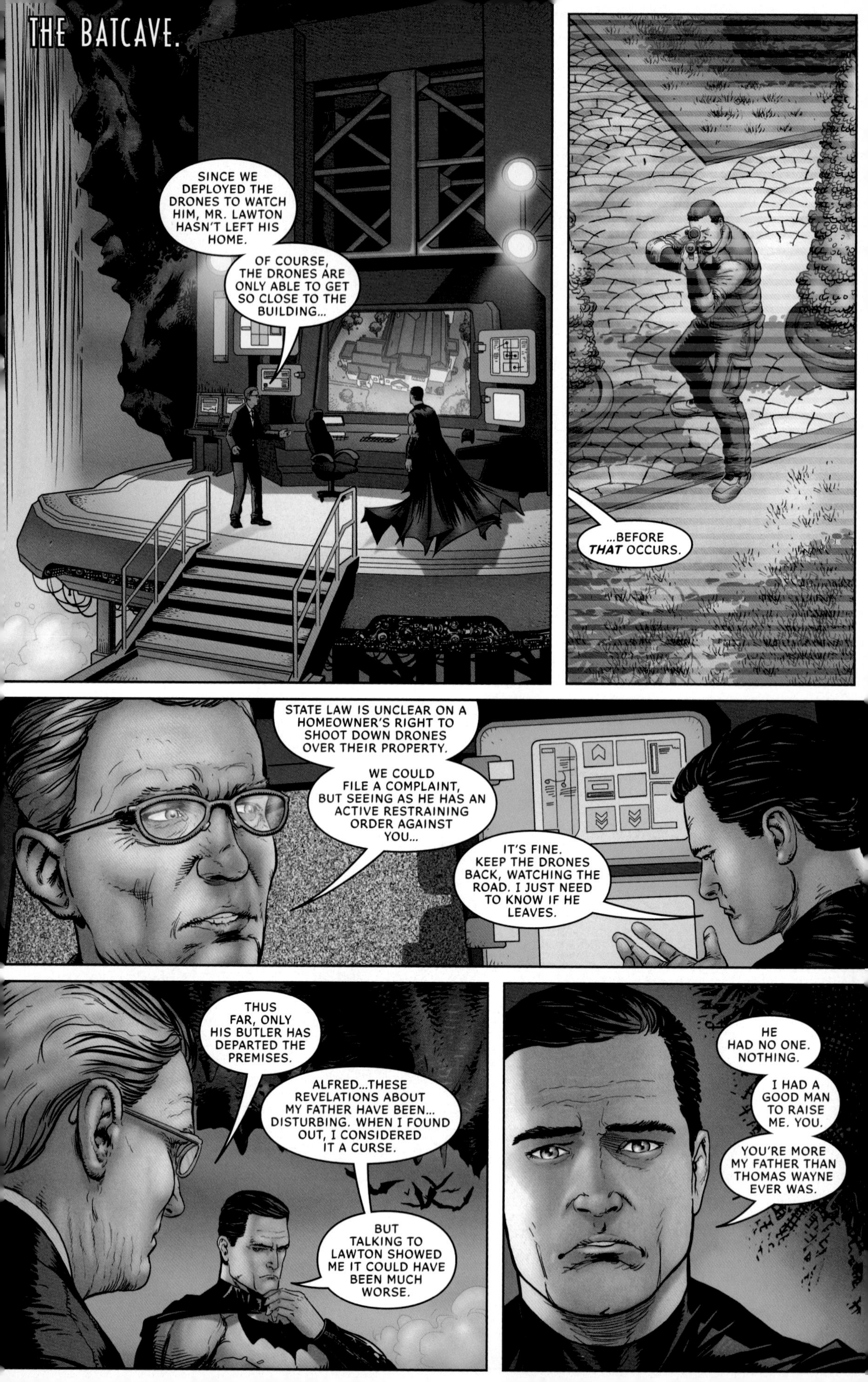
THE BATCAVE.
SINCE WE DEPLOYED THE DRONES TO WATCH HIM, MR. LAWTON HASN'T LEFT HIS HOME.
OF COURSE, THE DRONES ARE ONLY ABLE TO GET SO CLOSE TO THE BUILDING...
...BEFORE THAT OCCURS.
STATE LAW IS UNCLEAR ON A HOMEOWNER'S RIGHT TO SHOOT DOWN DRONES OVER THEIR PROPERTY.
WE COULD FILE A COMPLAINT, BUT SEEING AS HE HAS AN ACTIVE RESTRAINING ORDER AGAINST YOU...
IT'S FINE. KEEP THE DRONES BACK, WATCHING THE ROAD. I JUST NEED TO KNOW IF HE LEAVES.
THUS FAR, ONLY HIS BUTLER HAS DEPARTED THE PREMISES.
ALFRED...THESE REVELATIONS ABOUT MY FATHER HAVE BEEN... DISTURBING. WHEN I FOUND OUT, I CONSIDERED IT A CURSE.
BUT TALKING TO LAWTON SHOWED ME IT COULD HAVE BEEN MUCH WORSE.
HE HAD NO ONE. NOTHING.
I HAD A GOOD MAN TO RAISE ME. YOU.
YOU'RE MORE MY FATHER THAN THOMAS WAYNE EVER WAS.

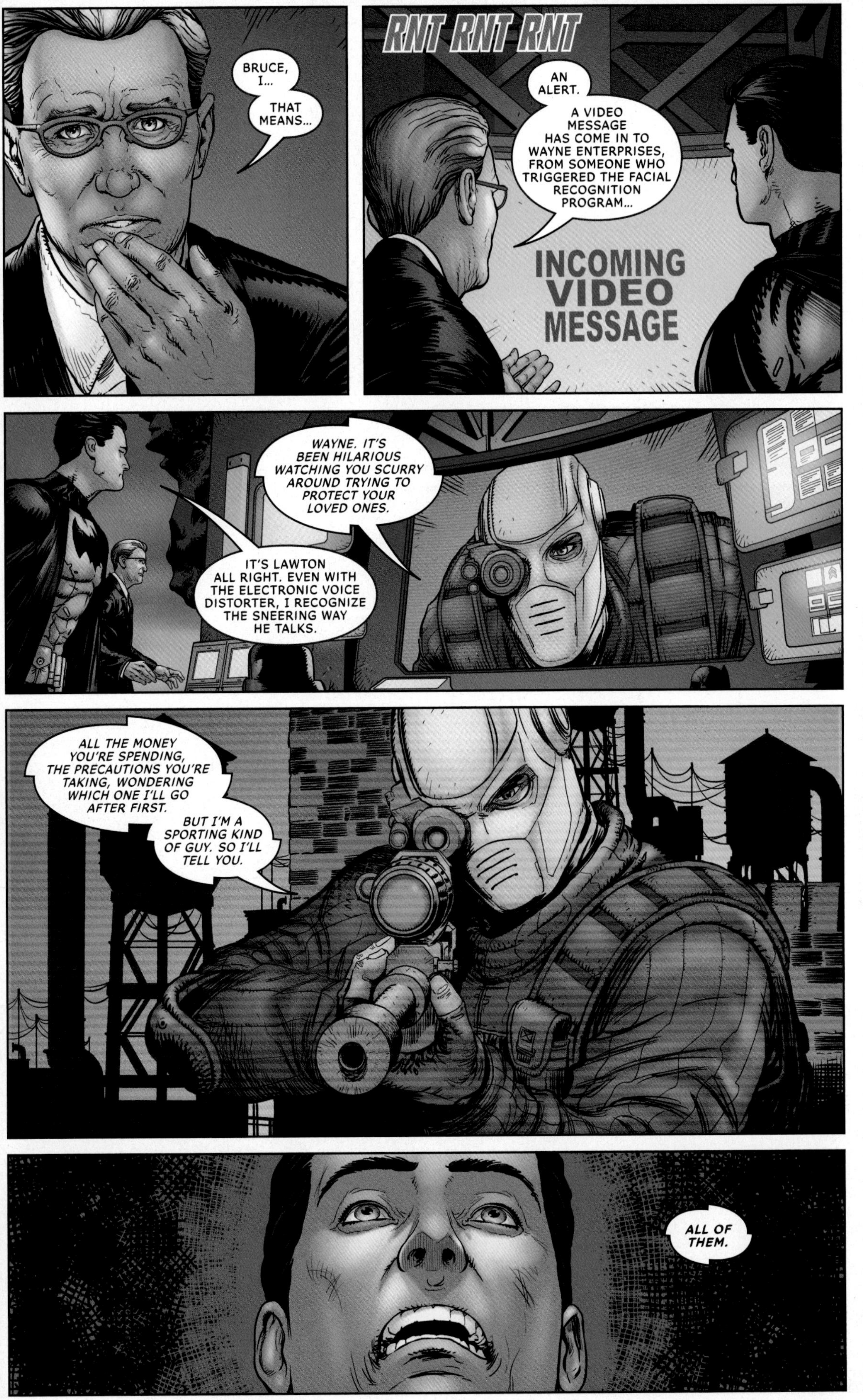

BRUCE, I... THAT MEANS...
RNT RNT RNT
AN ALERT.
A VIDEO MESSAGE HAS COME IN TO WAYNE ENTERPRISES, FROM SOMEONE WHO TRIGGERED THE FACIAL RECOGNITION PROGRAM...
INCOMING VIDEO MESSAGE
WAYNE. IT'S BEEN HILARIOUS WATCHING YOU SCURRY AROUND TRYING TO PROTECT YOUR LOVED ONES.
IT'S LAWTON ALL RIGHT. EVEN WITH THE ELECTRONIC VOICE DISTORTER, I RECOGNIZE THE SNEERING WAY HE TALKS.
ALL THE MONEY YOU'RE SPENDING, THE PRECAUTIONS YOU'RE TAKING, WONDERING WHICH ONE I'LL GO AFTER FIRST.
BUT I'M A SPORTING KIND OF GUY. SO I'LL TELL YOU.
ALL OF THEM.

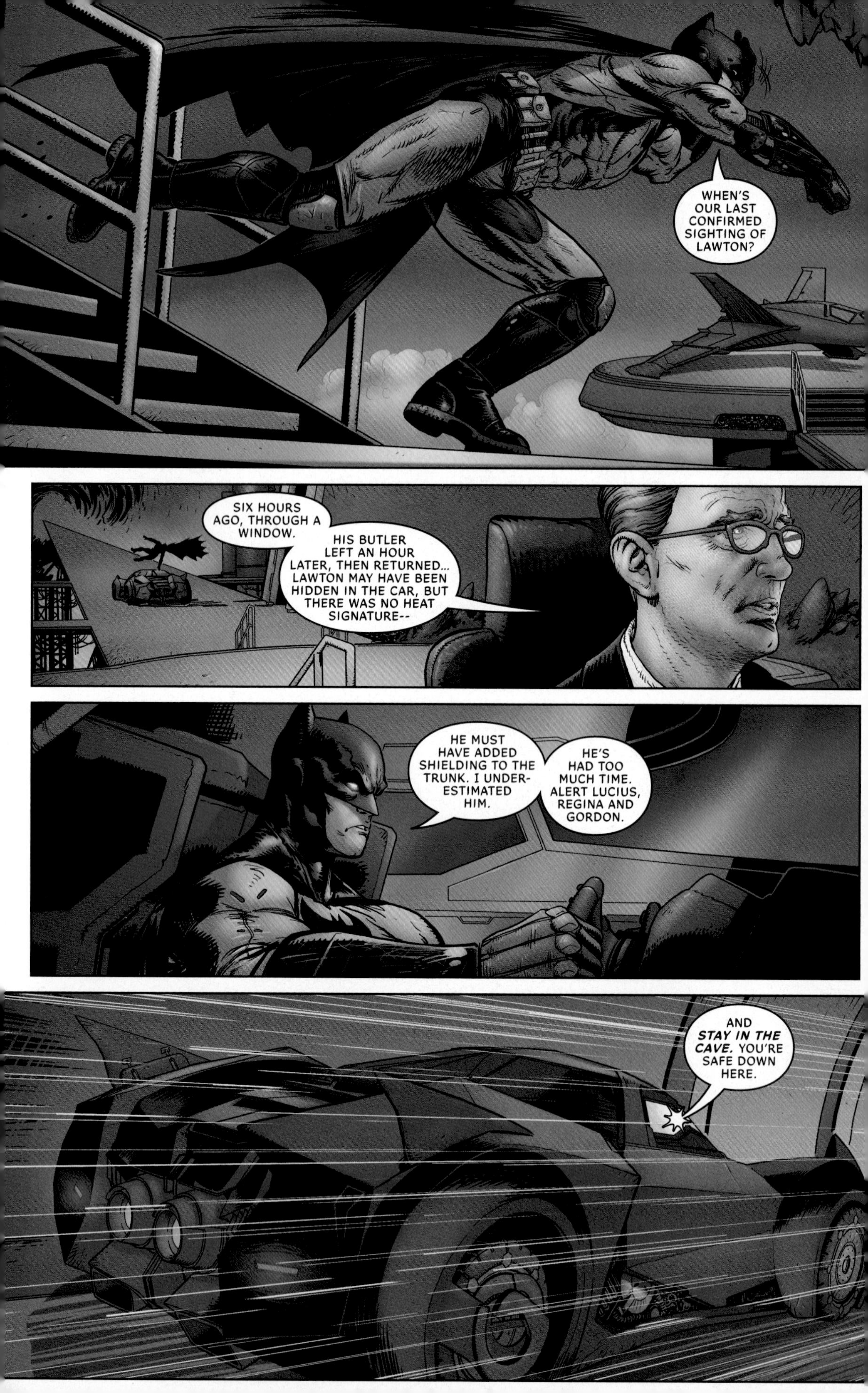
WHEN'S OUR LAST CONFIRMED SIGHTING OF LAWTON?
SIX HOURS AGO, THROUGH A WINDOW.
HIS BUTLER LEFT AN HOUR LATER, THEN RETURNED... LAWTON MAY HAVE BEEN HIDDEN IN THE CAR, BUT THERE WAS NO HEAT SIGNATURE--
HE MUST HAVE ADDED SHIELDING TO THE TRUNK. I UNDER-ESTIMATED HIM.
HE'S HAD TOO MUCH TIME. ALERT LUCIUS, REGINA AND GORDON.
AND *STAY IN THE CAVE.* YOU'RE SAFE DOWN HERE.

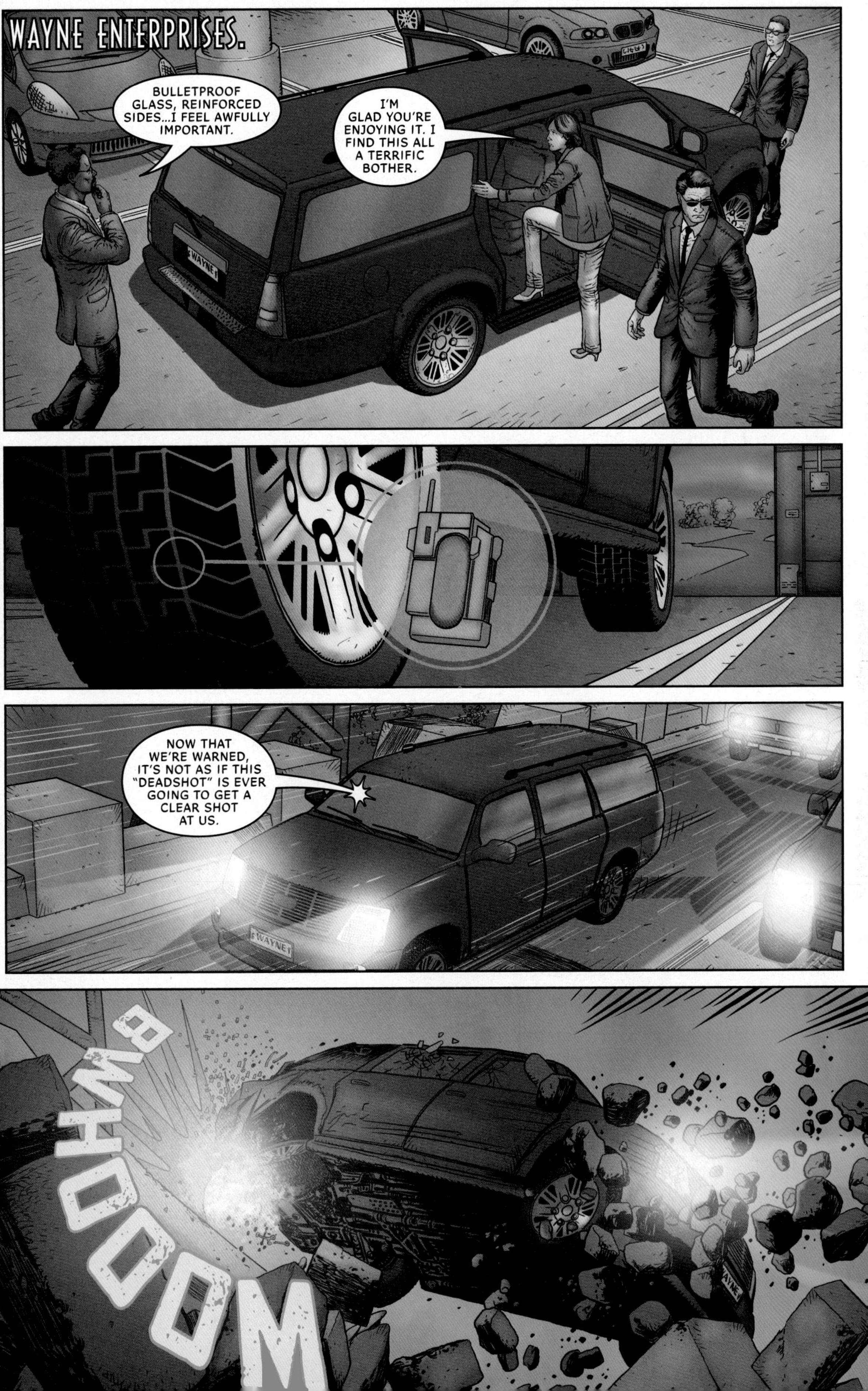
WAYNE ENTERPRISES.
BULLETPROOF GLASS, REINFORCED SIDES...I FEEL AWFULLY IMPORTANT.
I'M GLAD YOU'RE ENJOYING IT. I FIND THIS ALL A TERRIFIC BOTHER.
WAYNE 1
NOW THAT WE'RE WARNED, IT'S NOT AS IF THIS "DEADSHOT" IS EVER GOING TO GET A CLEAR SHOT AT US.
WAYNE 1
BWHOOOM

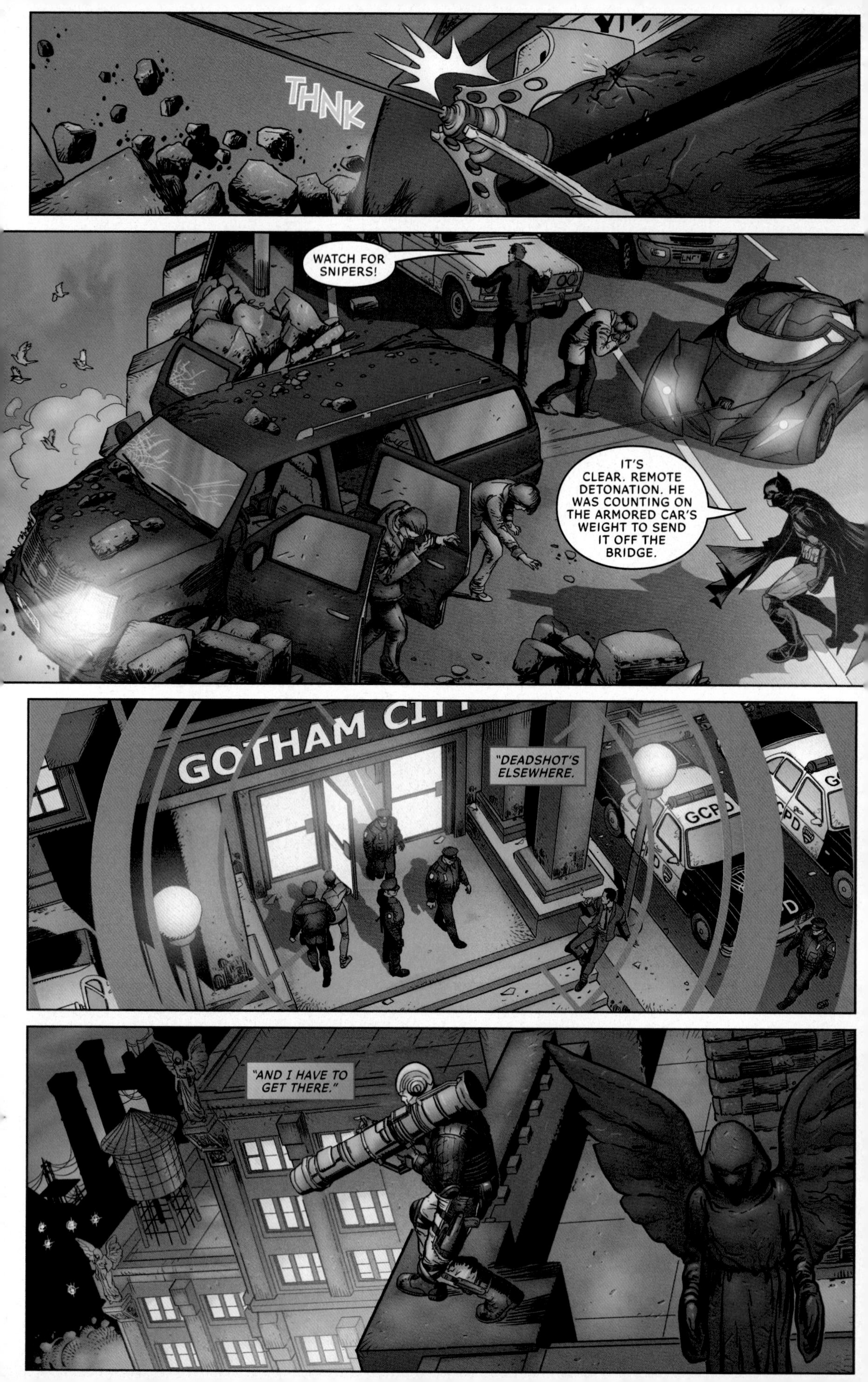
THNK
WATCH FOR SNIPERS!
IT'S CLEAR. REMOTE DETONATION. HE WAS COUNTING ON THE ARMORED CAR'S WEIGHT TO SEND IT OFF THE BRIDGE.
GOTHAM CIT
"DEADSHOT'S ELSEWHERE.
GCPD
"AND I HAVE TO GET THERE."

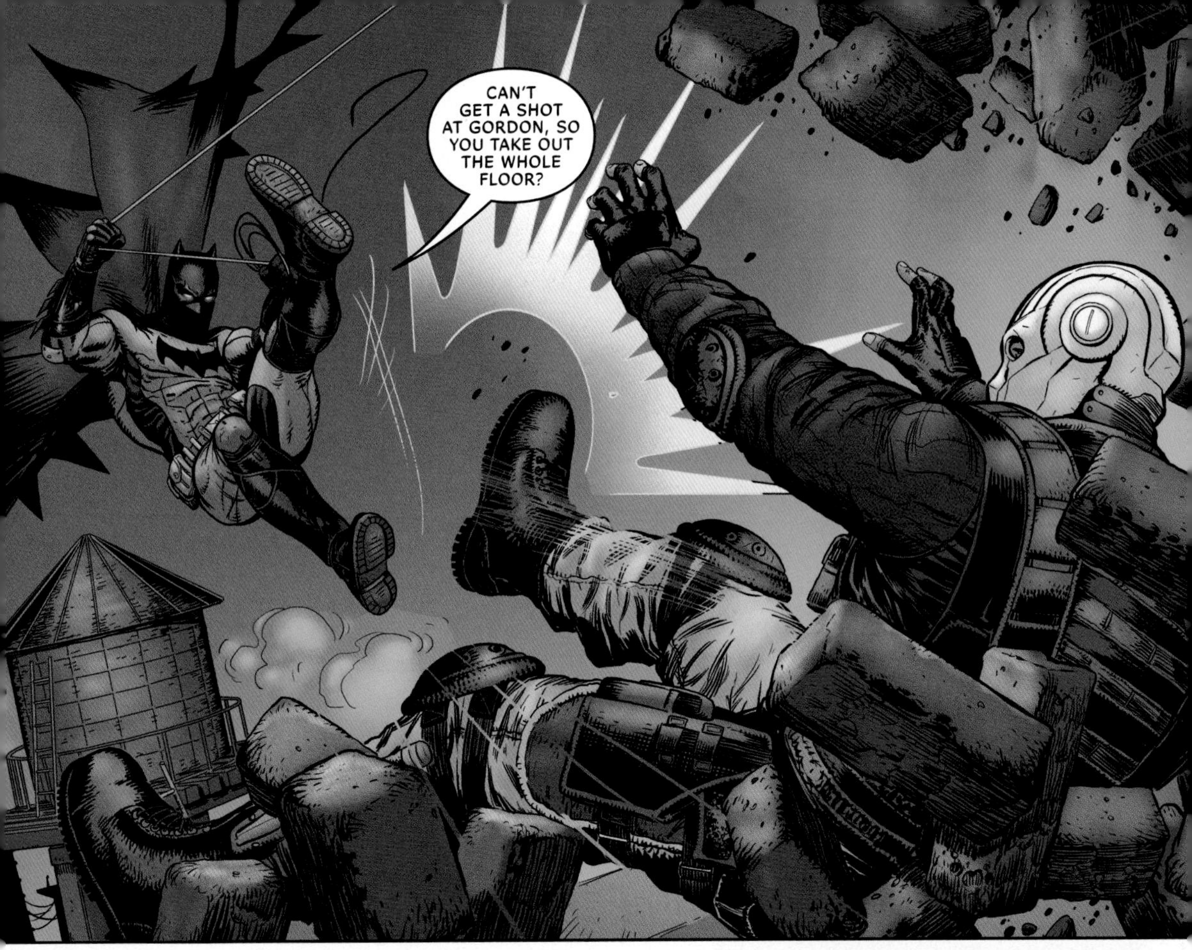
CAN'T GET A SHOT AT GORDON, SO YOU TAKE OUT THE WHOLE FLOOR?

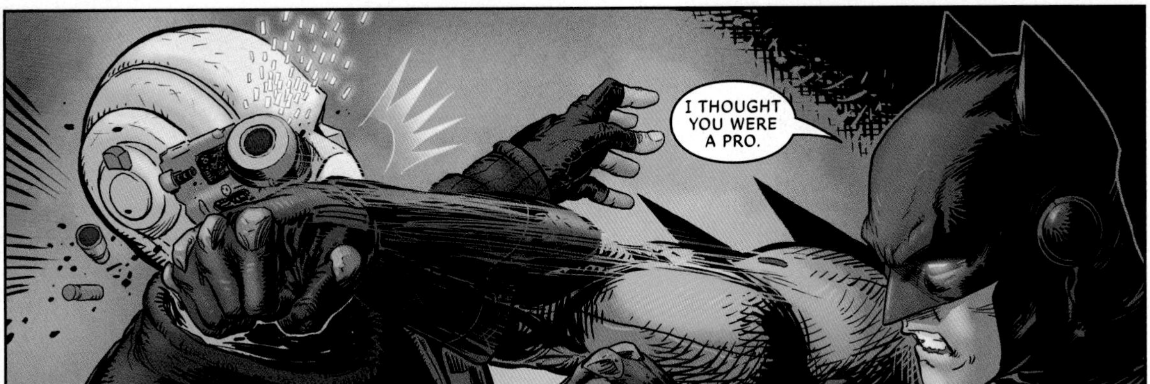
I THOUGHT YOU WERE A PRO.

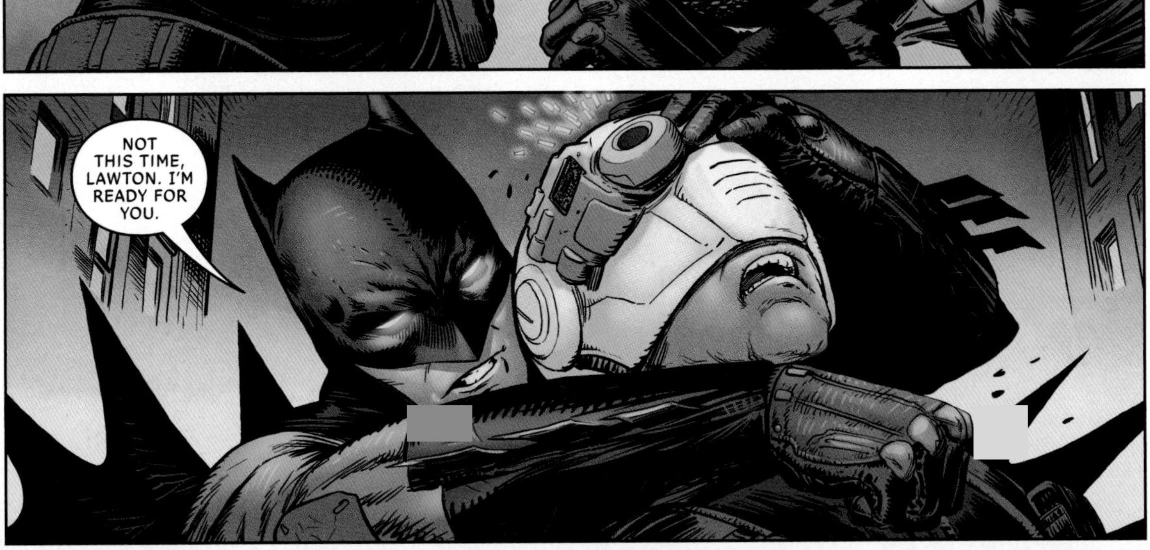
NOT THIS TIME, LAWTON. I'M READY FOR YOU.

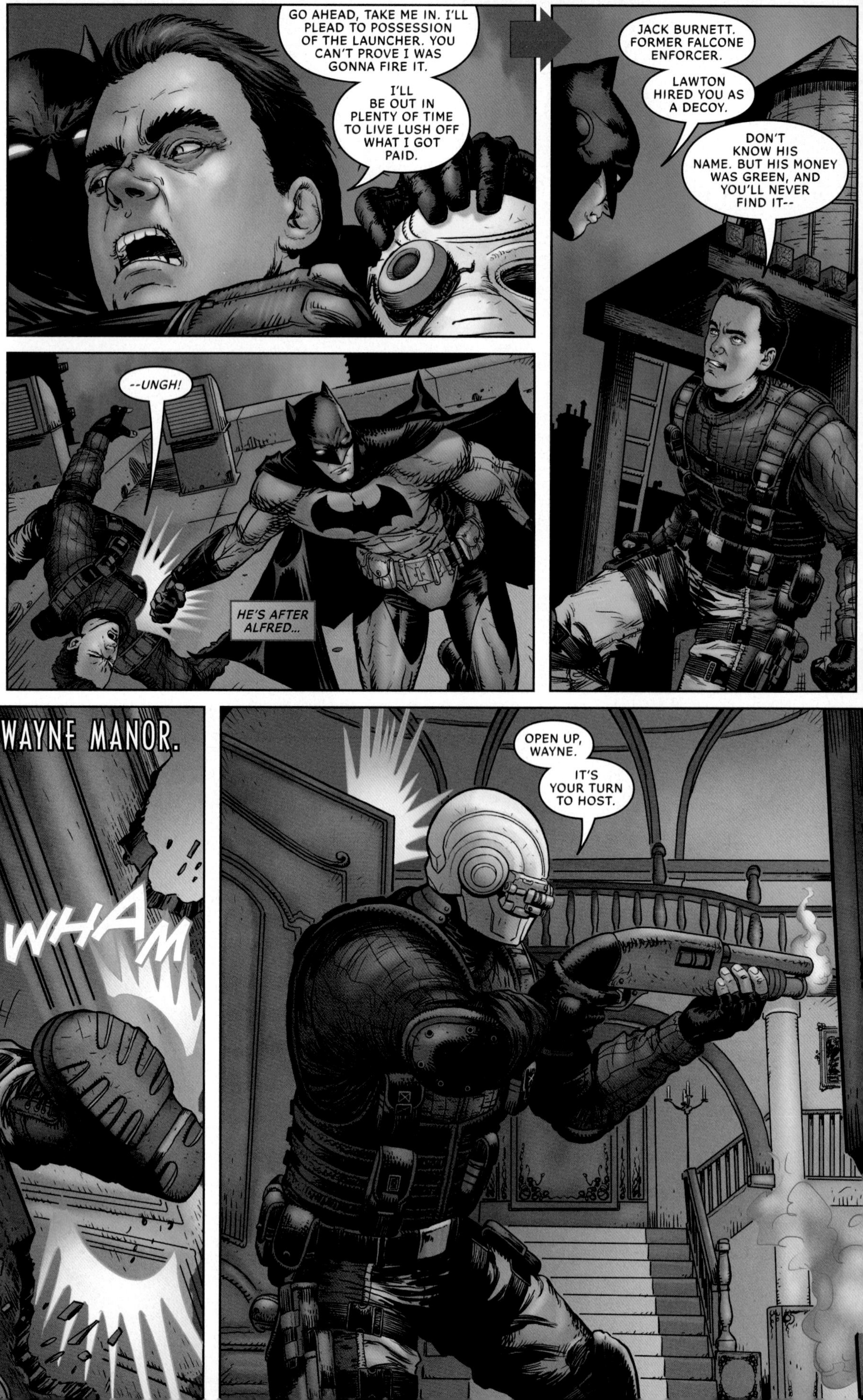
GO AHEAD, TAKE ME IN. I'LL PLEAD TO POSSESSION OF THE LAUNCHER. YOU CAN'T PROVE I WAS GONNA FIRE IT.
I'LL BE OUT IN PLENTY OF TIME TO LIVE LUSH OFF WHAT I GOT PAID.
JACK BURNETT. FORMER FALCONE ENFORCER.
LAWTON HIRED YOU AS A DECOY.
DON'T KNOW HIS NAME. BUT HIS MONEY WAS GREEN, AND YOU'LL NEVER FIND IT--
--UNGH!
HE'S AFTER ALFRED...
WAYNE MANOR.
WHAM
OPEN UP, WAYNE.
IT'S YOUR TURN TO HOST.

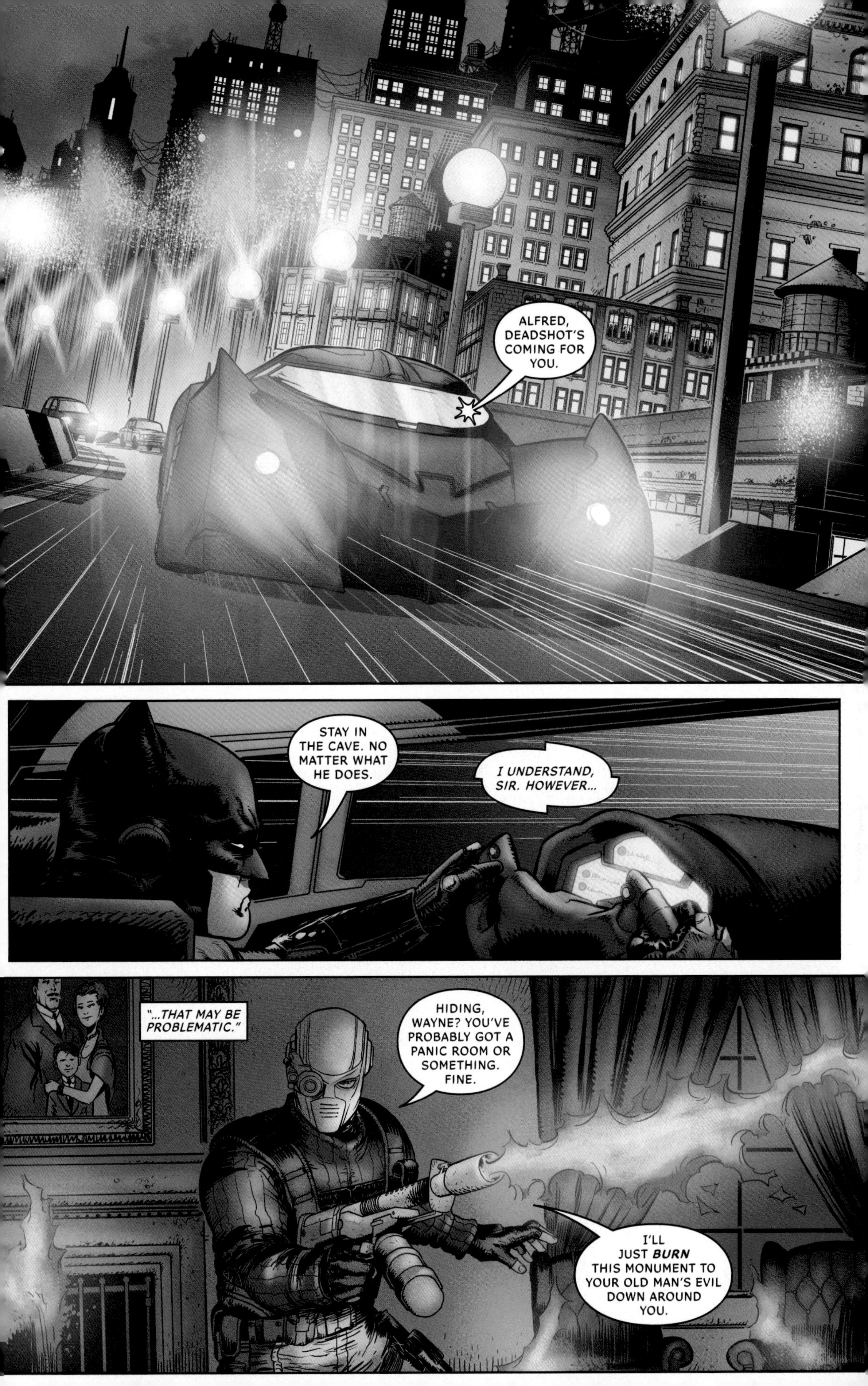
ALFRED, DEADSHOT'S COMING FOR YOU.
STAY IN THE CAVE. NO MATTER WHAT HE DOES.
I UNDERSTAND, SIR. HOWEVER...
"...THAT MAY BE PROBLEMATIC."
HIDING, WAYNE? YOU'VE PROBABLY GOT A PANIC ROOM OR SOMETHING. FINE.
I'LL JUST **BURN** THIS MONUMENT TO YOUR OLD MAN'S EVIL DOWN AROUND YOU.

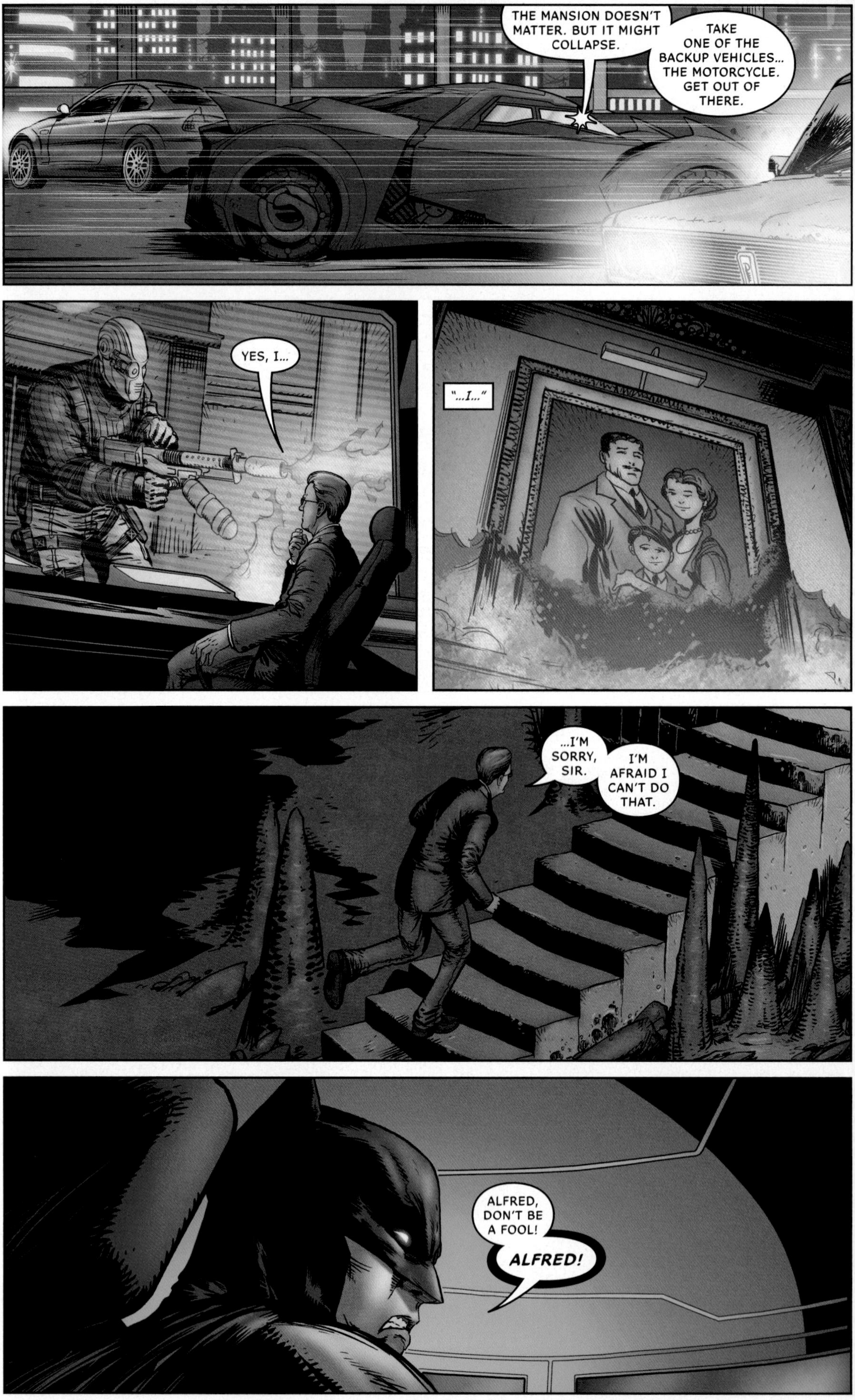
THE MANSION DOESN'T MATTER. BUT IT MIGHT COLLAPSE.
TAKE ONE OF THE BACKUP VEHICLES... THE MOTORCYCLE. GET OUT OF THERE.
YES, I...
"...I..."
...I'M SORRY, SIR.
I'M AFRAID I CAN'T DO THAT.
ALFRED, DON'T BE A FOOL!
ALFRED!

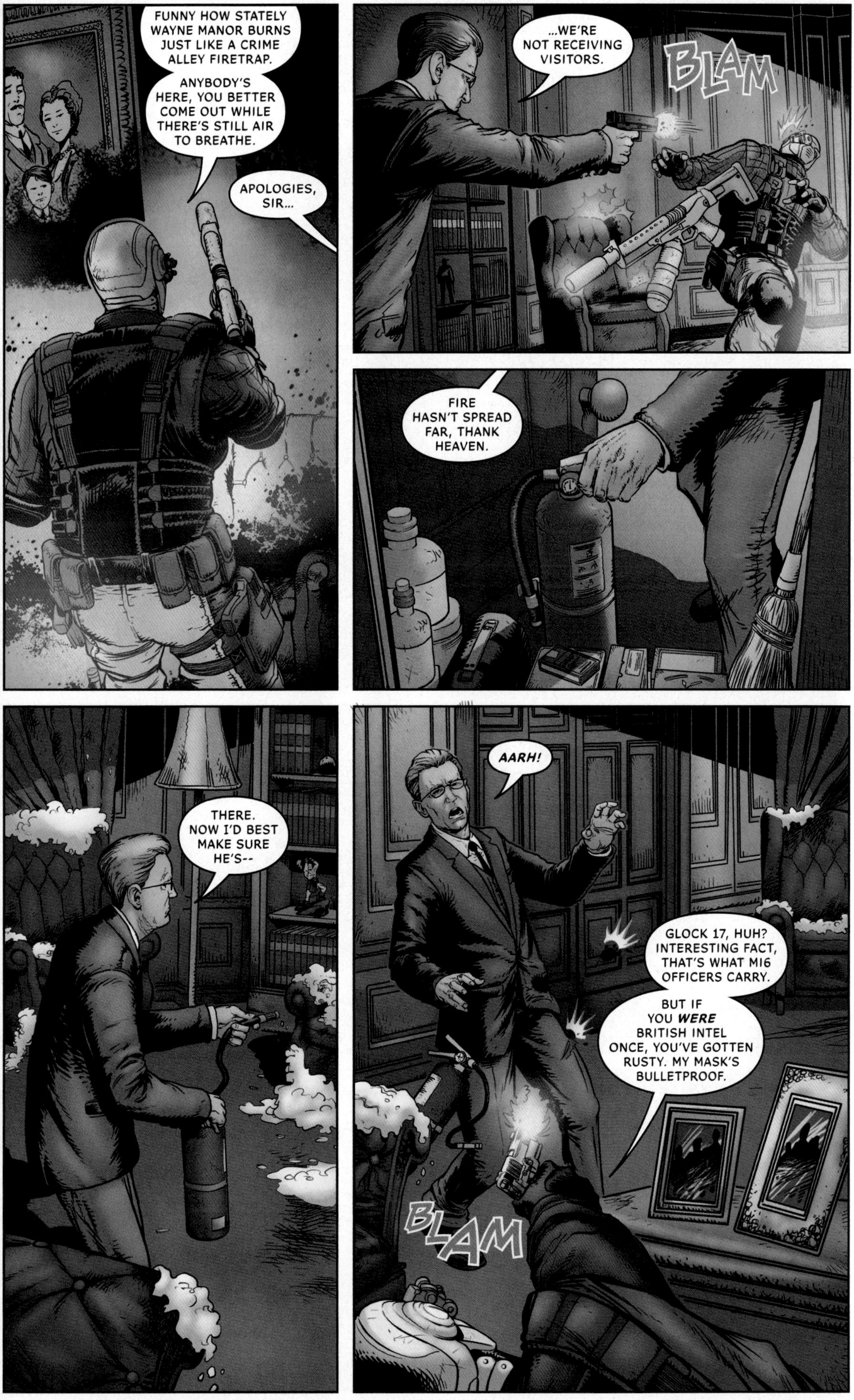
FUNNY HOW STATELY WAYNE MANOR BURNS JUST LIKE A CRIME ALLEY FIRETRAP.
ANYBODY'S HERE, YOU BETTER COME OUT WHILE THERE'S STILL AIR TO BREATHE.
APOLOGIES, SIR...
...WE'RE NOT RECEIVING VISITORS.
BLAM
FIRE HASN'T SPREAD FAR, THANK HEAVEN.
THERE. NOW I'D BEST MAKE SURE HE'S--
AARH!
GLOCK 17, HUH? INTERESTING FACT, THAT'S WHAT MI6 OFFICERS CARRY.
BUT IF YOU *WERE* BRITISH INTEL ONCE, YOU'VE GOTTEN RUSTY. MY MASK'S BULLETPROOF.
BLAM

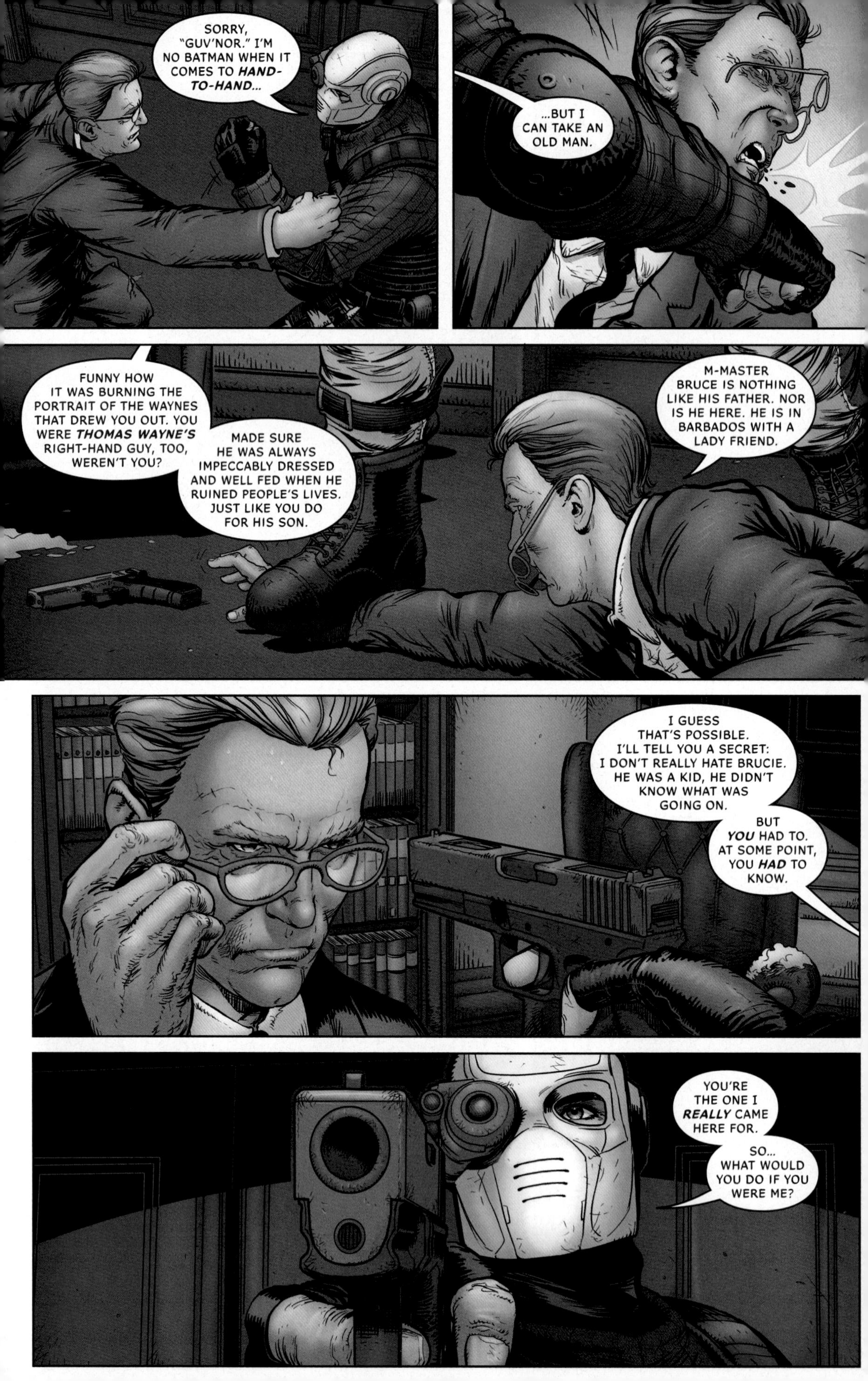
SORRY, "GUV'NOR." I'M NO BATMAN WHEN IT COMES TO ***HAND-TO-HAND***...
...BUT I CAN TAKE AN OLD MAN.
FUNNY HOW IT WAS BURNING THE PORTRAIT OF THE WAYNES THAT DREW YOU OUT. YOU WERE ***THOMAS WAYNE'S*** RIGHT-HAND GUY, TOO, WEREN'T YOU?
MADE SURE HE WAS ALWAYS IMPECCABLY DRESSED AND WELL FED WHEN HE RUINED PEOPLE'S LIVES. JUST LIKE YOU DO FOR HIS SON.
M-MASTER BRUCE IS NOTHING LIKE HIS FATHER. NOR IS HE HERE. HE IS IN BARBADOS WITH A LADY FRIEND.
I GUESS THAT'S POSSIBLE. I'LL TELL YOU A SECRET: I DON'T REALLY HATE BRUCIE. HE WAS A KID, HE DIDN'T KNOW WHAT WAS GOING ON.
BUT ***YOU*** HAD TO. AT SOME POINT, YOU ***HAD*** TO KNOW.
YOU'RE THE ONE I ***REALLY*** CAME HERE FOR.
SO... WHAT WOULD YOU DO IF YOU WERE ME?

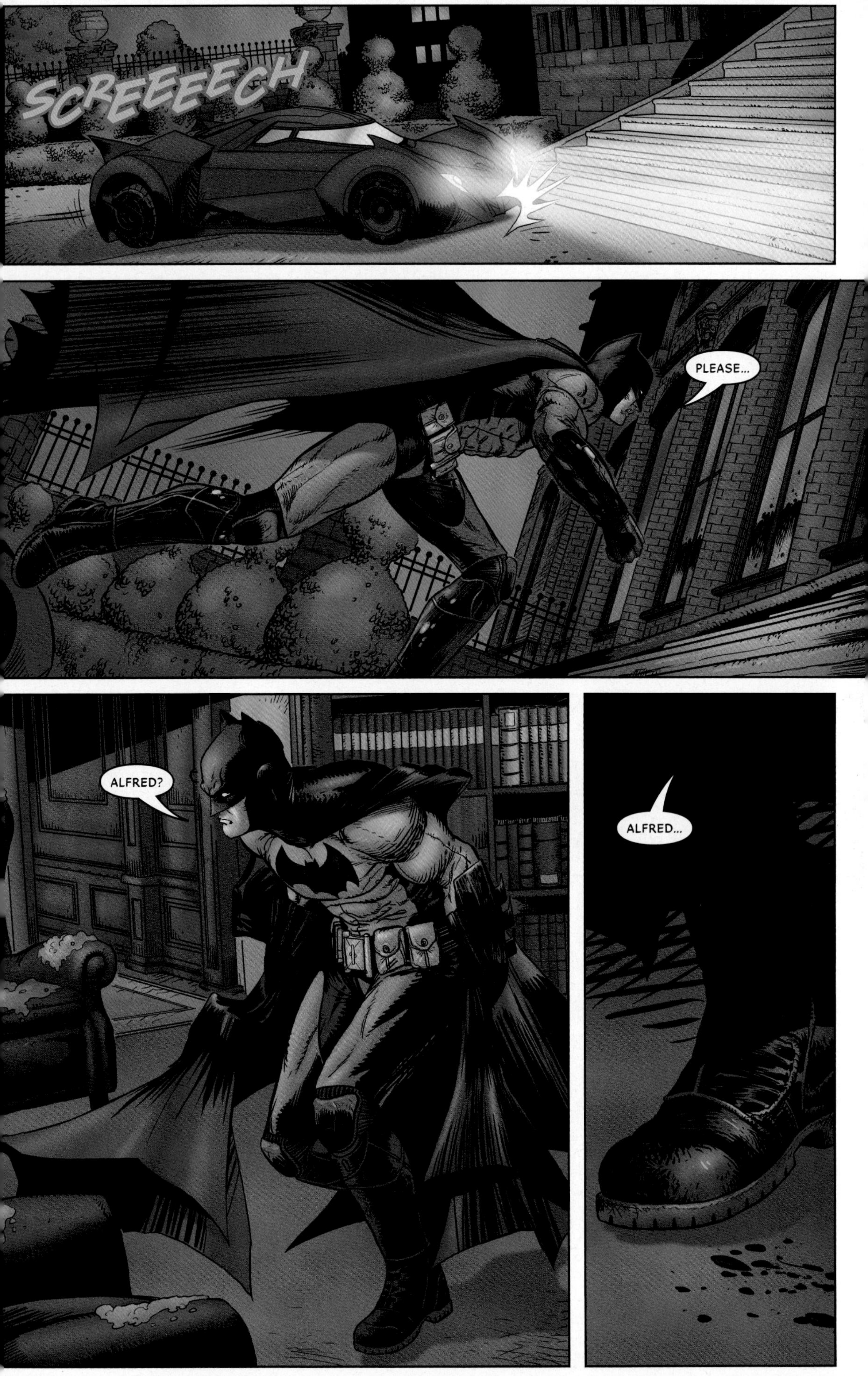
SCREEEECH
PLEASE...
ALFRED?
ALFRED...

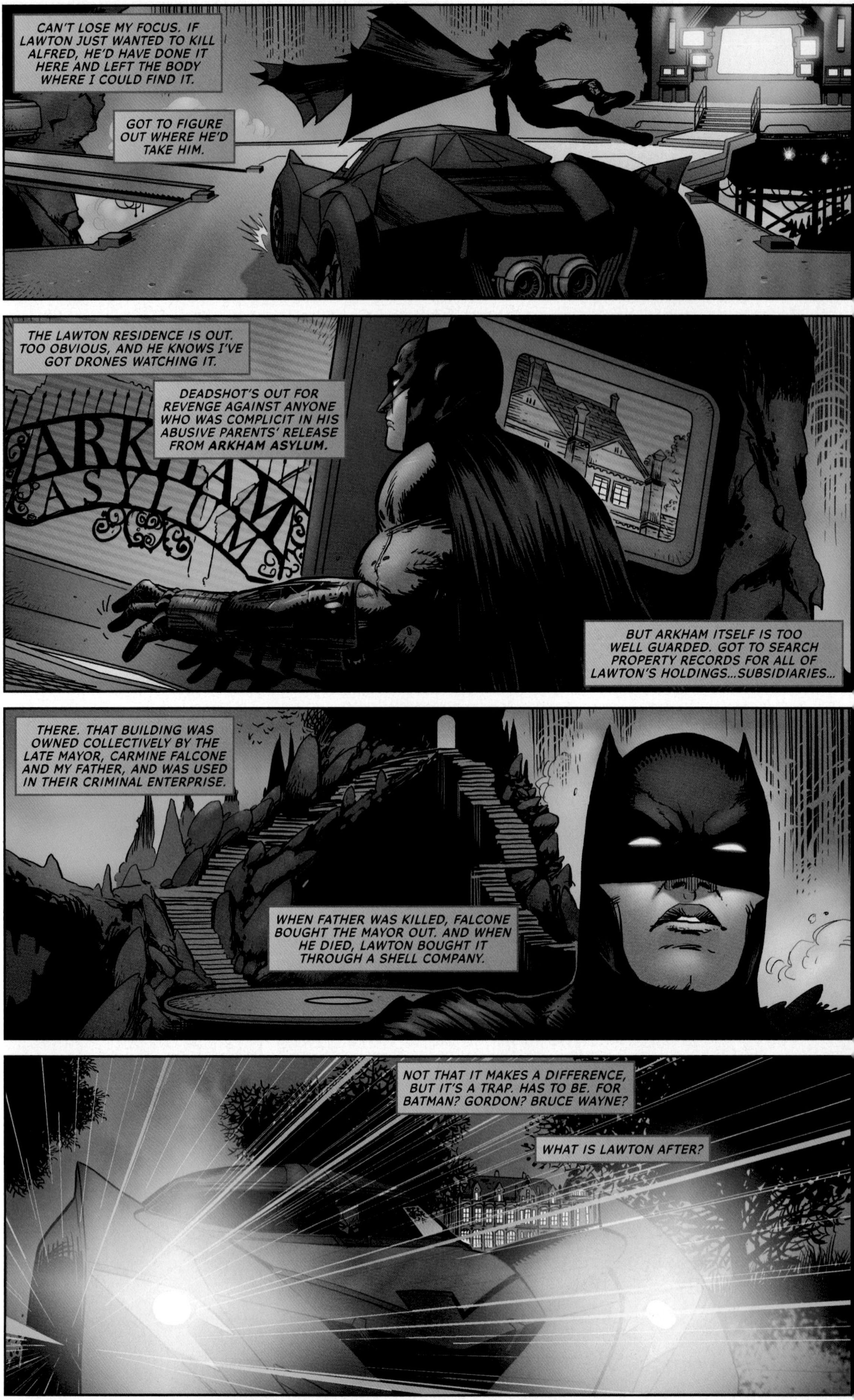
CAN'T LOSE MY FOCUS. IF LAWTON JUST WANTED TO KILL ALFRED, HE'D HAVE DONE IT HERE AND LEFT THE BODY WHERE I COULD FIND IT.
GOT TO FIGURE OUT WHERE HE'D TAKE HIM.
THE LAWTON RESIDENCE IS OUT. TOO OBVIOUS, AND HE KNOWS I'VE GOT DRONES WATCHING IT.
DEADSHOT'S OUT FOR REVENGE AGAINST ANYONE WHO WAS COMPLICIT IN HIS ABUSIVE PARENTS' RELEASE FROM ARKHAM ASYLUM.
ARKHAM ASYLUM
BUT ARKHAM ITSELF IS TOO WELL GUARDED. GOT TO SEARCH PROPERTY RECORDS FOR ALL OF LAWTON'S HOLDINGS...SUBSIDIARIES...
THERE. THAT BUILDING WAS OWNED COLLECTIVELY BY THE LATE MAYOR, CARMINE FALCONE AND MY FATHER, AND WAS USED IN THEIR CRIMINAL ENTERPRISE.
WHEN FATHER WAS KILLED, FALCONE BOUGHT THE MAYOR OUT. AND WHEN HE DIED, LAWTON BOUGHT IT THROUGH A SHELL COMPANY.
NOT THAT IT MAKES A DIFFERENCE, BUT IT'S A TRAP. HAS TO BE. FOR BATMAN? GORDON? BRUCE WAYNE?
WHAT IS LAWTON AFTER?

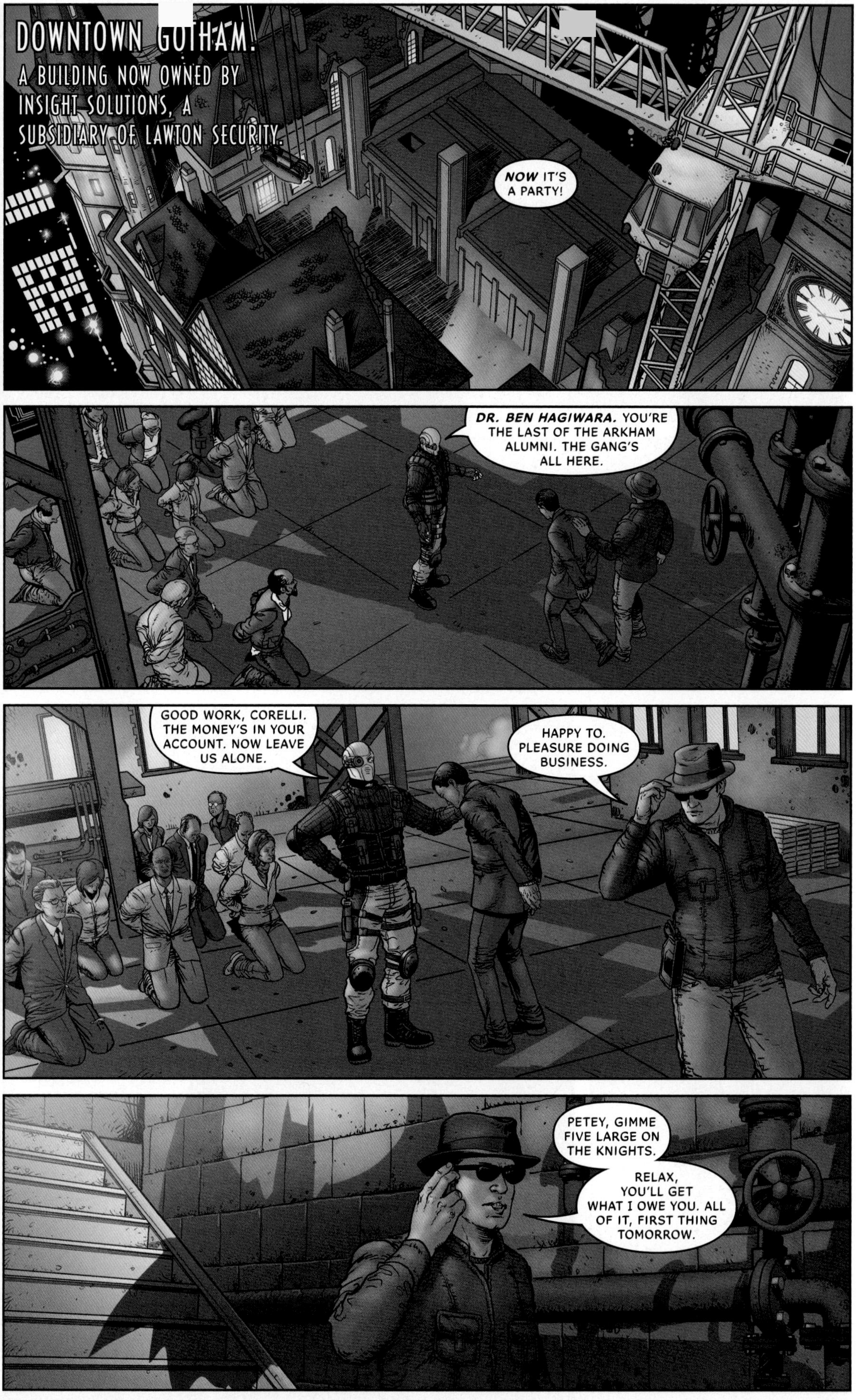
DOWNTOWN GOTHAM.
A BUILDING NOW OWNED BY INSIGHT SOLUTIONS, A SUBSIDIARY OF LAWTON SECURITY.
NOW IT'S A PARTY!
DR. BEN HAGIWARA. YOU'RE THE LAST OF THE ARKHAM ALUMNI. THE GANG'S ALL HERE.
GOOD WORK, CORELLI. THE MONEY'S IN YOUR ACCOUNT. NOW LEAVE US ALONE.
HAPPY TO. PLEASURE DOING BUSINESS.
PETEY, GIMME FIVE LARGE ON THE KNIGHTS.
RELAX, YOU'LL GET WHAT I OWE YOU. ALL OF IT, FIRST THING TOMORROW.

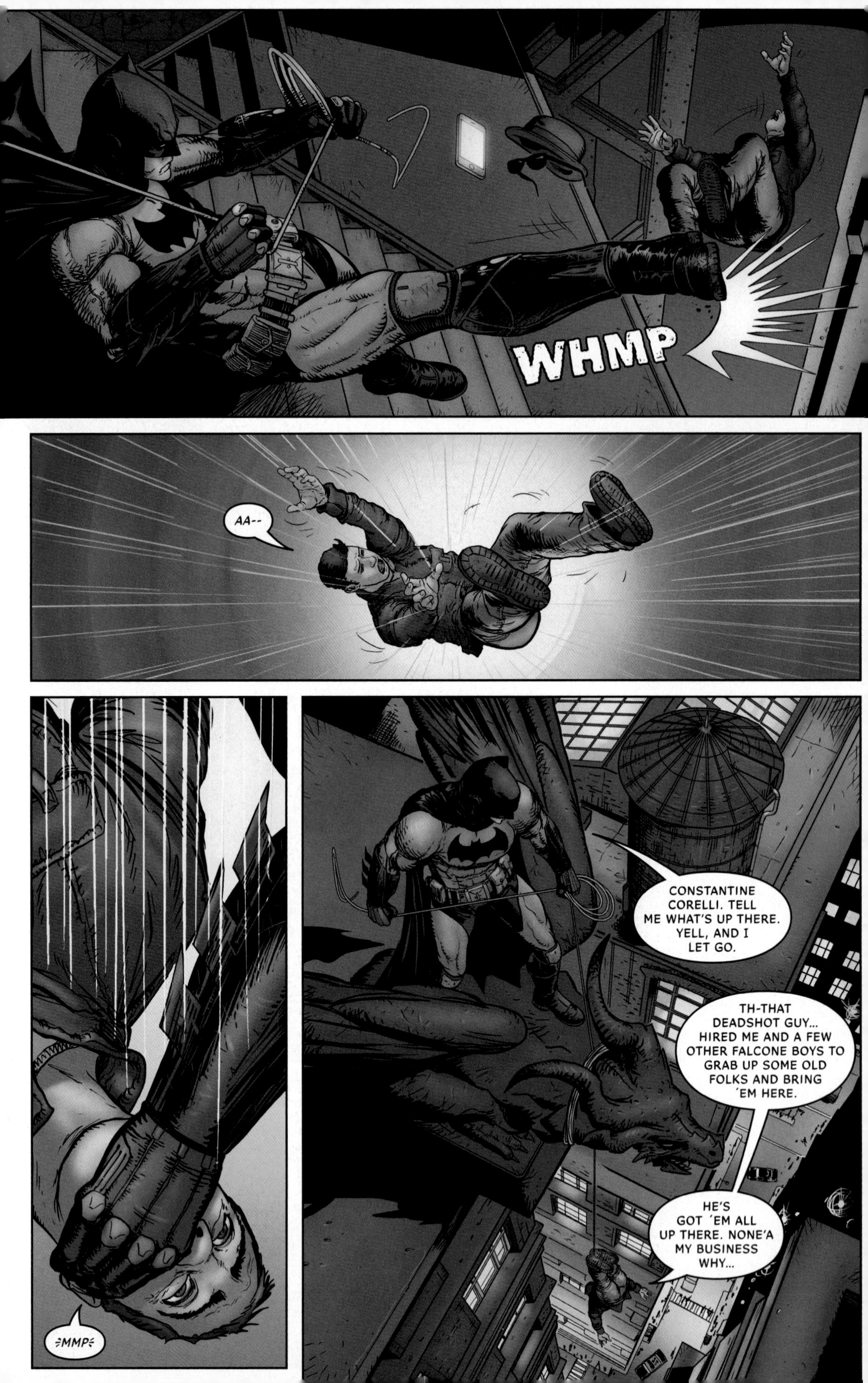
WHMP
AA--
MMP
CONSTANTINE CORELLI. TELL ME WHAT'S UP THERE. YELL, AND I LET GO.
TH-THAT DEADSHOT GUY... HIRED ME AND A FEW OTHER FALCONE BOYS TO GRAB UP SOME OLD FOLKS AND BRING 'EM HERE.
HE'S GOT 'EM ALL UP THERE. NONE'A MY BUSINESS WHY...

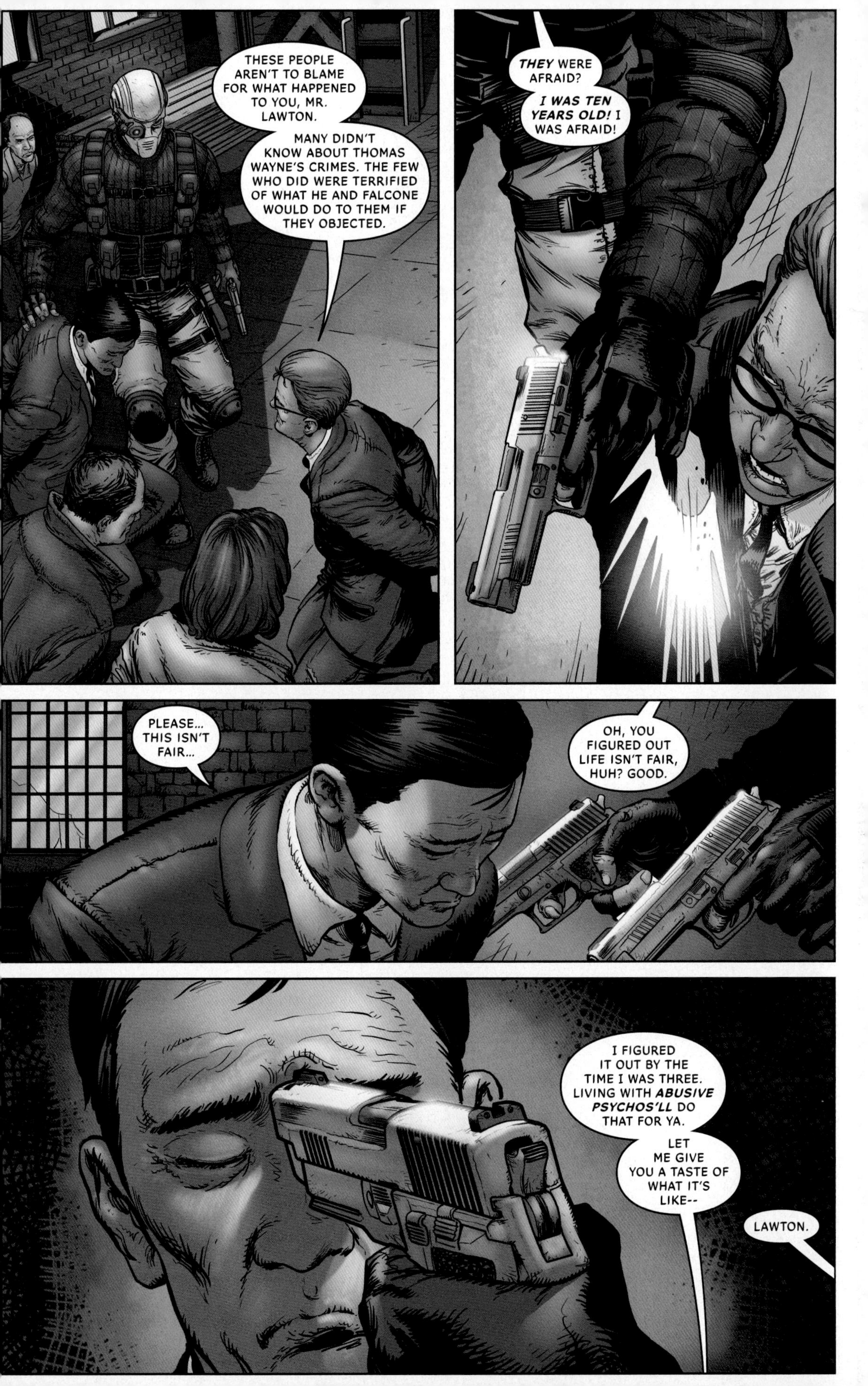
THESE PEOPLE AREN'T TO BLAME FOR WHAT HAPPENED TO YOU, MR. LAWTON.
MANY DIDN'T KNOW ABOUT THOMAS WAYNE'S CRIMES. THE FEW WHO DID WERE TERRIFIED OF WHAT HE AND FALCONE WOULD DO TO THEM IF THEY OBJECTED.
THEY WERE AFRAID?
I WAS TEN YEARS OLD! I WAS AFRAID!
PLEASE... THIS ISN'T FAIR...
OH, YOU FIGURED OUT LIFE ISN'T FAIR, HUH? GOOD.
I FIGURED IT OUT BY THE TIME I WAS THREE. LIVING WITH *ABUSIVE PSYCHOS'LL* DO THAT FOR YA.
LET ME GIVE YOU A TASTE OF WHAT IT'S LIKE--
LAWTON.

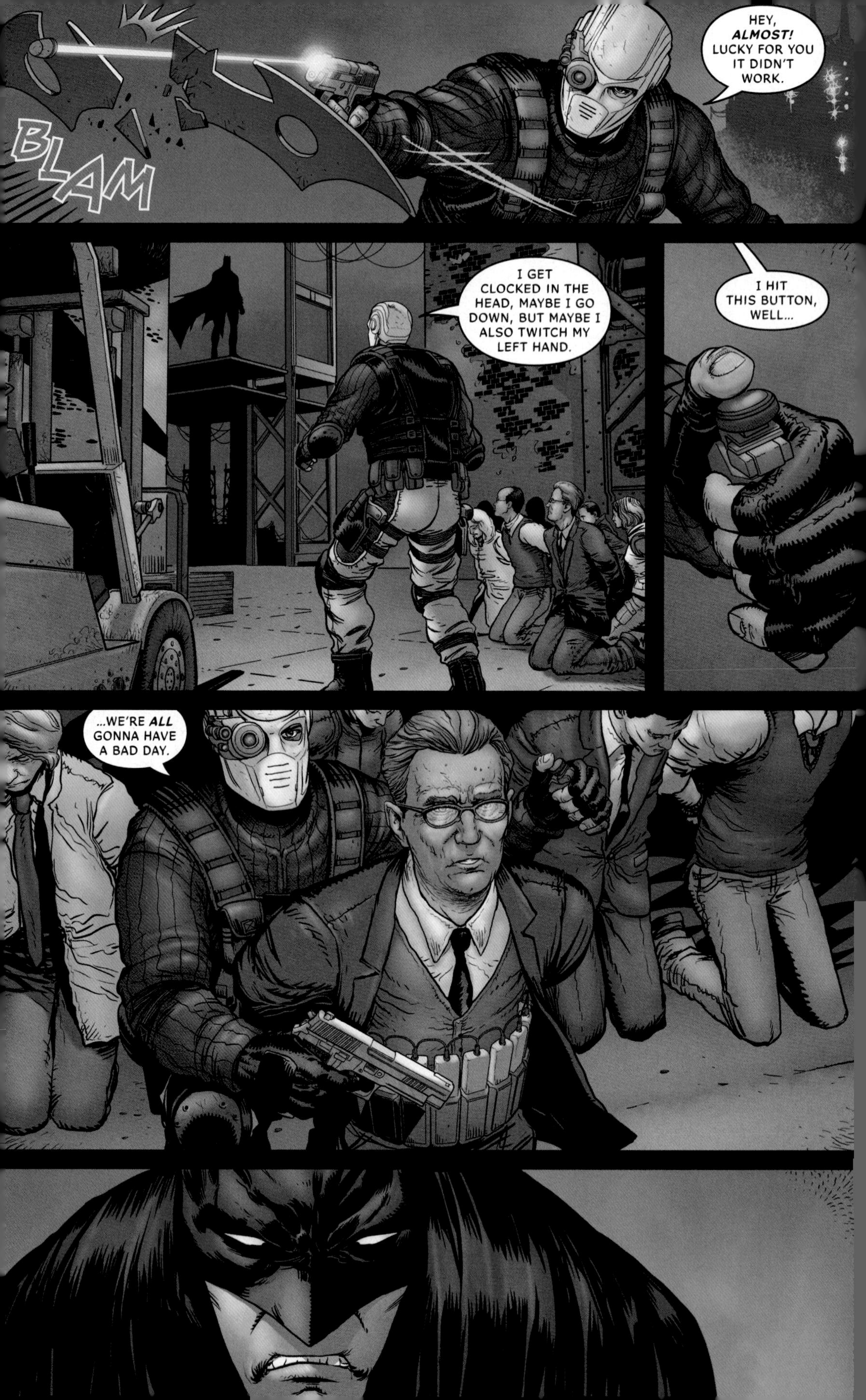

BLAM
HEY, **ALMOST!** LUCKY FOR YOU IT DIDN'T WORK.
I GET CLOCKED IN THE HEAD, MAYBE I GO DOWN, BUT MAYBE I ALSO TWITCH MY LEFT HAND.
I HIT THIS BUTTON, WELL...
...WE'RE **ALL** GONNA HAVE A BAD DAY.

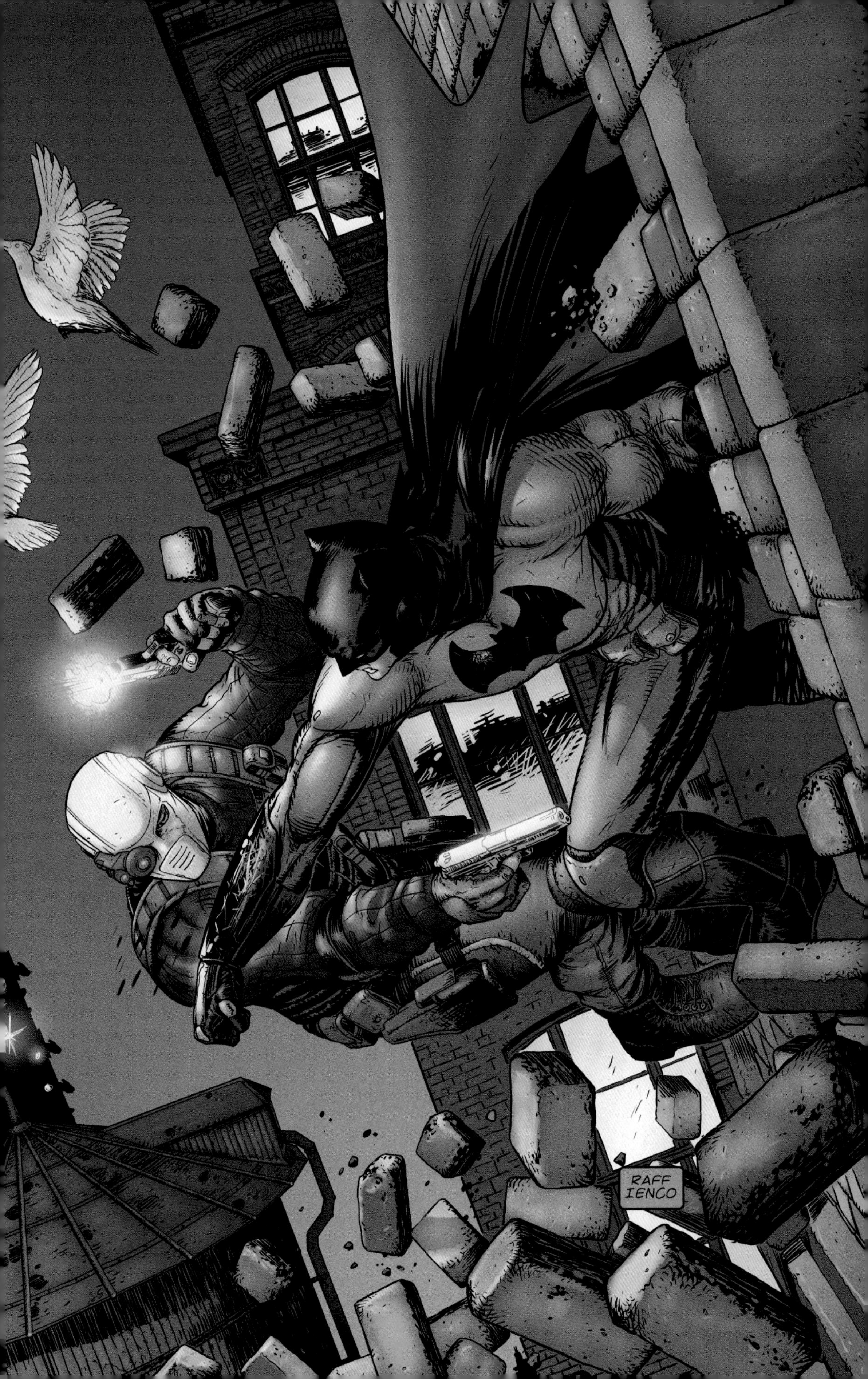
RAFF
IENCO

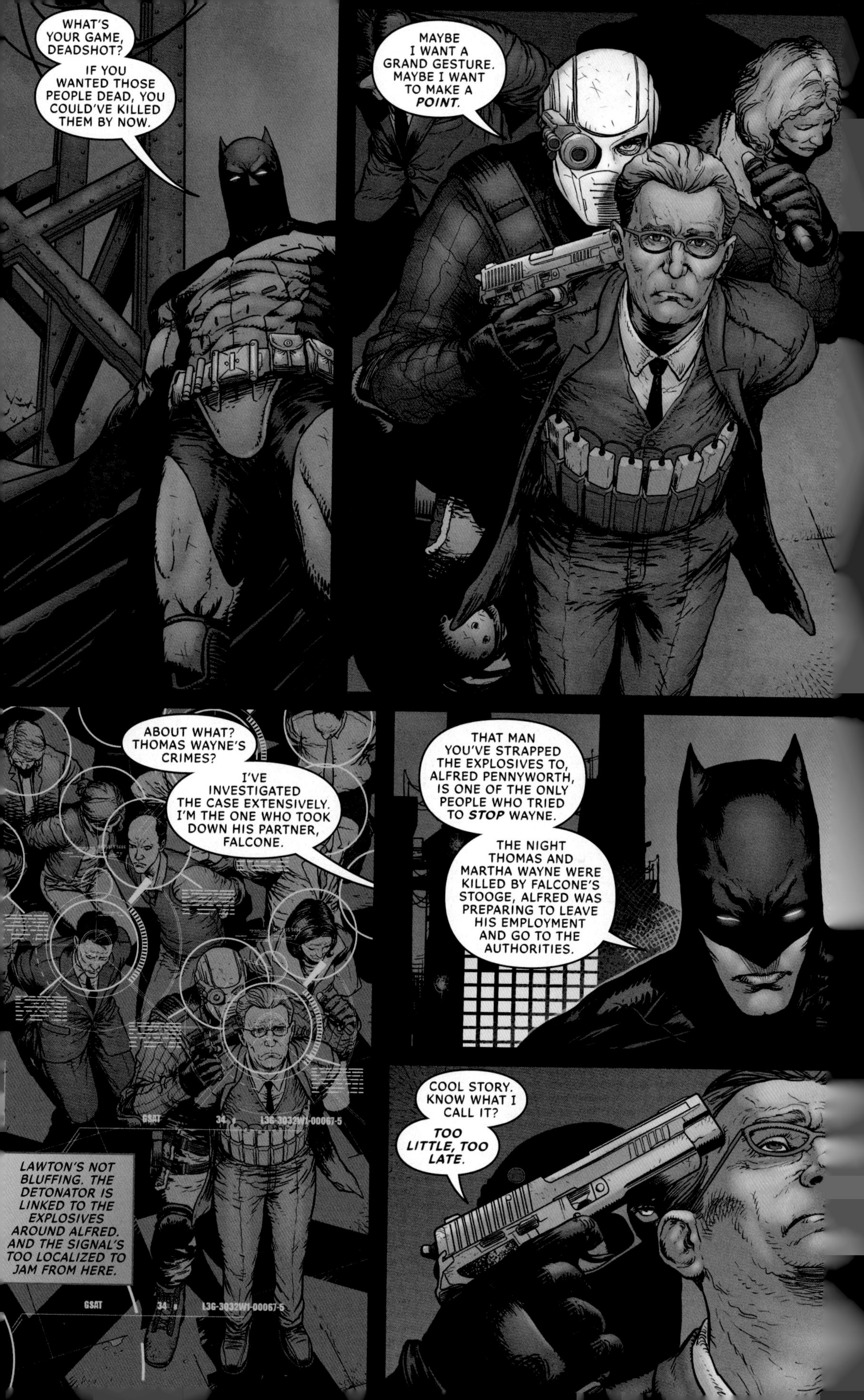
WHAT'S YOUR GAME, DEADSHOT?
IF YOU WANTED THOSE PEOPLE DEAD, YOU COULD'VE KILLED THEM BY NOW.
MAYBE I WANT A GRAND GESTURE. MAYBE I WANT TO MAKE A *POINT*.
ABOUT WHAT? THOMAS WAYNE'S CRIMES?
I'VE INVESTIGATED THE CASE EXTENSIVELY. I'M THE ONE WHO TOOK DOWN HIS PARTNER, FALCONE.
GSAT 34 L3G-3032W1-00067-5
LAWTON'S NOT BLUFFING. THE DETONATOR IS LINKED TO THE EXPLOSIVES AROUND ALFRED. AND THE SIGNAL'S TOO LOCALIZED TO JAM FROM HERE.
GSAT 34 L3G-3032W1-00067-5
THAT MAN YOU'VE STRAPPED THE EXPLOSIVES TO, ALFRED PENNYWORTH, IS ONE OF THE ONLY PEOPLE WHO TRIED TO *STOP* WAYNE.
THE NIGHT THOMAS AND MARTHA WAYNE WERE KILLED BY FALCONE'S STOOGE, ALFRED WAS PREPARING TO LEAVE HIS EMPLOYMENT AND GO TO THE AUTHORITIES.
COOL STORY. KNOW WHAT I CALL IT?
TOO LITTLE, TOO LATE.

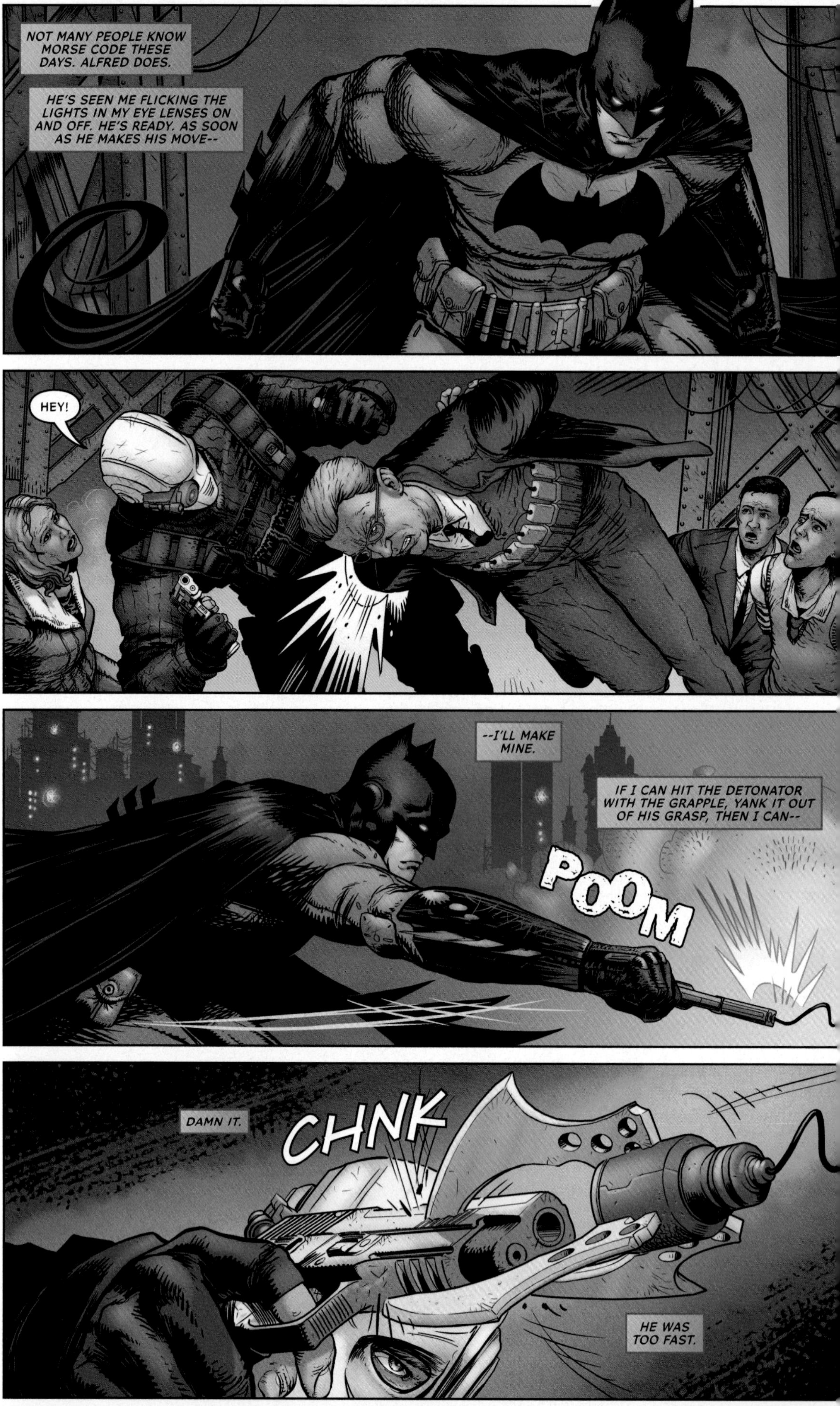
NOT MANY PEOPLE KNOW MORSE CODE THESE DAYS. ALFRED DOES.
HE'S SEEN ME FLICKING THE LIGHTS IN MY EYE LENSES ON AND OFF. HE'S READY. AS SOON AS HE MAKES HIS MOVE--
HEY!
--I'LL MAKE MINE.
IF I CAN HIT THE DETONATOR WITH THE GRAPPLE, YANK IT OUT OF HIS GRASP, THEN I CAN--
POOM
DAMN IT.
CHNK
HE WAS TOO FAST.

KEEP THAT GUN.

I'VE GOT MORE.

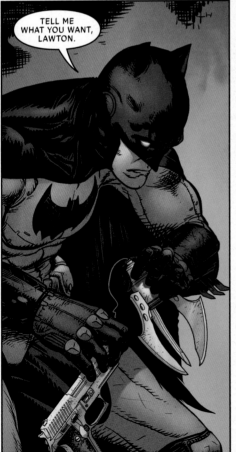

TELL ME WHAT YOU WANT, LAWTON.

WHAT KIND OF SICK POINT ARE YOU TRYING TO MAKE?

YOU'RE GOING TO MAKE IT FOR ME.

I'LL ONLY TELL YOU ONCE: DO EXACTLY AS I SAY, OR I KILL THE OLD MAN.

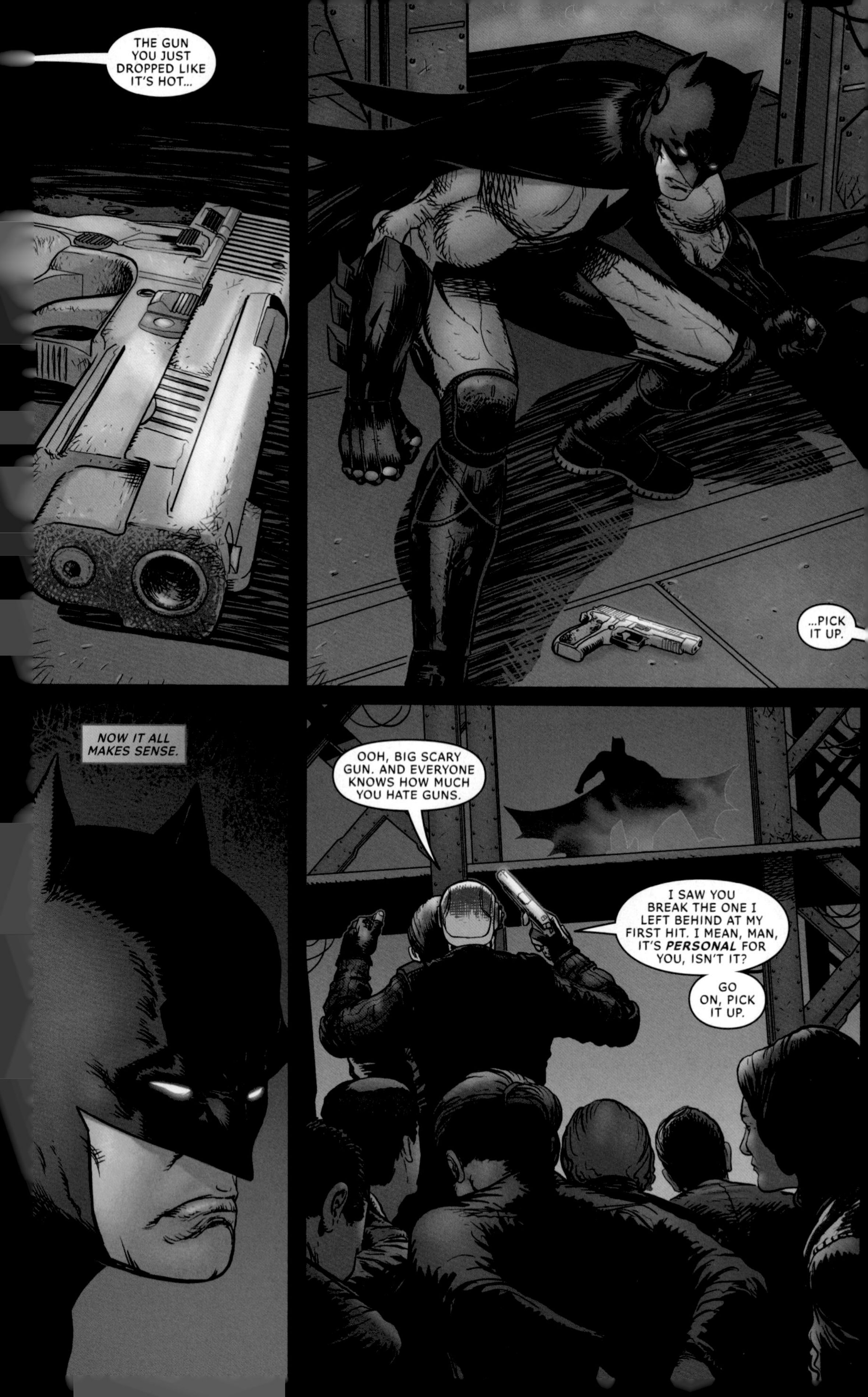
THE GUN YOU JUST DROPPED LIKE IT'S HOT...
...PICK IT UP.
NOW IT ALL MAKES SENSE.
OOH, BIG SCARY GUN. AND EVERYONE KNOWS HOW MUCH YOU HATE GUNS.
I SAW YOU BREAK THE ONE I LEFT BEHIND AT MY FIRST HIT. I MEAN, MAN, IT'S ***PERSONAL*** FOR YOU, ISN'T IT?
GO ON, PICK IT UP.

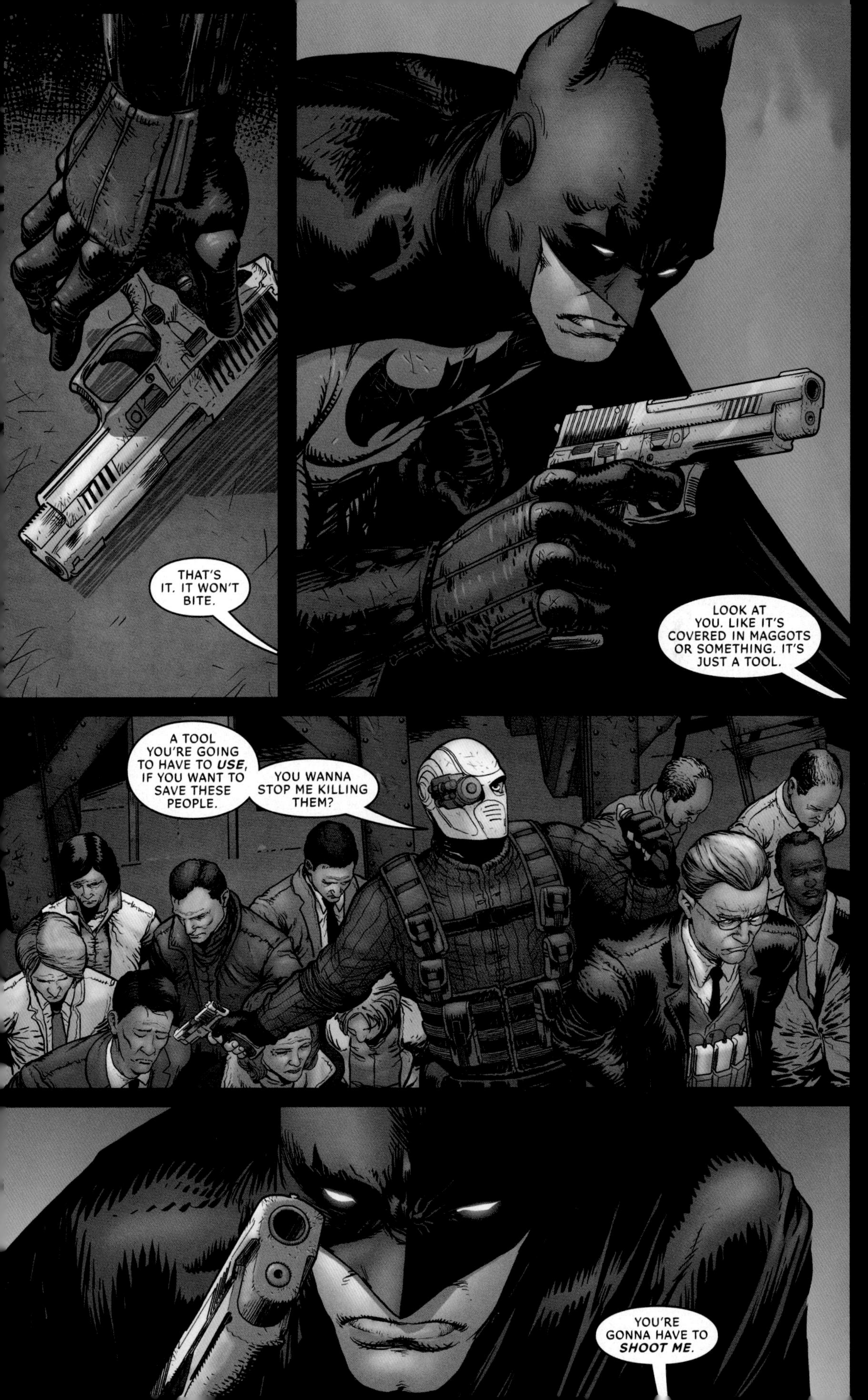
THAT'S IT. IT WON'T BITE.
LOOK AT YOU. LIKE IT'S COVERED IN MAGGOTS OR SOMETHING. IT'S JUST A TOOL.
A TOOL YOU'RE GOING TO HAVE TO USE, IF YOU WANT TO SAVE THESE PEOPLE.
YOU WANNA STOP ME KILLING THEM?
YOU'RE GONNA HAVE TO SHOOT ME.

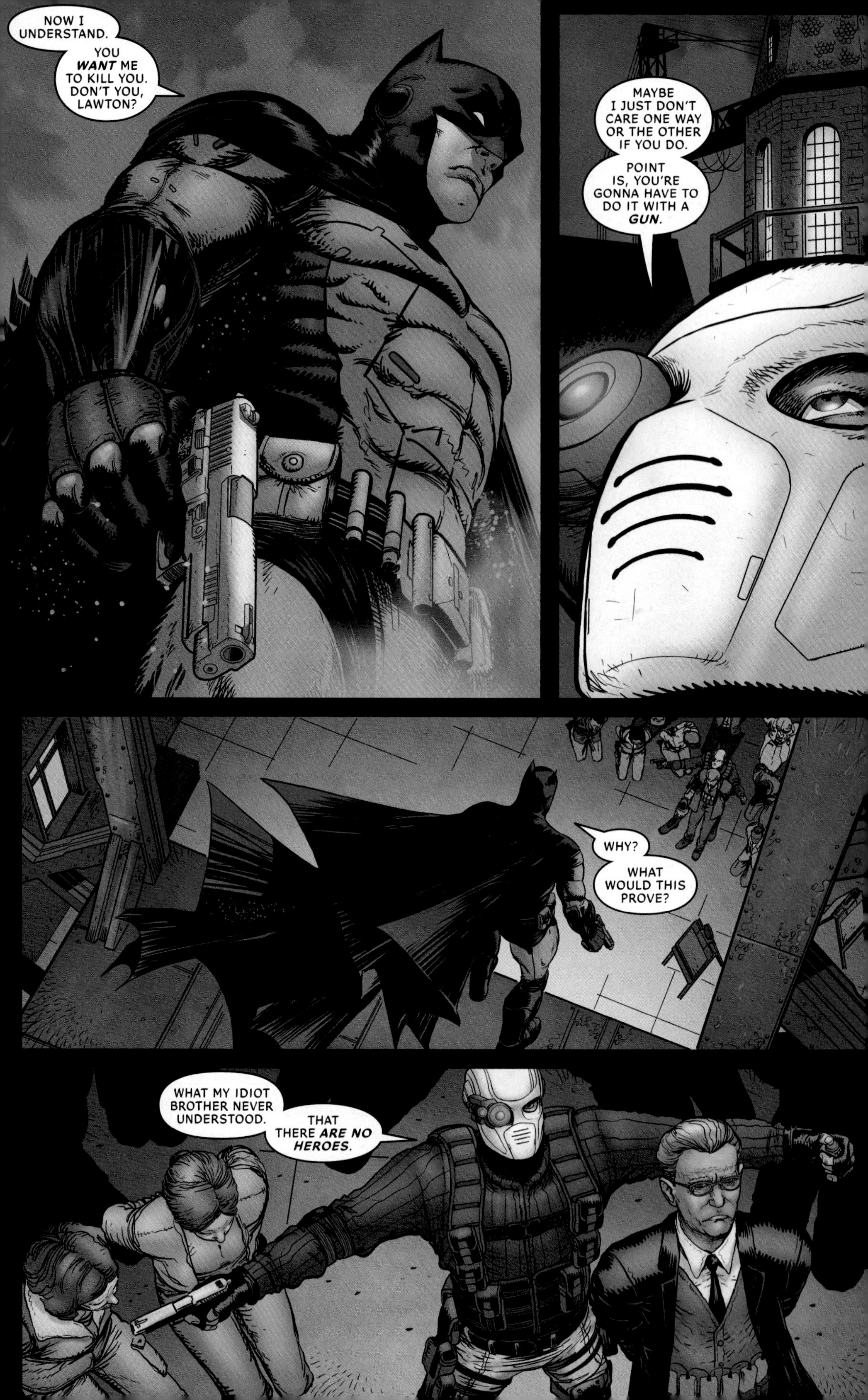
NOW I UNDERSTAND.
YOU *WANT* ME TO KILL YOU. DON'T YOU, LAWTON?
MAYBE I JUST DON'T CARE ONE WAY OR THE OTHER IF YOU DO.
POINT IS, YOU'RE GONNA HAVE TO DO IT WITH A *GUN*.
WHY?
WHAT WOULD THIS PROVE?
WHAT MY IDIOT BROTHER NEVER UNDERSTOOD.
THAT THERE *ARE NO HEROES*.

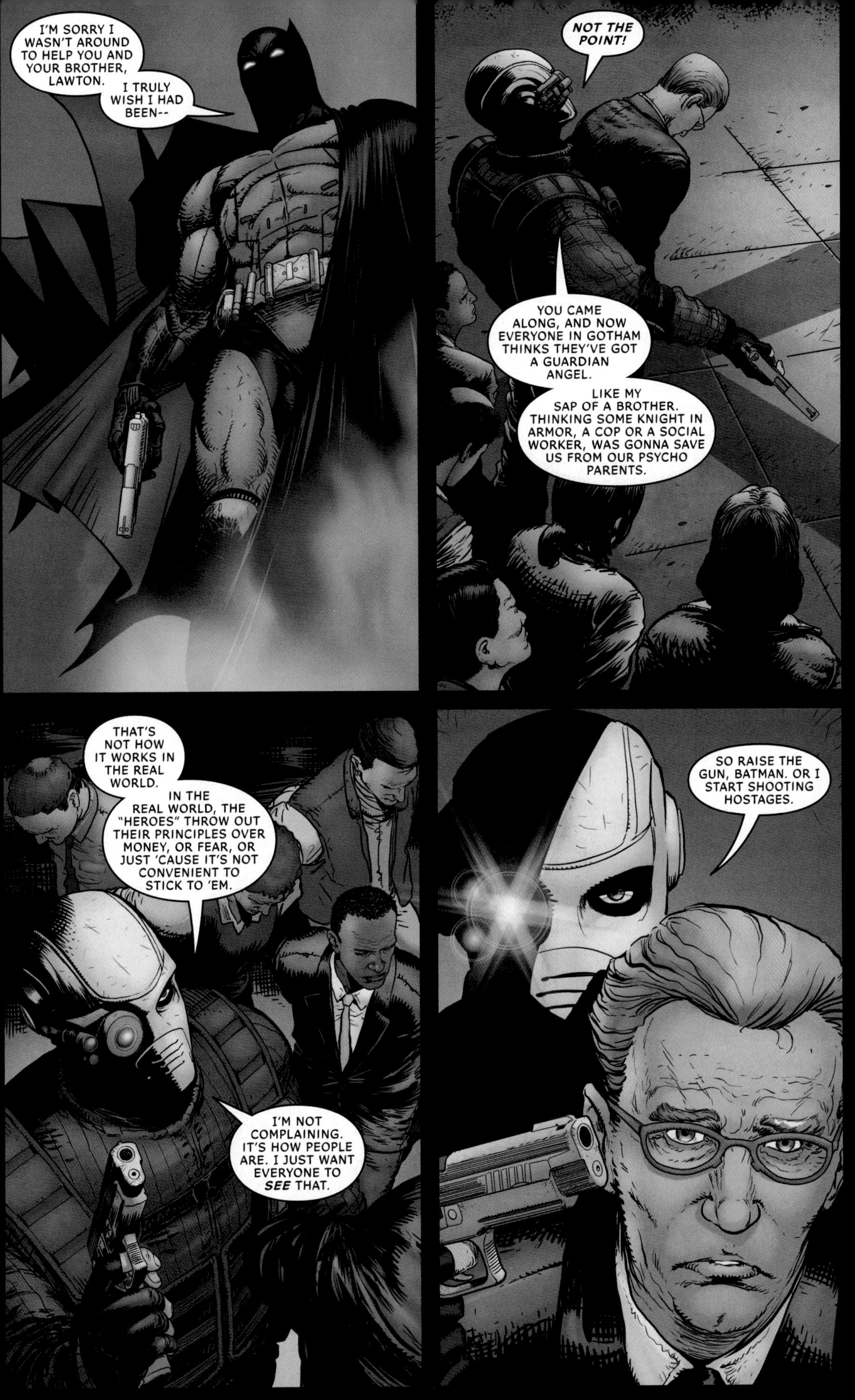
I'M SORRY I WASN'T AROUND TO HELP YOU AND YOUR BROTHER, LAWTON.
I TRULY WISH I HAD BEEN--
NOT THE POINT!
YOU CAME ALONG, AND NOW EVERYONE IN GOTHAM THINKS THEY'VE GOT A GUARDIAN ANGEL.
LIKE MY SAP OF A BROTHER. THINKING SOME KNIGHT IN ARMOR, A COP OR A SOCIAL WORKER, WAS GONNA SAVE US FROM OUR PSYCHO PARENTS.
THAT'S NOT HOW IT WORKS IN THE REAL WORLD.
IN THE REAL WORLD, THE "HEROES" THROW OUT THEIR PRINCIPLES OVER MONEY, OR FEAR, OR JUST 'CAUSE IT'S NOT CONVENIENT TO STICK TO 'EM.
I'M NOT COMPLAINING. IT'S HOW PEOPLE ARE. I JUST WANT EVERYONE TO *SEE* THAT.
SO RAISE THE GUN, BATMAN. OR I START SHOOTING HOSTAGES.

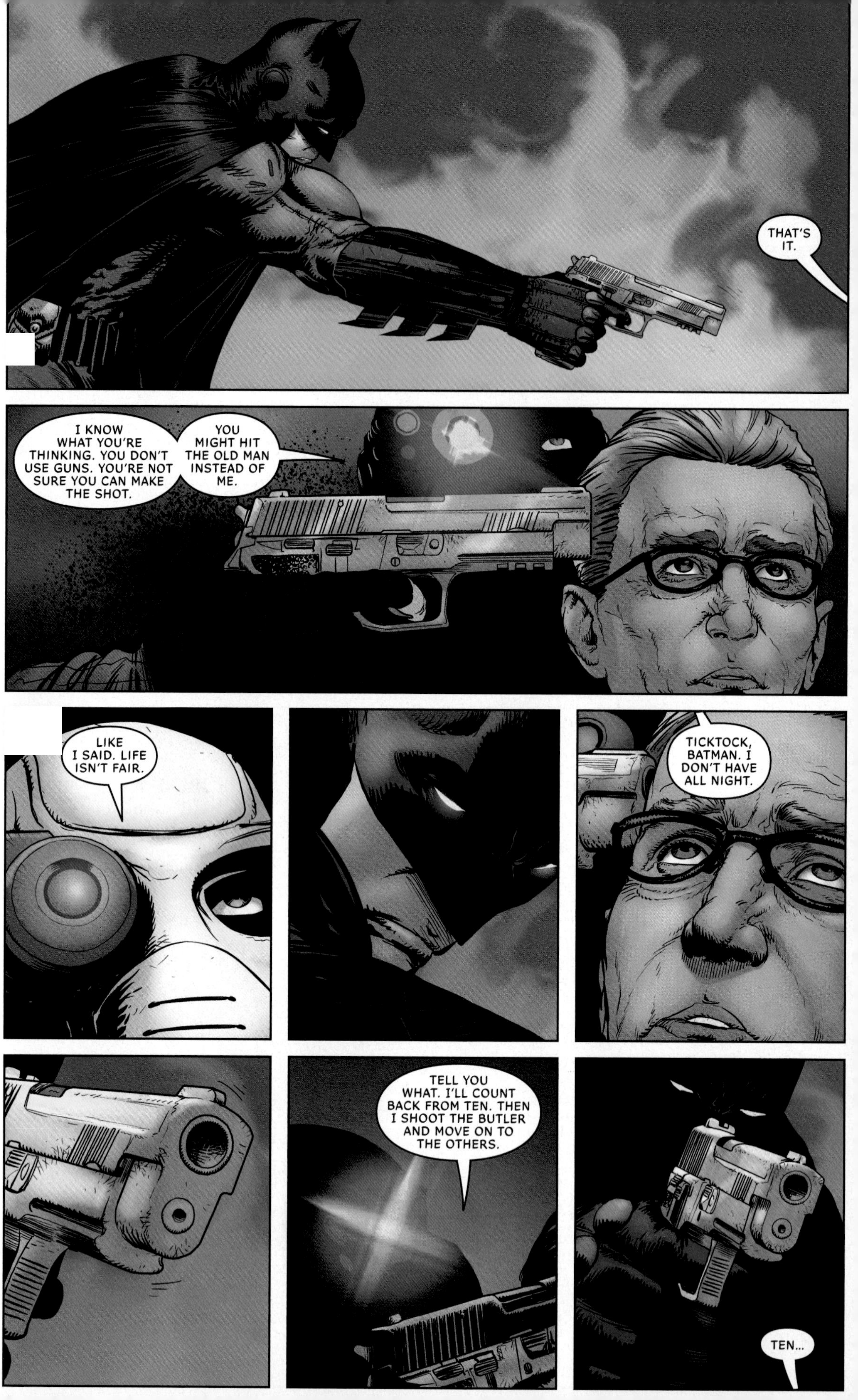
THAT'S IT.
I KNOW WHAT YOU'RE THINKING. YOU DON'T USE GUNS. YOU'RE NOT SURE YOU CAN MAKE THE SHOT.
YOU MIGHT HIT THE OLD MAN INSTEAD OF ME.
LIKE I SAID. LIFE ISN'T FAIR.
TICKTOCK, BATMAN. I DON'T HAVE ALL NIGHT.
TELL YOU WHAT. I'LL COUNT BACK FROM TEN. THEN I SHOOT THE BUTLER AND MOVE ON TO THE OTHERS.
TEN...

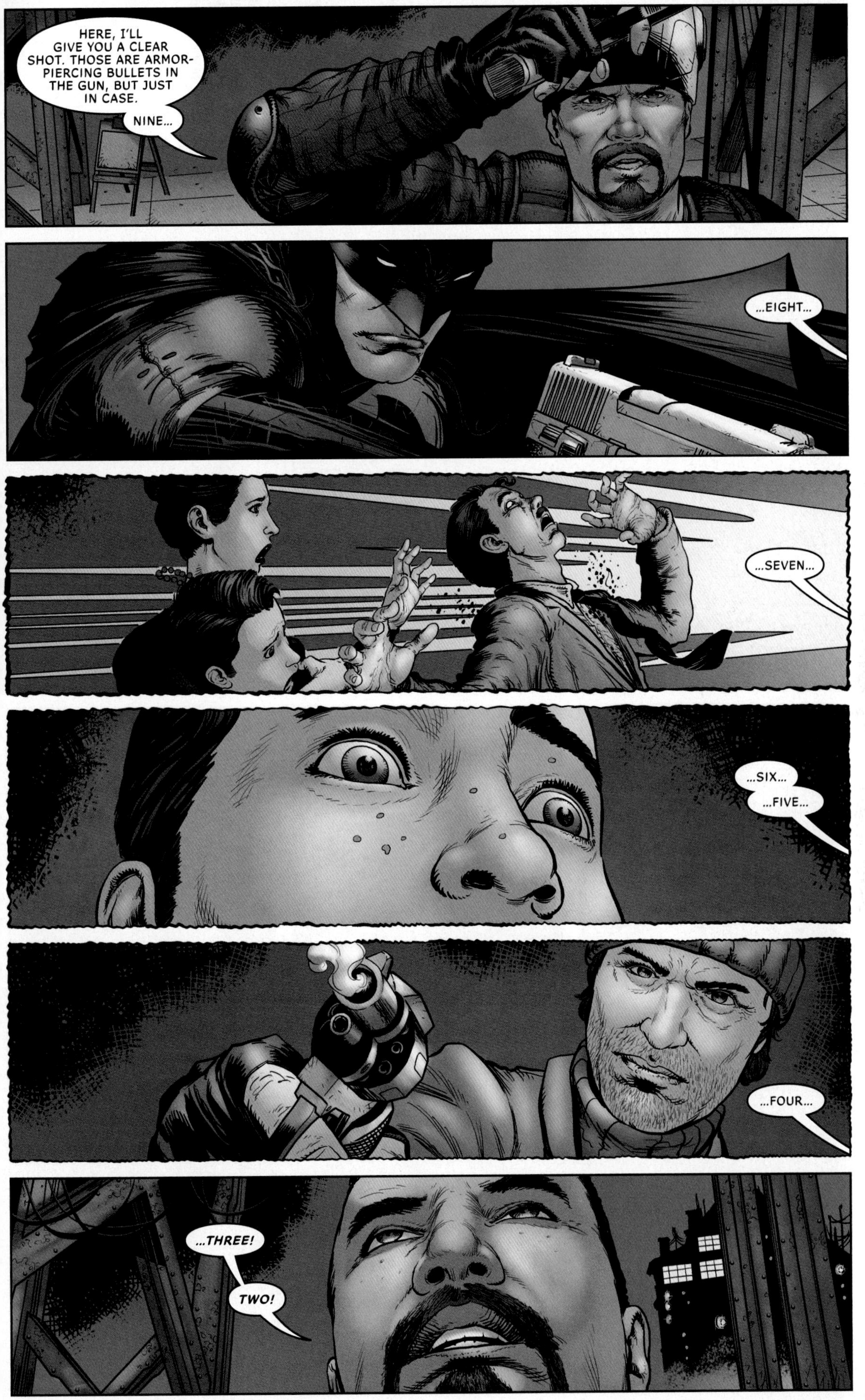
HERE, I'LL GIVE YOU A CLEAR SHOT. THOSE ARE ARMOR-PIERCING BULLETS IN THE GUN, BUT JUST IN CASE.
NINE...
...EIGHT...
...SEVEN...
...SIX...
...FIVE...
...FOUR...
...THREE!
TWO!

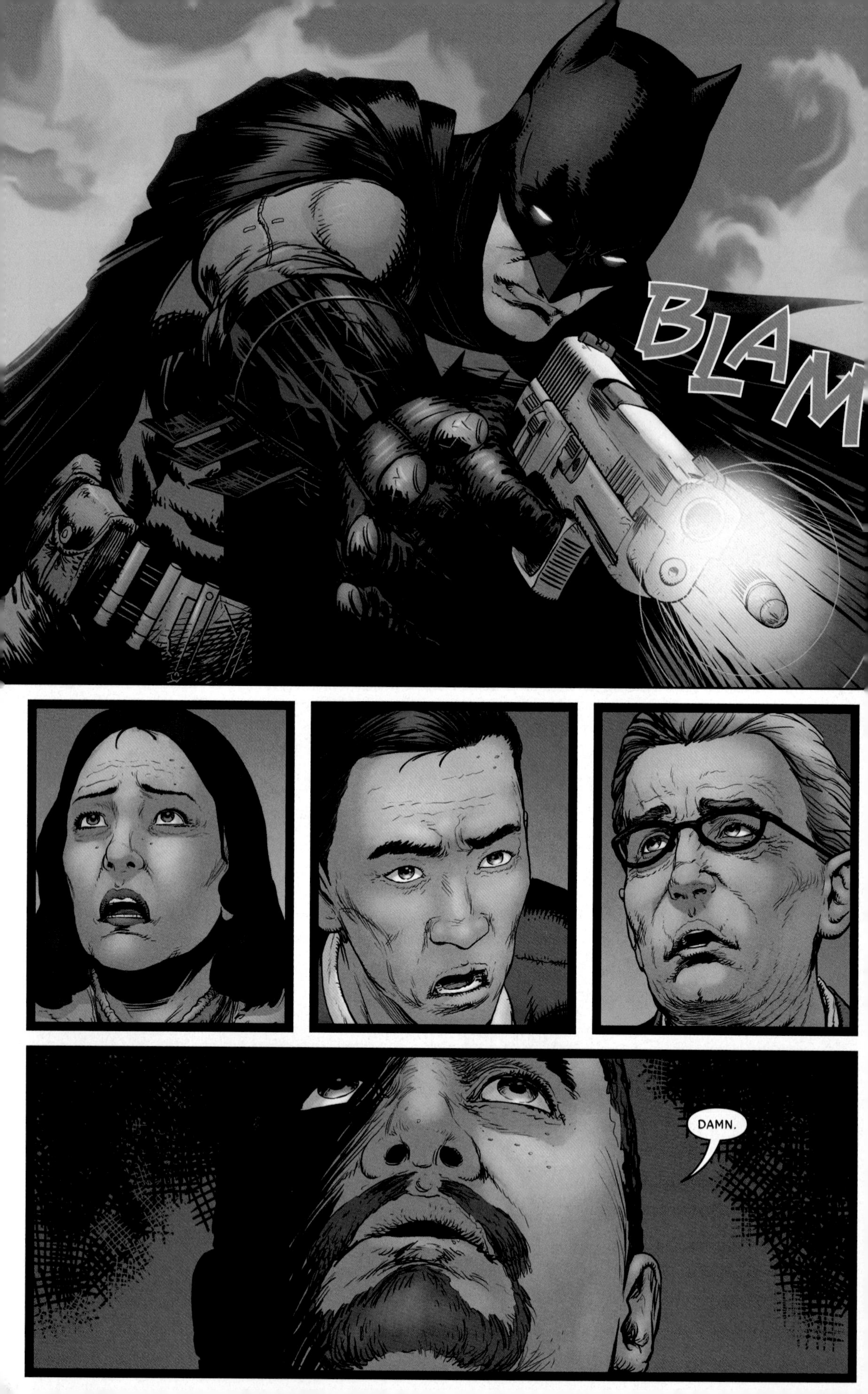
BLAM
DAMN.

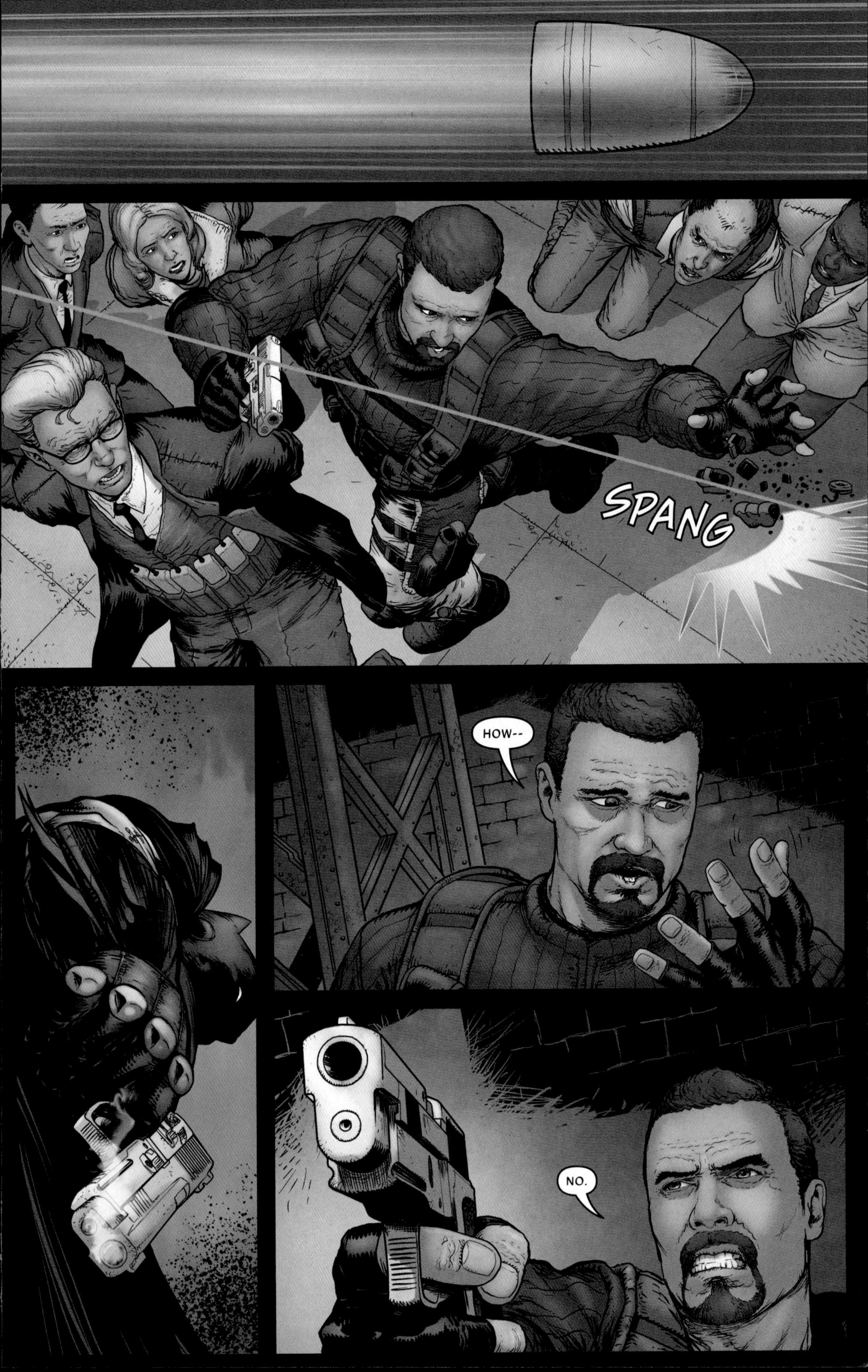
SPANG
HOW--
NO.

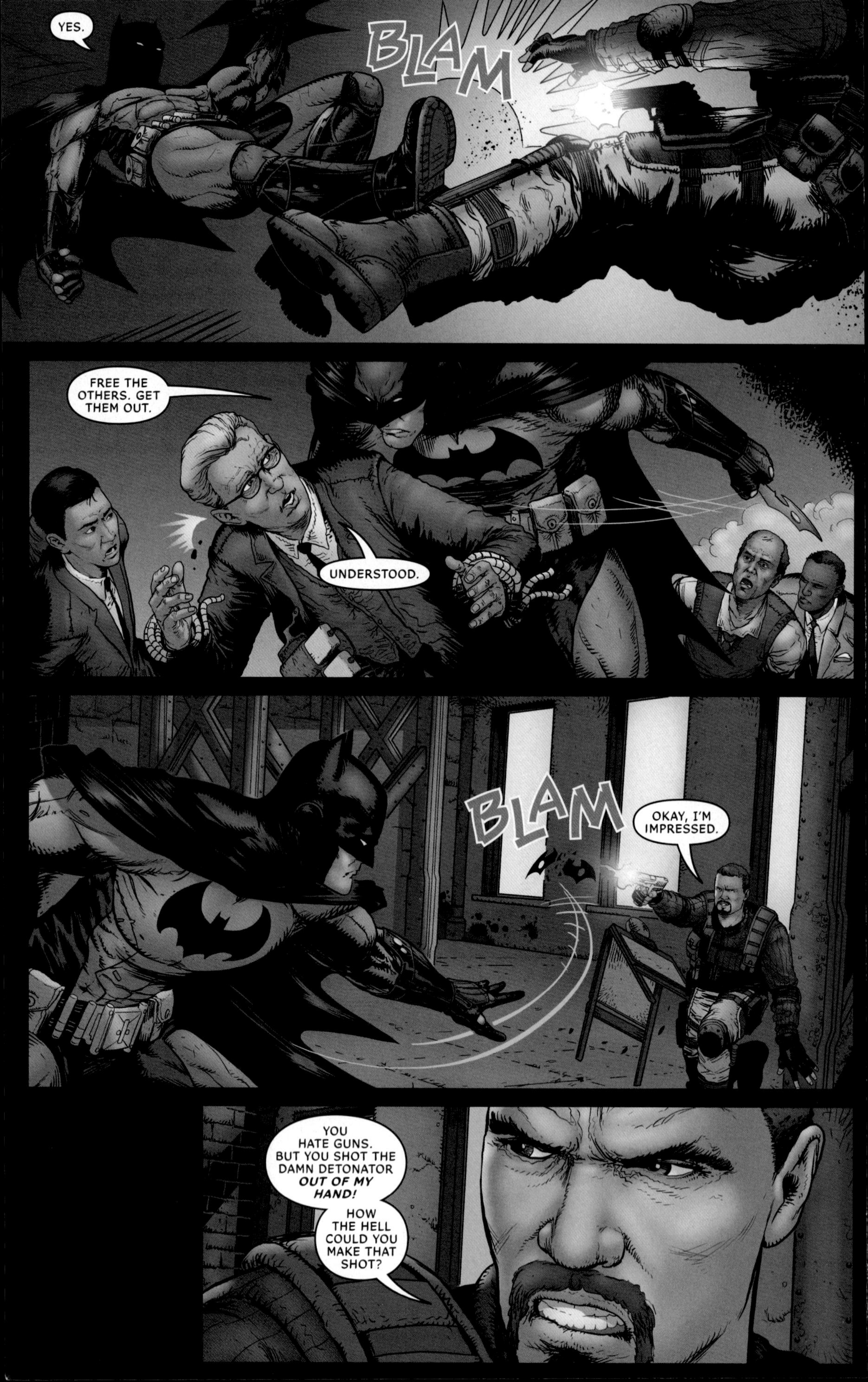
YES.
BLAM
FREE THE OTHERS. GET THEM OUT.
UNDERSTOOD.
BLAM
OKAY, I'M IMPRESSED.
YOU HATE GUNS. BUT YOU SHOT THE DAMN DETONATOR ***OUT OF MY HAND!***
HOW THE HELL COULD YOU MAKE THAT SHOT?

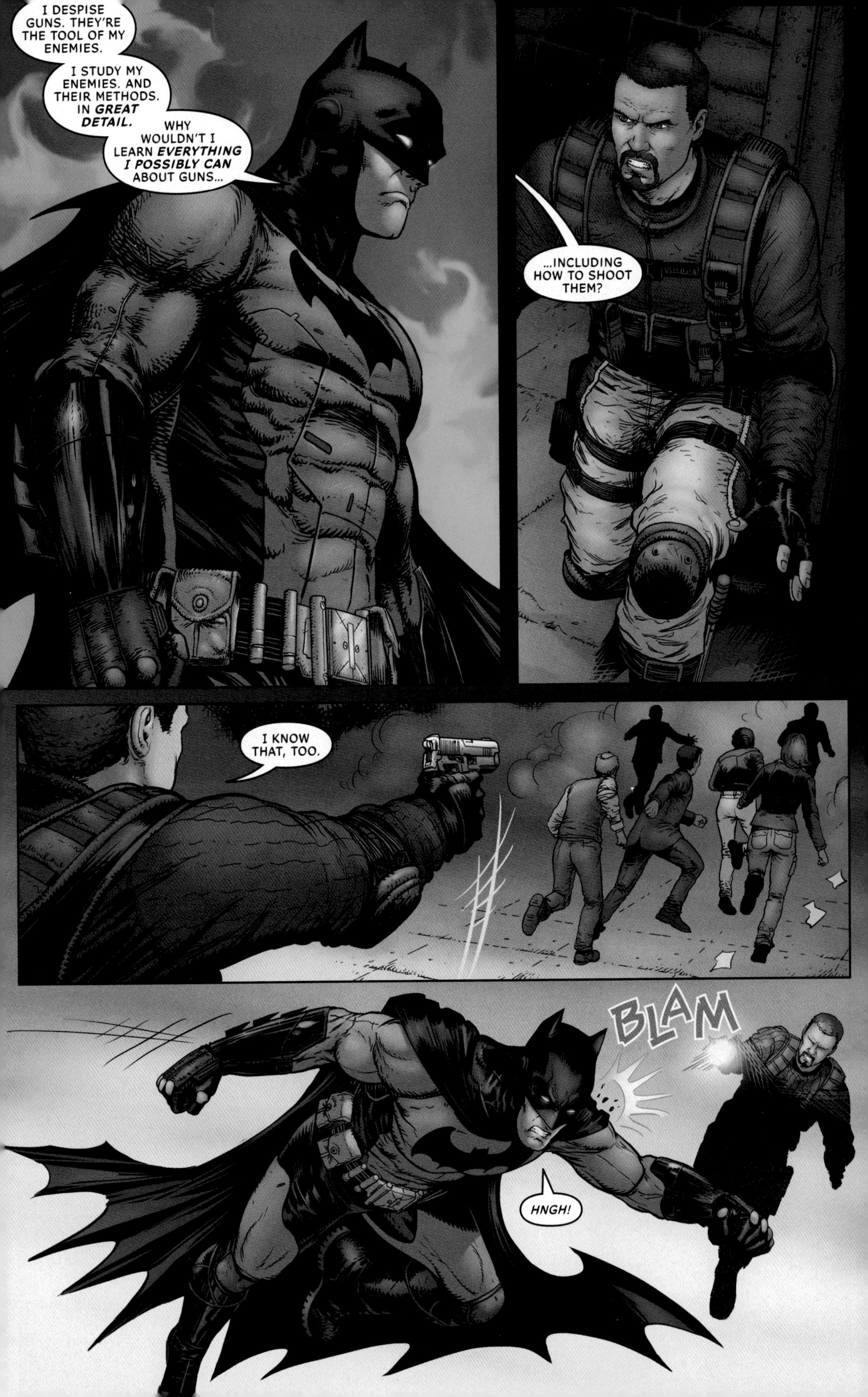
I DESPISE GUNS. THEY'RE THE TOOL OF MY ENEMIES.
I STUDY MY ENEMIES. AND THEIR METHODS. IN *GREAT DETAIL.*
WHY WOULDN'T I LEARN *EVERYTHING I POSSIBLY CAN* ABOUT GUNS...
...INCLUDING HOW TO SHOOT THEM?
I KNOW THAT, TOO.
BLAM
HNGH!

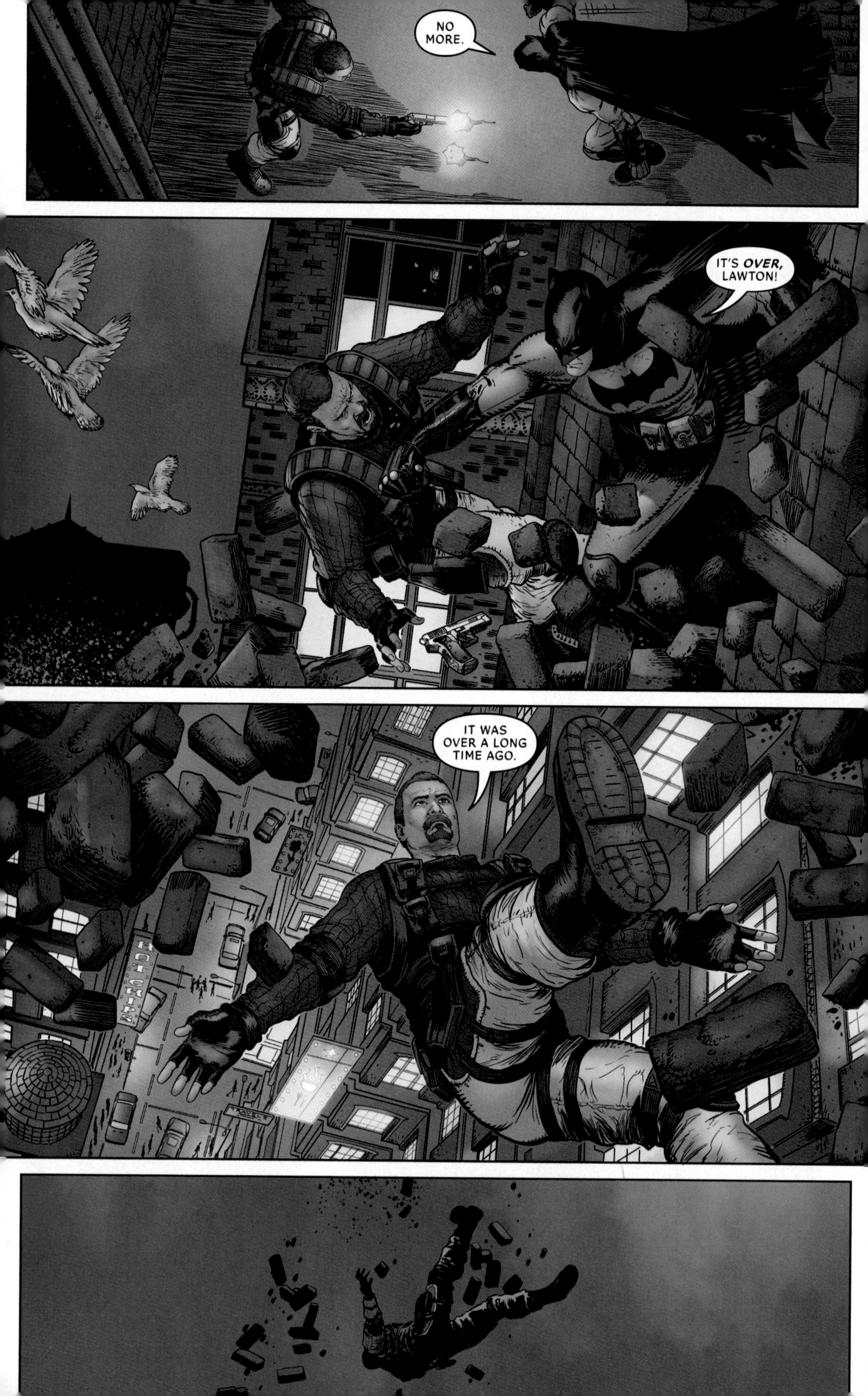
NO MORE.
IT'S *OVER*, LAWTON!
IT WAS OVER A LONG TIME AGO.

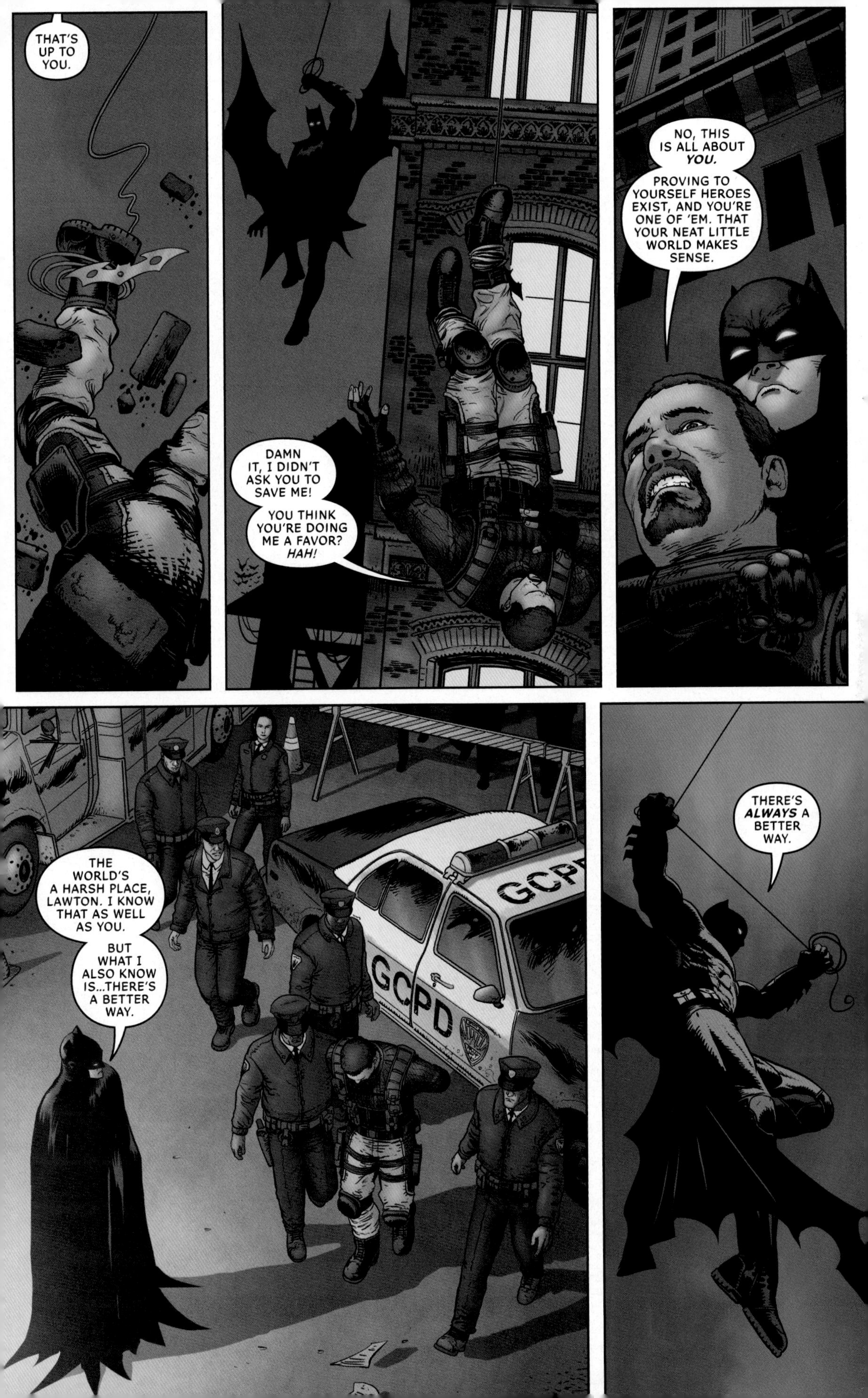
THAT'S UP TO YOU.
DAMN IT, I DIDN'T ASK YOU TO SAVE ME!
YOU THINK YOU'RE DOING ME A FAVOR? *HAH!*
NO, THIS IS ALL ABOUT *YOU.*
PROVING TO YOURSELF HEROES EXIST, AND YOU'RE ONE OF 'EM. THAT YOUR NEAT LITTLE WORLD MAKES SENSE.
THE WORLD'S A HARSH PLACE, LAWTON. I KNOW THAT AS WELL AS YOU.
BUT WHAT I ALSO KNOW IS...THERE'S A BETTER WAY.
GCPD
GCPD
THERE'S *ALWAYS* A BETTER WAY.

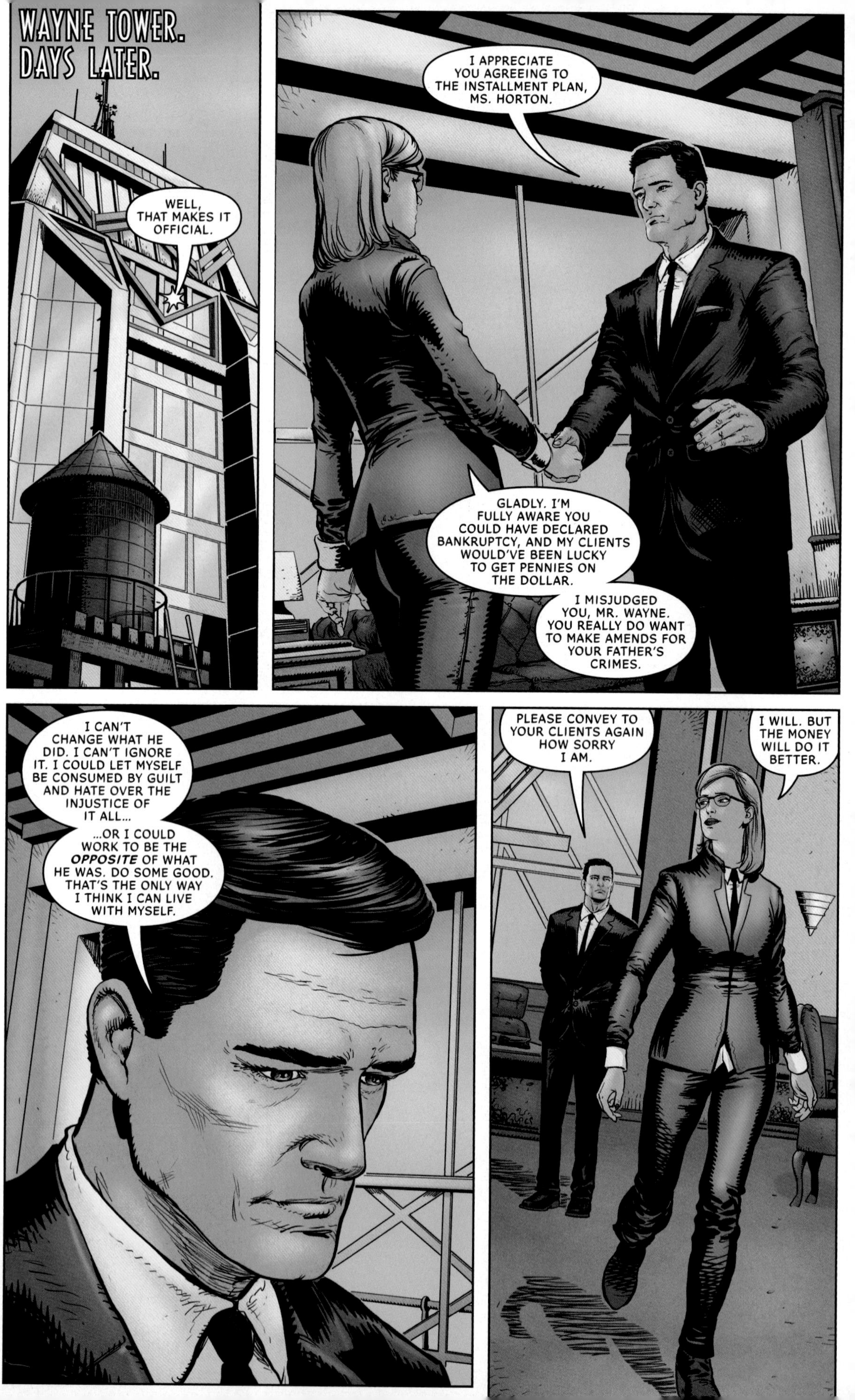
WAYNE TOWER. DAYS LATER.
WELL, THAT MAKES IT OFFICIAL.
I APPRECIATE YOU AGREEING TO THE INSTALLMENT PLAN, MS. HORTON.
GLADLY. I'M FULLY AWARE YOU COULD HAVE DECLARED BANKRUPTCY, AND MY CLIENTS WOULD'VE BEEN LUCKY TO GET PENNIES ON THE DOLLAR.
I MISJUDGED YOU, MR. WAYNE. YOU REALLY DO WANT TO MAKE AMENDS FOR YOUR FATHER'S CRIMES.
I CAN'T CHANGE WHAT HE DID. I CAN'T IGNORE IT. I COULD LET MYSELF BE CONSUMED BY GUILT AND HATE OVER THE INJUSTICE OF IT ALL...
...OR I COULD WORK TO BE THE *OPPOSITE* OF WHAT HE WAS. DO SOME GOOD. THAT'S THE ONLY WAY I THINK I CAN LIVE WITH MYSELF.
PLEASE CONVEY TO YOUR CLIENTS AGAIN HOW SORRY I AM.
I WILL. BUT THE MONEY WILL DO IT BETTER.

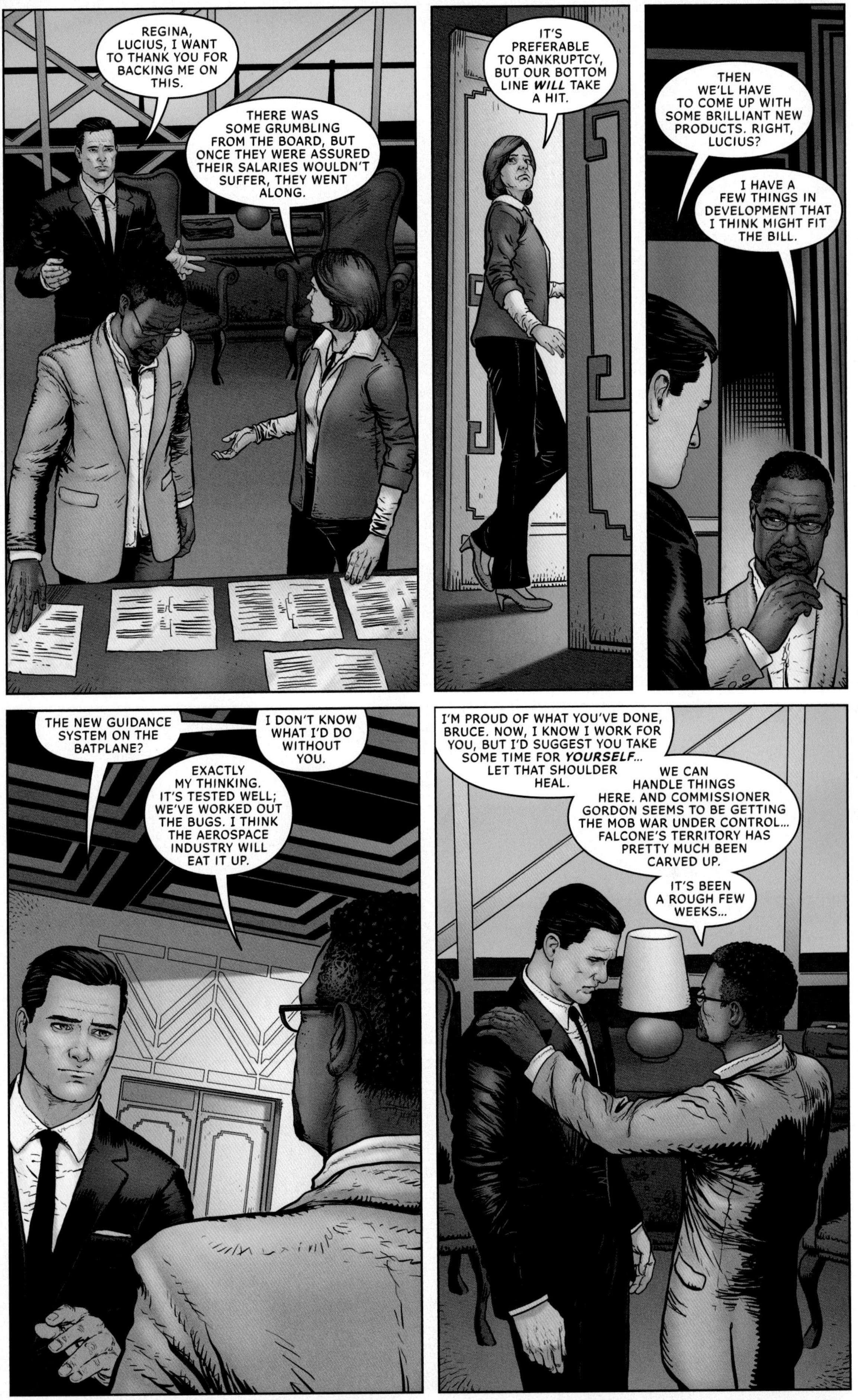
REGINA, LUCIUS, I WANT TO THANK YOU FOR BACKING ME ON THIS.
THERE WAS SOME GRUMBLING FROM THE BOARD, BUT ONCE THEY WERE ASSURED THEIR SALARIES WOULDN'T SUFFER, THEY WENT ALONG.
IT'S PREFERABLE TO BANKRUPTCY, BUT OUR BOTTOM LINE ***WILL*** TAKE A HIT.
THEN WE'LL HAVE TO COME UP WITH SOME BRILLIANT NEW PRODUCTS. RIGHT, LUCIUS?
I HAVE A FEW THINGS IN DEVELOPMENT THAT I THINK MIGHT FIT THE BILL.
THE NEW GUIDANCE SYSTEM ON THE BATPLANE?
EXACTLY MY THINKING. IT'S TESTED WELL; WE'VE WORKED OUT THE BUGS. I THINK THE AEROSPACE INDUSTRY WILL EAT IT UP.
I DON'T KNOW WHAT I'D DO WITHOUT YOU.
I'M PROUD OF WHAT YOU'VE DONE, BRUCE. NOW, I KNOW I WORK FOR YOU, BUT I'D SUGGEST YOU TAKE SOME TIME FOR ***YOURSELF***... LET THAT SHOULDER HEAL.
WE CAN HANDLE THINGS HERE. AND COMMISSIONER GORDON SEEMS TO BE GETTING THE MOB WAR UNDER CONTROL... FALCONE'S TERRITORY HAS PRETTY MUCH BEEN CARVED UP.
IT'S BEEN A ROUGH FEW WEEKS...

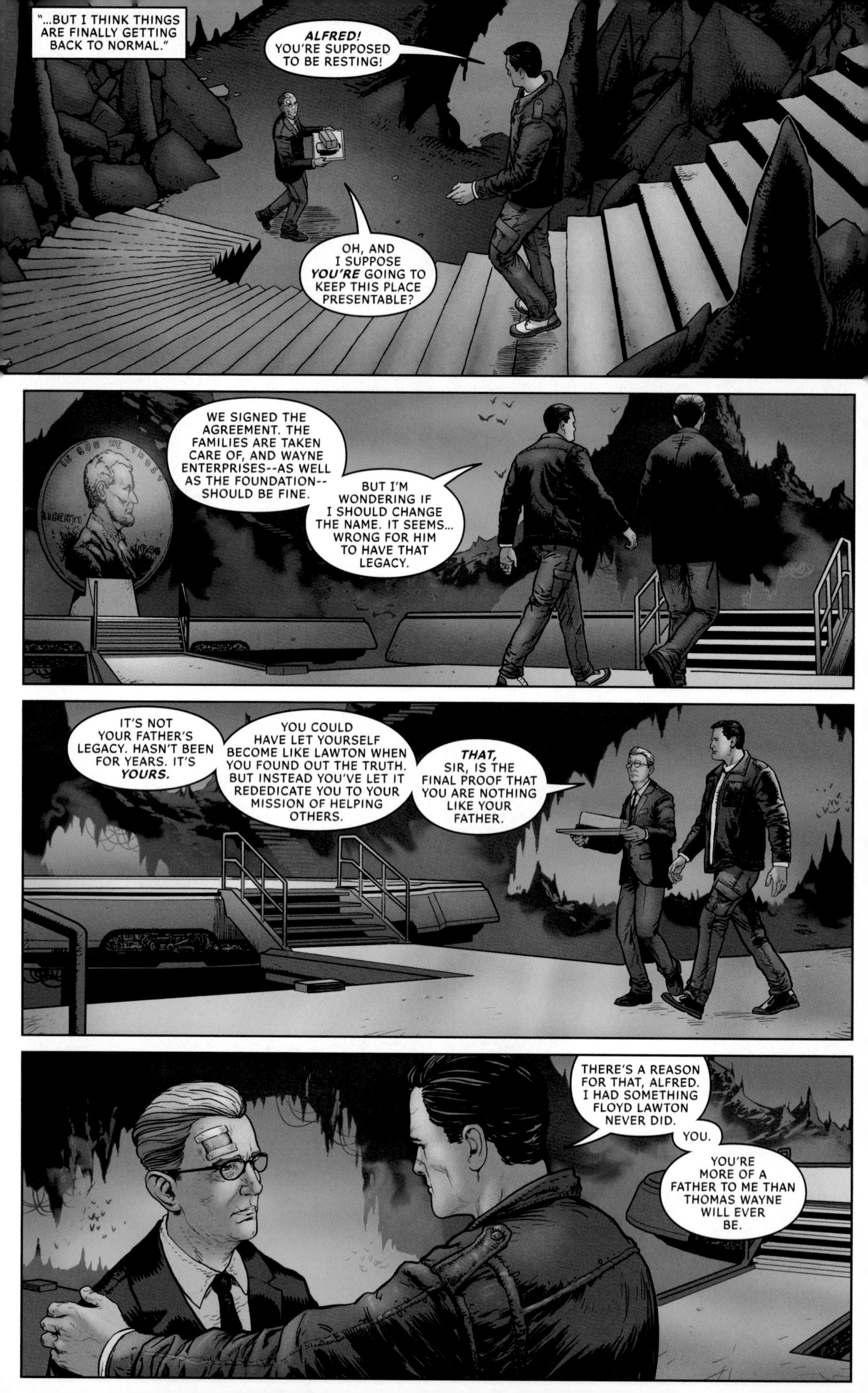
"...BUT I THINK THINGS ARE FINALLY GETTING BACK TO NORMAL."
ALFRED! YOU'RE SUPPOSED TO BE RESTING!
OH, AND I SUPPOSE YOU'RE GOING TO KEEP THIS PLACE PRESENTABLE?
WE SIGNED THE AGREEMENT. THE FAMILIES ARE TAKEN CARE OF, AND WAYNE ENTERPRISES--AS WELL AS THE FOUNDATION--SHOULD BE FINE.
BUT I'M WONDERING IF I SHOULD CHANGE THE NAME. IT SEEMS... WRONG FOR HIM TO HAVE THAT LEGACY.
IT'S NOT YOUR FATHER'S LEGACY. HASN'T BEEN FOR YEARS. IT'S YOURS.
YOU COULD HAVE LET YOURSELF BECOME LIKE LAWTON WHEN YOU FOUND OUT THE TRUTH. BUT INSTEAD YOU'VE LET IT REDEDICATE YOU TO YOUR MISSION OF HELPING OTHERS.
THAT, SIR, IS THE FINAL PROOF THAT YOU ARE NOTHING LIKE YOUR FATHER.
THERE'S A REASON FOR THAT, ALFRED. I HAD SOMETHING FLOYD LAWTON NEVER DID.
YOU.
YOU'RE MORE OF A FATHER TO ME THAN THOMAS WAYNE WILL EVER BE.

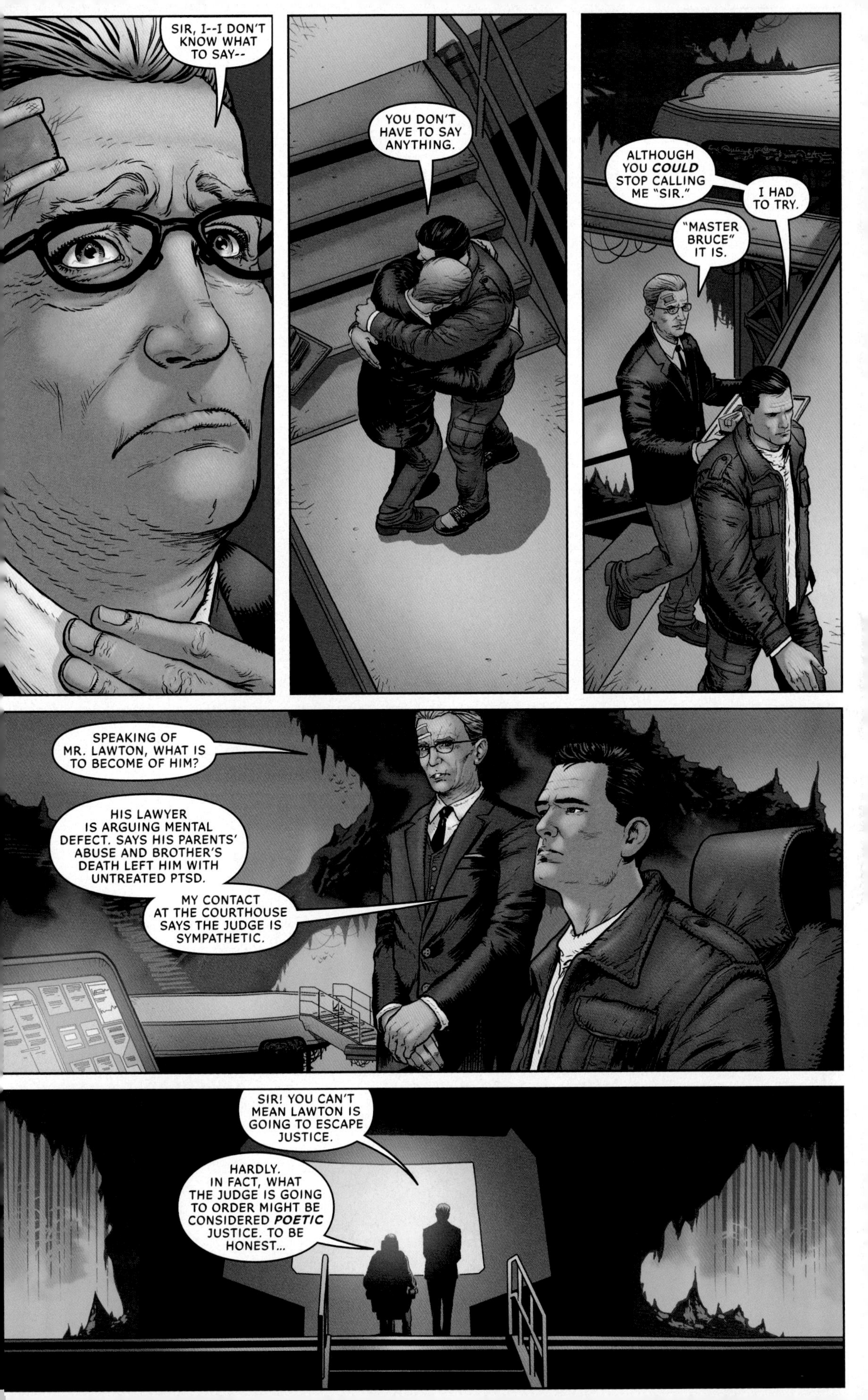
SIR, I--I DON'T KNOW WHAT TO SAY--
YOU DON'T HAVE TO SAY ANYTHING.
ALTHOUGH YOU *COULD* STOP CALLING ME "SIR."
I HAD TO TRY.
"MASTER BRUCE" IT IS.
SPEAKING OF MR. LAWTON, WHAT IS TO BECOME OF HIM?
HIS LAWYER IS ARGUING MENTAL DEFECT. SAYS HIS PARENTS' ABUSE AND BROTHER'S DEATH LEFT HIM WITH UNTREATED PTSD.
MY CONTACT AT THE COURTHOUSE SAYS THE JUDGE IS SYMPATHETIC.
SIR! YOU CAN'T MEAN LAWTON IS GOING TO ESCAPE JUSTICE.
HARDLY. IN FACT, WHAT THE JUDGE IS GOING TO ORDER MIGHT BE CONSIDERED *POETIC* JUSTICE. TO BE HONEST...

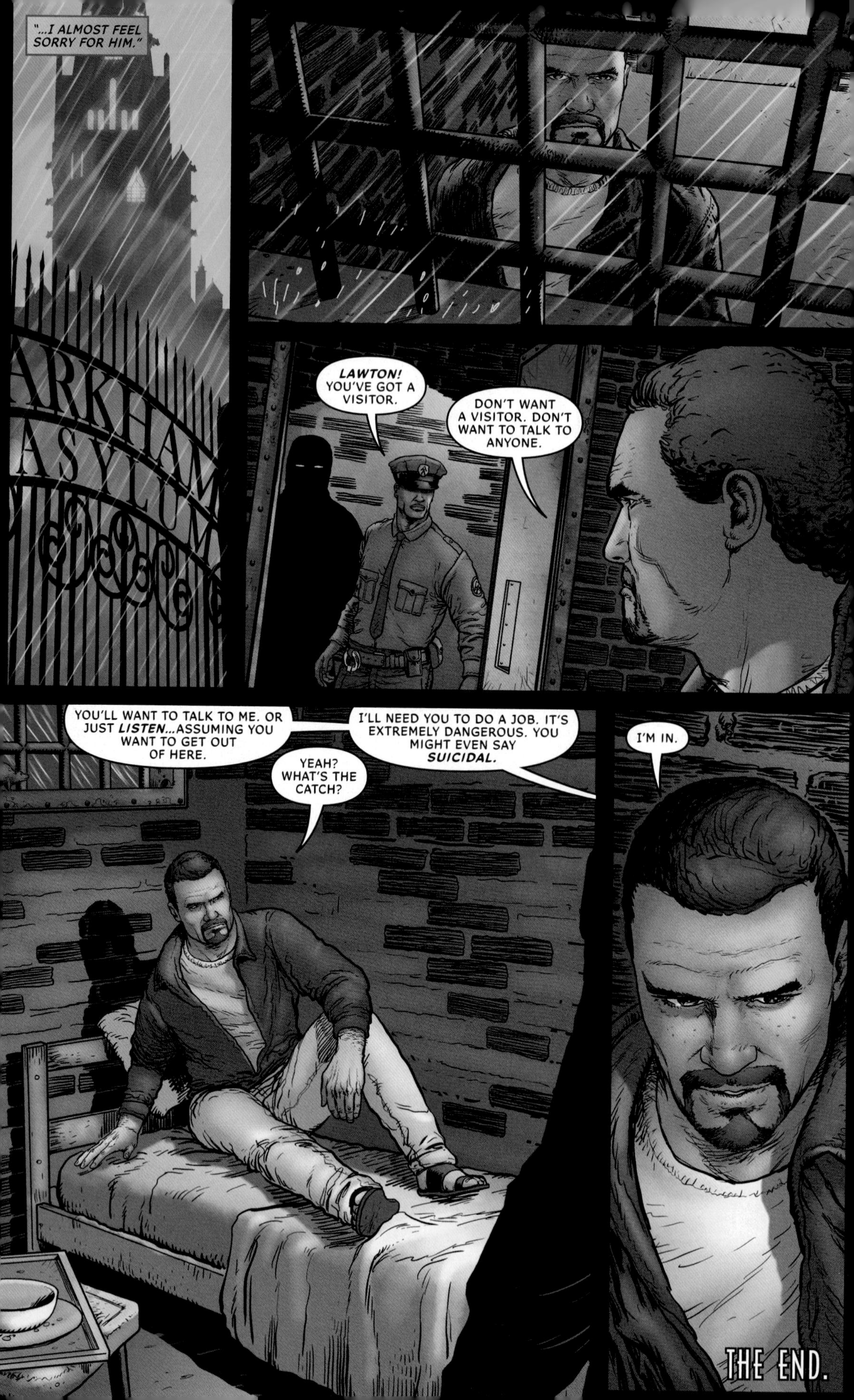
"...I ALMOST FEEL SORRY FOR HIM."
ARKHAM ASYLUM
LAWTON! YOU'VE GOT A VISITOR.
DON'T WANT A VISITOR. DON'T WANT TO TALK TO ANYONE.
YOU'LL WANT TO TALK TO ME. OR JUST LISTEN...ASSUMING YOU WANT TO GET OUT OF HERE.
YEAH? WHAT'S THE CATCH?
I'LL NEED YOU TO DO A JOB. IT'S EXTREMELY DANGEROUS. YOU MIGHT EVEN SAY SUICIDAL.
I'M IN.
THE END.

BATMAN: SINS OF THE FATHER #1 game art variant cover

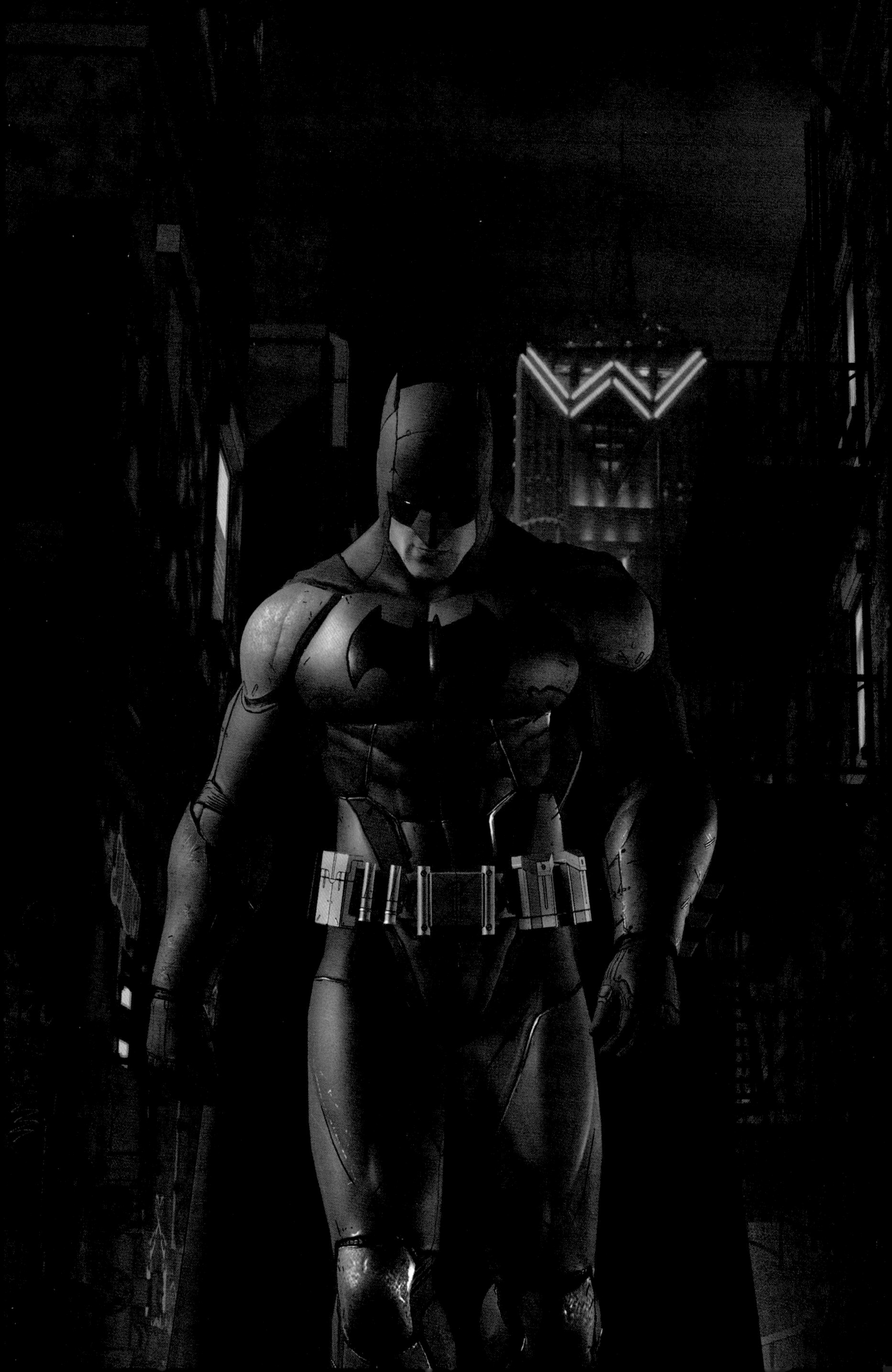

Cover roughs for **BATMAN: SINS OF THE FATHER #1** by **RAFFAELE IENCO**

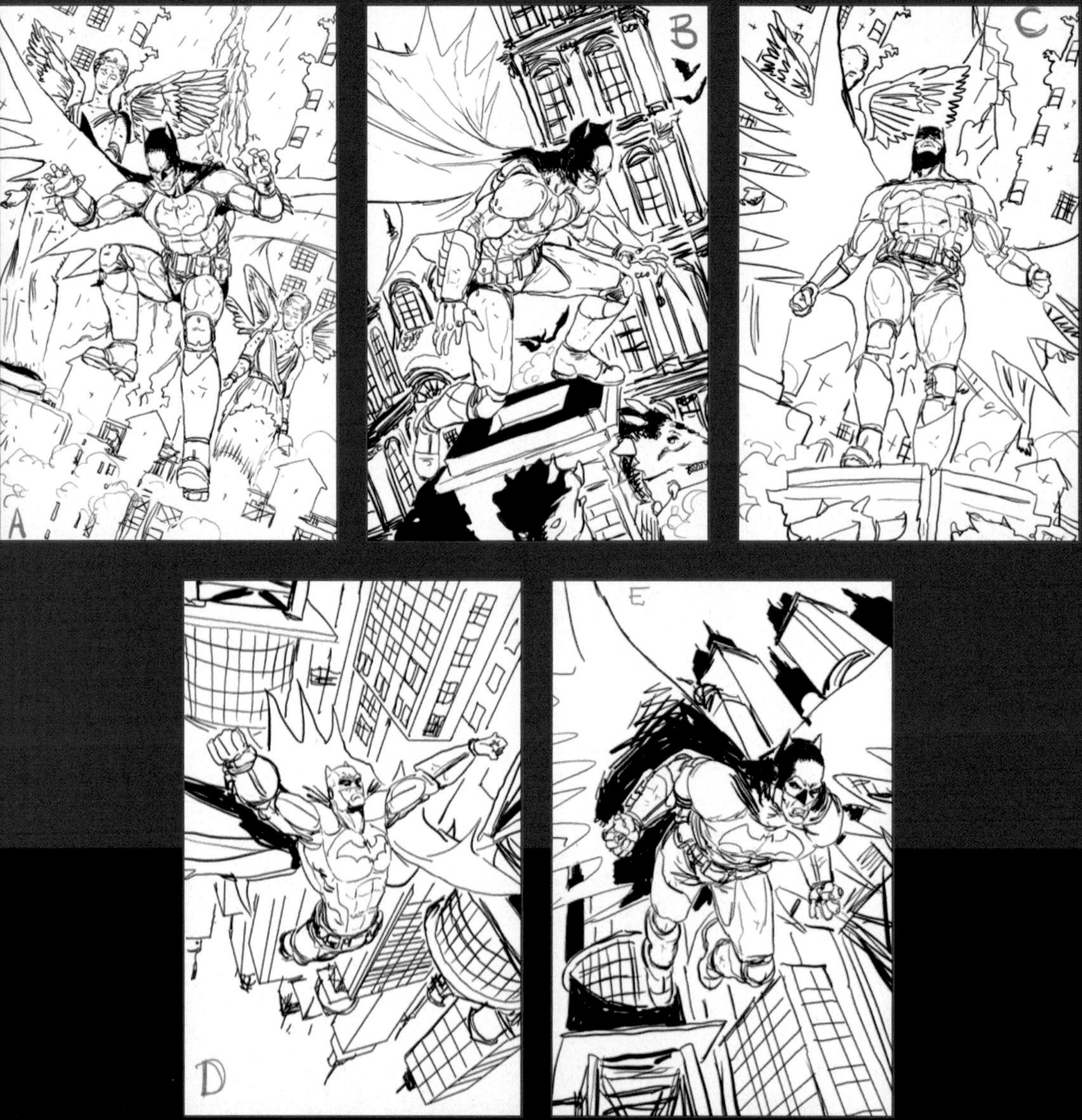
A
B
C
D
E

Cover roughs for **BATMAN: SINS OF THE FATHER #2** by **RAFFAELE IENCO**

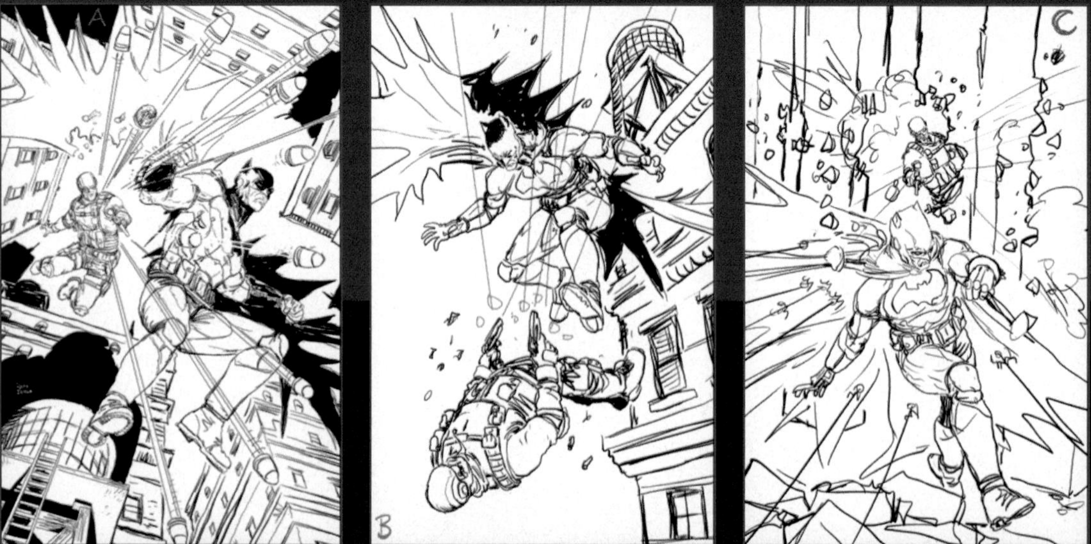
A
B
C

Cover roughs for **BATMAN: SINS OF THE FATHER #3** by **RAFFAELE IENCO**

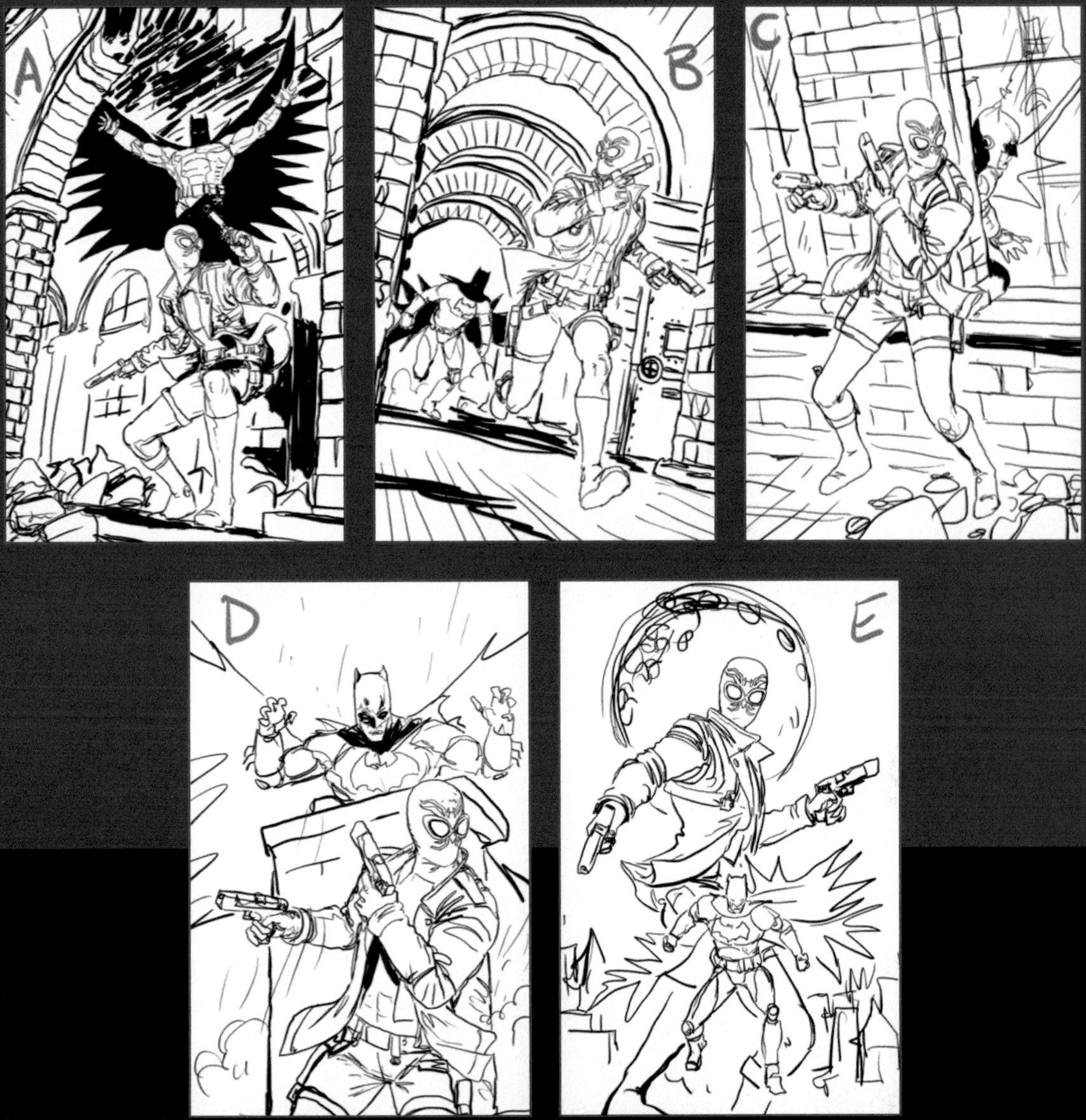
A
B
C
D
E

Cover roughs for **BATMAN: SINS OF THE FATHER #4** by **RAFFAELE IENCO**

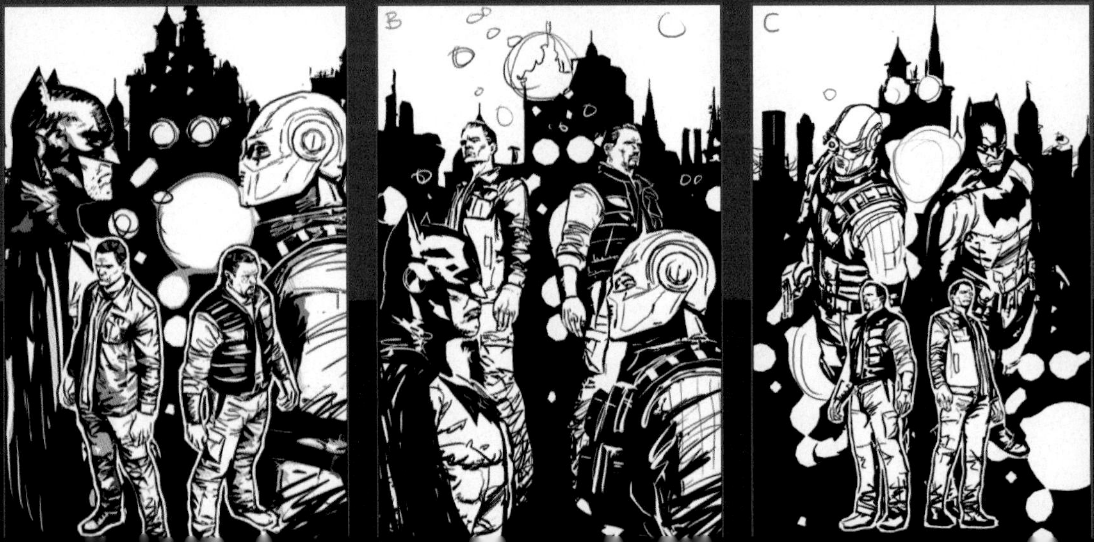
B
C

Cover roughs for **BATMAN: SINS OF THE FATHER #5** by **RAFFAELE IENCO**

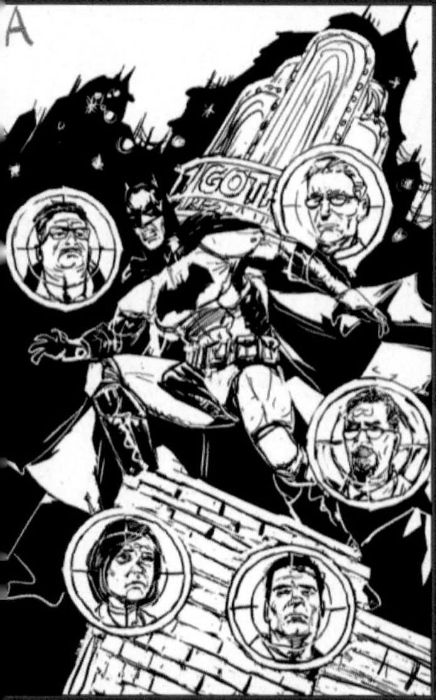
A

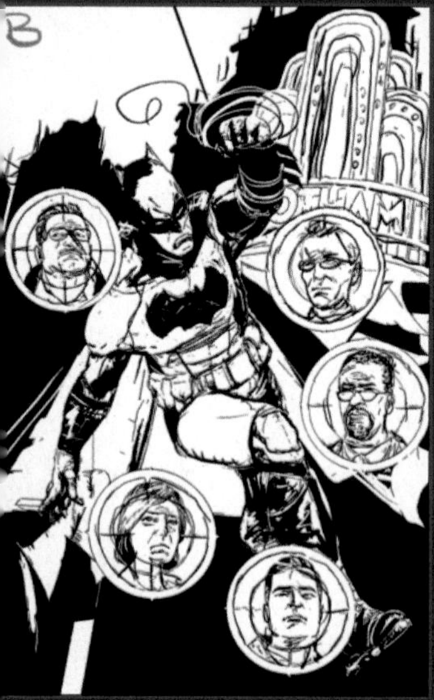
B

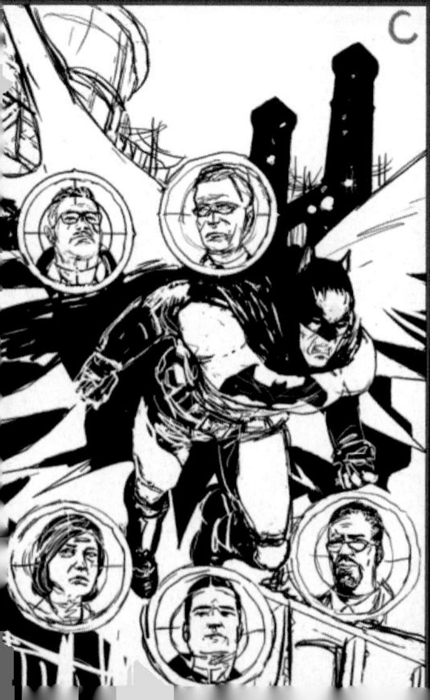
C

Cover roughs for **BATMAN: SINS OF THE FATHER #6** by **RAFFAELE IENCO**

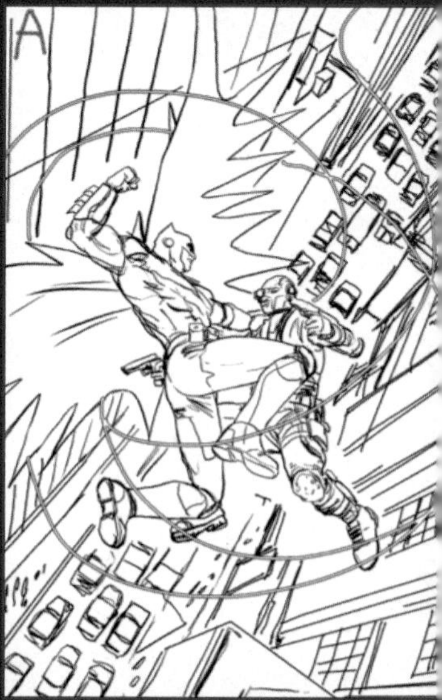
A

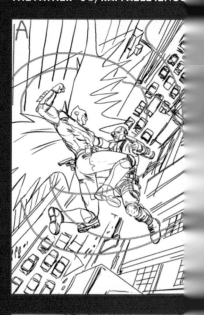

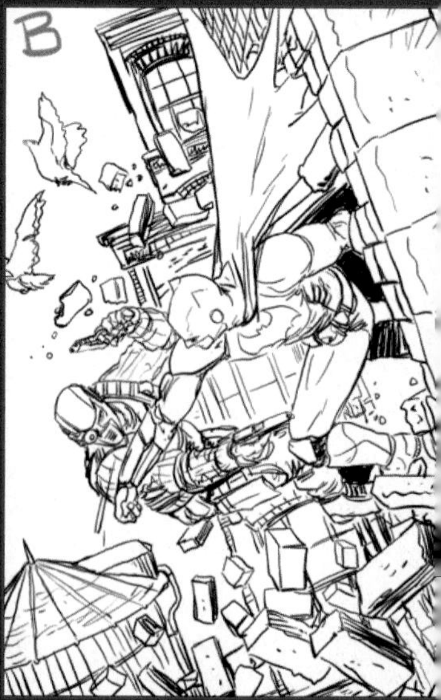
B

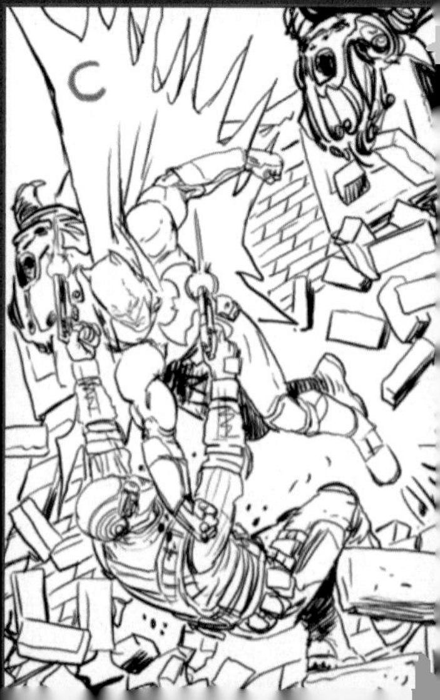
C

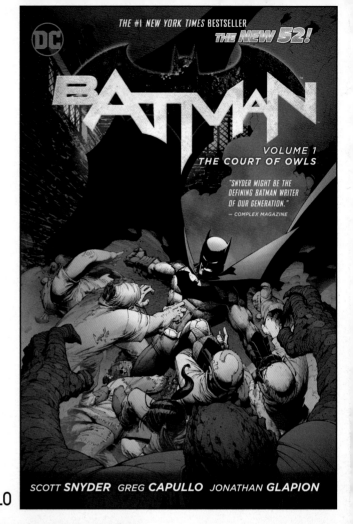

BATMAN

VOLUME 1
THE COURT OF OWLS

SCOTT **SNYDER** GREG **CAPULLO** Jonathan **GLAPION**

START AT THE BEGINNING!

BATMAN

VOL. 1: THE COURT OF OWLS
SCOTT SNYDER with GREG CAPULLO

BATMAN

VOLUME 2
THE CITY OF OWLS

SCOTT **SNYDER** GREG **CAPULLO** JONATHAN **GLAPION** JAMES **TYNION IV** RAFAEL **ALBUQUERQUE** JASON **FABOK**

**BATMAN VOL. 2:
THE CITY OF OWLS**

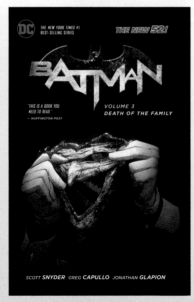

BATMAN

VOLUME 3
DEATH OF THE FAMILY

SCOTT **SNYDER** GREG **CAPULLO** JONATHAN **GLAPION**

**BATMAN VOL. 3:
DEATH OF THE FAMILY**

READ THE ENTIRE EPIC!

BATMAN VOL. 4:
ZERO YEAR – SECRET CITY

BATMAN VOL. 5:
ZERO YEAR – DARK CITY

BATMAN VOL. 6:
GRAVEYARD SHIFT

BATMAN VOL. 7:
ENDGAME

BATMAN VOL. 8:
SUPERHEAVY

BATMAN VOL. 9:
BLOOM

BATMAN VOL. 10:
EPILOGUE

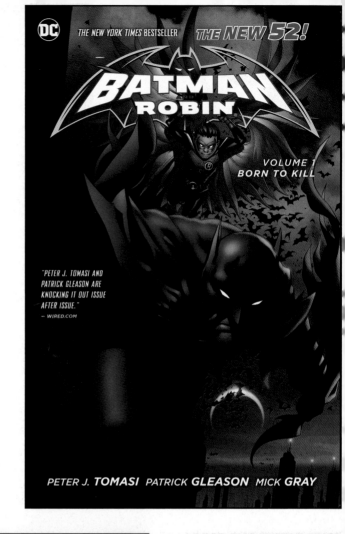

"Batman is getting a brand-new voice."
– USA TODAY

"A great showcase for the new team as well as offering a taste of the new flavor they'll be bringing to Gotham City." **– IGN**

DC UNIVERSE REBIRTH

BATMAN

VOL. 1: I AM GOTHAM
TOM KING
with DAVID FINCH

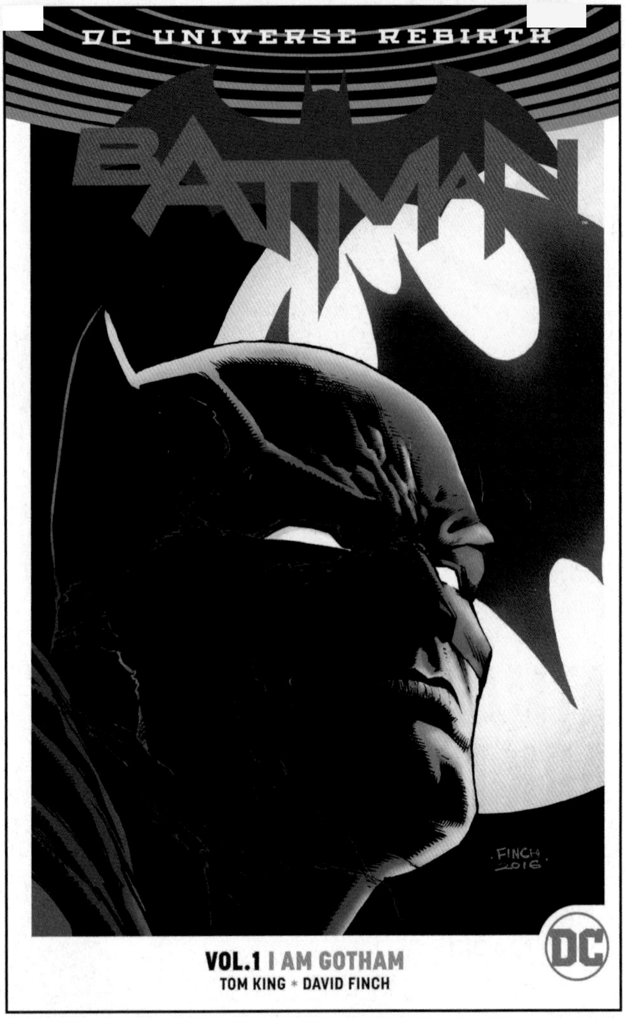
DC UNIVERSE REBIRTH
BATMAN
FINCH 2016
VOL.1 I AM GOTHAM
TOM KING ✶ DAVID FINCH

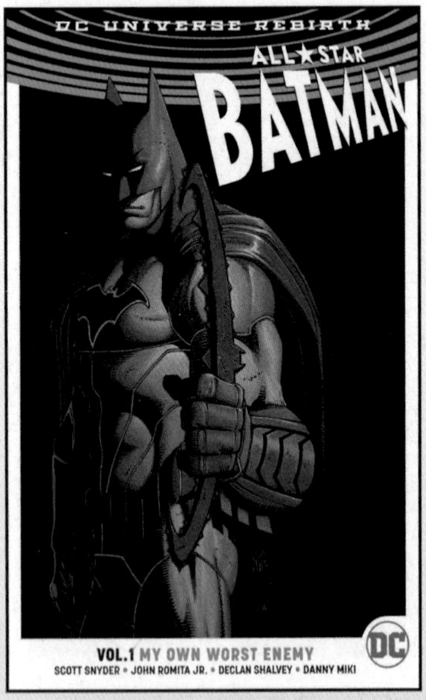
DC UNIVERSE REBIRTH
ALL★STAR
BATMAN
VOL.1 MY OWN WORST ENEMY
SCOTT SNYDER • JOHN ROMITA JR. • DECLAN SHALVEY • DANNY MIKI

ALL-STAR BATMAN VOL. 1:
MY OWN WORST ENEMY

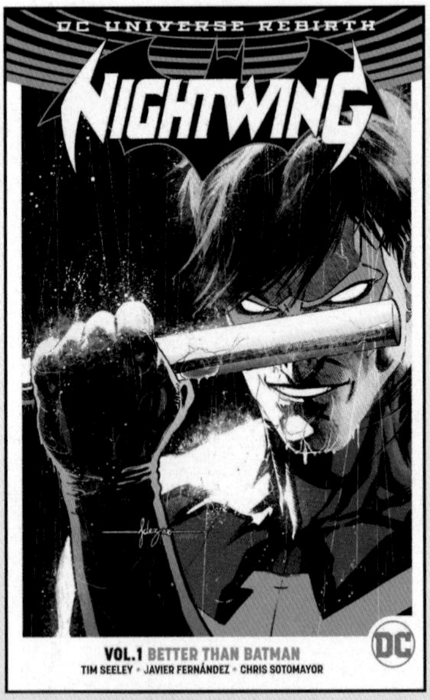
DC UNIVERSE REBIRTH
NIGHTWING
VOL.1 BETTER THAN BATMAN
TIM SEELEY • JAVIER FERNÁNDEZ • CHRIS SOTOMAYOR

NIGHTWING VOL. 1:
BETTER THAN BATMAN

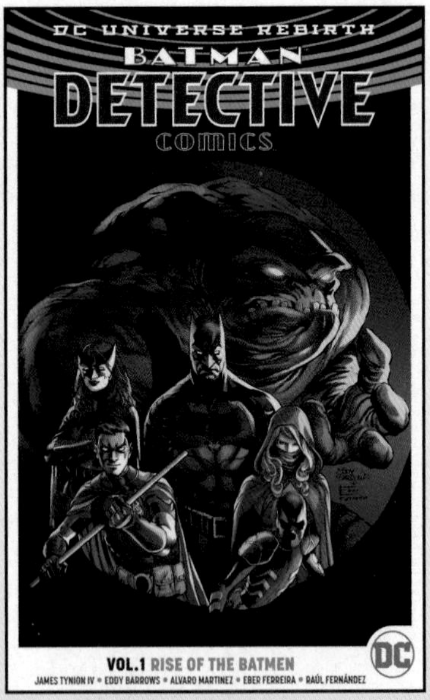
DC UNIVERSE REBIRTH
BATMAN
DETECTIVE
COMICS
VOL.1 RISE OF THE BATMEN
JAMES TYNION IV • EDDY BARROWS • ALVARO MARTINEZ • EBER FERREIRA • RAÚL FERNÁNDEZ

DETECTIVE COMICS VOL. 1:
RISE OF THE BATMEN

Get more DC graphic novels wherever comics and books are sold!